Markets and Managers

Public Policy and Management

Series Editor: Professor R.A.W. Rhodes, Department of Politics, University of York.
Series Advisers: Professor Peter Jackson, University of Leicester and Professor Mike Connolly, University of Ulster.

The effectiveness of public policies is a matter of public concern and the efficiency with which policies are put into practice is a continuing problem for governments of all political persuasions. This series contributes to these debates by publishing informed, in-depth and contemporary analyses of public administration, public policy and public management.

The intention is to go beyond the usual textbook approach to the analysis of public policy and management and to encourage authors to move debate about their issue forward. In this sense, each book both describes current thinking and research, and explores future policy directions. Accessibility is a key feature and, as a result, the series will appeal to academics and their students as well as to the informed practitioner.

Current and Forthcoming Titles Include:

Delivering Welfare
T. Butcher

Implementing Thatcherite Policies: Audit of an Era
David Marsh and R.A.W. Rhodes (eds)

British Aid and International Trade
O. Morrissey, B. Smith and E. Horesh

Markets and Managers: New Issues in the Delivery of Welfare
Peter Taylor-Gooby and Robyn Lawson (eds)

Markets and Managers

New Issues in the Delivery of Welfare

Edited by
Peter Taylor-Gooby and Robyn Lawson

Open University Press
Buckingham · Philadelphia

Open University Press
Celtic Court
22 Ballmoor
Buckingham
MK18 1XW

and
1900 Frost Road, Suite 101
Bristol, PA 19007, USA

First Published 1993

A catalogue record of this book is available from the British Library

0 335 15789 0 (Paperback)   0 335 15790 4 (Hardback)

Library of Congress Cataloging-in-Publication Data

Markets and managers: new issues in the delivery of welfare/edited
    by Peter Taylor-Gooby and Robyn Lawson.
        p.   cm.
    Includes bibliographical references (p. 192) and index.
    ISBN 0–335–15790–4 (Hardback) ISBN 0–335–15789–0 (Paperback)
    1. Public welfare administration – Great Britain.
    2. Privatization – Great Britain.   I. Taylor-Gooby, Peter.
    II. Lawson, Robyn, 1958–
    HV248.M35   1993
    361'.0068–dc20   92–43087
                                                                CIP

Typeset by Inforum, Rowlands Castle, Hants
Printed in Great Britain by Biddles Ltd, Guildford and Kings Lynn

Contents

Notes on contributors

Pat Ainley is a writer and researcher on education and training based at the University of Kent. Currently undertaking a comparative study of student experiences at a Home Counties university and an inner-city polytechnic. Co-author (with M. Corney) of *Training for the Future: The Rise and Fall of the Manpower Services Commission* (Cassell, 1990) and a number of books on education and training.

John Baldock is Lecturer in Social Policy, University of Kent. Currently engaged in two projects to evaluate the community care response for people who suffer strokes and heart attacks. Has conducted research and published in the areas of penal policy, social work methods and the care of elderly people. Co-author of *Care for the Elderly: Significant Innovations in Three European Countries* (Campus Verlag and Westview Press, 1991).

John Butler is Professor of Health Service Studies, University of Kent. Currently researching organizational changes in the NHS. Author of *Patients, Policies and Politics: Before and After 'Working for Patients'* (Open University Press, 1992) and a number of other books and studies of the NHS, primary health care and of health and lifestyle.

Hartley Dean is Senior Lecturer in Government and Social Policy, Luton College of Higher Education, formerly Research Fellow in Social Policy, University of Kent. Previously Director of Brixton Advice Centre. Co-author (with Peter Taylor-Gooby) of *Dependency Culture: The Explosion of a Myth* (Wheatsheaf, 1992) and a number of books and articles on social security.

Ray Forrest is Senior Research Fellow, School of Advanced Urban Studies, University of Bristol. Co-author (with A. Murie) of *Moving the Housing Market: State Housing after Privatisation* (Avebury, 1990), another book and numerous articles and reports on recent developments in housing policy. One of the foremost researchers in this field.

Andrew Gray is Reader in Public Management and Accountability, University of Kent. Currently researching new policy initiatives including the establishment of Next Steps Agencies, and value-for-money auditing. Co-author (with Bill Jenkins) of *Administrative Politics in Britain* (Wheatsheaf, 1985) and numerous studies of developments in central and local government.

Bill Jenkins is Reader in Public Policy and Management, University of Kent. Currently researching new policy initiatives including the establishment of Next Step Agencies and value-for-money auditing. Co-author (with Andrew Gray) of *Administrative Politics in Britain* (Wheatsheaf, 1985).

Robyn Lawson is Research Officer, Personal Social Services Research Unit, University of Kent. Has worked in the NHS and has researched European health systems and primary health care in South America. Currently researching the structure, function and regulation of social care markets for elderly people resulting from community care legislation. Author of reports and papers on this subject.

Peter Taylor-Gooby is Professor of Social Policy, University of Kent. Author of *Social Change, Social Welfare and Social Science* (Wheatsheaf, 1991) and numerous books and articles on the Welfare State, to which he is rather attached.

Abbreviations

ADSS	Association of Directors of Social Services
CBI	Confederation of British Industry
CCT	Compulsory Competitive Tendering
CCWP	Community Care White Paper, *Caring for People*, 1989
CLSSAF	Central London Social Security Advisers' Forum
COMP	Contracted Out Money Purchase Scheme
CPAG	Child Poverty Action Group
CPRS	Central Policy Review Staff
CSO	Central Statistical Office
CTC	City Technical College
DES	Department of Education and Science
DHA	District Health Authority
DHSS	Department of Health and Social Security
DSS	Department of Social Security
EC	European Community
FMI	Financial Management Initiative
FMU	Financial Management Unit
GCSE	General Certificate of Secondary Education
GDP	Gross Domestic Product
GHS	General Household Survey
GP	General Practitioner
HAT	Housing Action Trust
HBAI	Households Below Average Income
HEFC	Higher Education Funding Council

HMI	Her Majesty's Inspectors
HRA	Housing Revenue Account
IAEEA	International Association for the Evaluation of Educational Achievement
IEA	Institute of Economic Affairs
ILEA	Inner London Education Authority
LEA	Local Education Authority
LEC	Local Enterprise Company
MINIS	Management Information System for Ministers
MSC	Manpower Services Commission
NACAB	National Association of Citizens' Advice Bureaux
NACRO	National Association for the Care and Resettlement of Offenders
NAO	National Audit Office
NFER	National Foundation for Education Research
NFSESB	National Federation of Small Employers and Small Businesses
NHS	National Health Service
NHSME	National Health Service Management Executive
NIC	National Insurance Contribution
NISB	National Insurance Sickness Benefit
NPM	New Public Management
NTTF	National Training Task Force
NVQ	National Vocational Qualification
OECD	Organization for Economic Cooperation and Development
OPB	Occupational Pension Board
OS	Operational Strategy
OSP	Occupational Sick Pay
PAR	Programme Analysis and Review
PCFC	Polytechnics and Colleges Funding Council
PES	Public Expenditure Survey
PIC	Private Industry Councils
PPP	Personal Pension Plan
PSS	Personal Social Services
RHA	Regional Health Authority
SERPS	State Earnings Related Pension Scheme
SIB	Securities and Investment Board
SMP	Statutory Maternity Pay
SSA	Standard Spending Assessment
SSC	Social Security Consortium
SSD	Social Services Department
SSI	Social Services Inspectorate
SSP	Statutory Sick Pay
SSSC	Social Security Select Committee
TEC	Training and Enterprise Council
TEED	Training Enterprise Education Division
TSA	Training Services Agency

TUC	Trades Union Congress
TVEI	Training and Vocational Education Initiative
UFC	University Funding Council
UGC	University Grants Committee
YOP	Youth Opportunities Programme
YT	Youth Training
YTS	Youth Training Scheme

Introduction

Since 1979, the Conservative government has pursued an ambitious programme of reform covering the whole of public provision in the UK. The
resulting welfare settlement is the most far-reaching change in British social
policy for half a century. Four immediate considerations lie behind the new
departure in policy: antipathy to large bureaucracies and the structured planning of services; an ideological commitment to privatization and the extension
of market systems; the vigorous endorsement of monetarist economic theory,
which places great emphasis on the control of inflation through the reduction
of state borrowing; and the determination to cut taxation for electoral advantage. However, the impetus for change in the structure of public provision also
derives from long-run factors operating beyond the immediate control or
enthusiasms of a particular party in government. These include: the continuing
economic decline of the UK, which calls into question the future of expansive
state services; increasing inequality, which threatens the solidarity of support
for mass welfare; and changes in household structure and family life, which
demand more sensitive and flexible provision.

   These issues have been extensively analysed elsewhere (see, for example,
Hills 1990; Pierson 1991, Taylor-Gooby 1991a; Wilson and Wilson 1991).
Much discussion of welfare policy has concerned itself with the general issues of
state spending and the role of government, and has dismissed the organization
and delivery of services as mere detail. This book argues that the organizational
changes of the past decade are of fundamental importance in determining who
gets what, who foots the bill, and perhaps most important, who gets nothing.
The grand pattern of spending constraint, of the extension of privatization from

nationalized industries into the welfare sector and of the marginalization of poorer groups forms the backdrop. However, organizational detail determines exactly where these policies bite.

Since the mid-1980s and particularly since the 1987 election victory, a new agenda has emerged which emphasizes the reform of state welfare services rather than a simple 'rolling back of the state'. The key policies are the decentralization of day-to-day administration, the use of markets as the chief mechanism for resource allocation, greater responsiveness to the demands of consumers and an expanded role for the private and voluntary sectors. This 'new managerialism' has emerged under Conservative governments and has been put into practice in a way that reflects that party's commitment to spending constraint, selectivity and the widening of inequalities. However, all main parties endorse the key themes of the new managerialism and the use of markets in state welfare. The pressures of continuing economic difficulty, the demand for more flexible services and the widespread public dissatisfaction with state bureaucracies suggest that the process of restructuring will continue into the next millennium, whichever party is in power. In the circumstances of the 1980s and 1990s, the new state managerialism has been implemented by a government committed to the diminution of the state, to be achieved by spending cuts and privatization. This agenda has had a determining impact on how the managerial programme of decentralization, choice and consumerism has been interpreted in practice.

The context of the 1990s: Spending cuts and privatization

Spending constraint and privatization have been central themes in policy debate throughout the past fifteen years. The 1979 Public Expenditure white paper opened with the words: 'public spending is at the heart of Britain's present economic difficulties' (Her Majesty's Treasury 1979). Although state programmes have been cut substantially and nationalized industries have been sold, public spending continues to rise. Welfare programmes are the most rapidly growing area of expenditure and the Welfare State is resistant to privatization. The most recent official estimates indicate an increase from £196 billion to £221 billion between 1979–80 and 1991–92, calculated at constant 1990–91 prices (Her Majesty's Treasury 1992, table 2.3). However, the economy has continued to grow through much of this period, so that spending as a proportion of gross domestic product (GDP) has fallen from 47 to 42 per cent (Her Majesty's Treasury 1992, chart 1.1).

Spending in the welfare sector accounts for all of the increase and more – in fact, this sector continues to grow more rapidly than the economy as a whole. Spending on social security, education, the National Health Service (NHS), housing, personal social services and training taken together increased from £107 billion to £137 billion over the period (Her Majesty's Treasury 1992, table 2.3), or from 62 to nearly 70 per cent of state spending (excluding privatization proceeds, debt repayments and other items not attributed to individual spending areas). Only in the relatively minor area of social housing has there been a real fall in spending. In the most substantial areas there has been a rapid increase – social security has grown from £43.5 billion to £64.8 billion, health from £20.3 billion to £29.4 billion and education from £24.4 billion to £29.0 billion. Concern at the scale of public spending has led to an urgent review of high-spending departments in 1993. Privatization appears unlikely to make substantial inroads on these figures, except in the case of the pensions element in social security, where real savings are not anticipated for at least two decades. There is a strong incentive for a government committed to spending restraint and tax cuts to pursue new approaches to management in the state sector.

Privatization has been of limited impact except in relation to the sale of council housing and the transfer of people from state to personal earnings-related pensions. Both policies required large state subsidies to achieve progress. Even so, there are indications that different policies will be required to dismantle state services in these areas further. By the early 1990s, over a quarter of the most desirable council properties had been sold off. The poverty of the tenants and the unattractiveness of the properties suggest that the remainder will be more difficult to sell. As Ray Forrest points out in Chapter 3, the removal of social housing responsibilities from the state requires a new approach involving transfer of estates mainly to the voluntary sector.

In the case of pensions, a range of financial institutions were willing to provide assurance-based schemes, once regulations concerning the size and inflation proofing of the benefits were relaxed (see Chapter 6). Contribution subsidies plus cuts in the state scheme provide a carrot-and-stick incentive for people to transfer, so that government is likely to be more successful in withdrawing from this area. In the long run, substantial savings in state earnings-related pension spending will appear, but these will take several decades to realize. Switching to private pensions is most attractive to young people who have not yet established state pension entitlements. However, in other areas, such as private medicine and health care, there is little evidence of a shift to private provision. The subsidies to private alternatives to state services provided by government in the 1980s (tax relief on some private health insurance policies, the Assisted Places bursary scheme for private schooling) were relatively small. However, the existence of private services and the division between private and state sector consumers raises the question of whether a move towards greater diversity in provision will result in greater inequality in access.

Over the period of Conservative government, British society has become markedly more unequal. This is brought out most clearly in official statistics: between 1979 and 1988–89 (the most recent period for which figures are available), the income of the poorest tenth of the population fell by some 6 per cent, taking housing costs and inflation into account. In contrast, average incomes rose by over 30 per cent, and increases at the top end are probably even greater (DSS 1992b). These statistics should be taken as an underestimate.

The shift from direct to indirect tax is likely to bear more heavily on poorer groups, so that living standards will have fallen by more than average inflation-based estimates indicate. The numbers in poverty (understood as having an income at or below last resort means-tested benefit level) more than doubled to nearly 11 million between 1979 and 1987 (Dean and Taylor-Gooby 1992: 9).

In part, the growth of inequality is a result of government policies that cut benefits, especially for poorer groups, and shift the burden of taxation from better off to poorer people. Thus the means-tested benefit claimed by most unemployed people – supplementary benefit/income support – has fallen in value from about a third to about 22 per cent of average wages between 1979 and 1989, taking employment costs and inflation into account (Dean and Taylor-Gooby 1992: 59). Tax and national insurance contributions as a proportion of income rose from 2.5 to 7.4 per cent for a married couple at half national average earnings between 1978–89 and 1990–91. For a couple at twice average earnings, the proportion fell from 28 to 25 per cent, and at five times from 48 to 35 per cent (*Hansard*, House of Commons, vol. 176, WA, cols 700–708).

Shifts in the economy only partly resulting from government policies have exacerbated inequalities. Of particular importance are the continuing high levels of unemployment throughout the period and the increasing division between well-paid stable employment in the 'core' of the economy and in-secure often part-time work at the periphery (Ball *et al.* 1989: 169). Changes in the family also played a part. Throughout the 1980s, the proportion of retired people continued to rise, putting pressure on pensions. The number of families headed by a single parent more than doubled from 8 to 19 per cent between 1971 and 1991 (CSO 1993, Chart 2.10). This group is at particular risk of poverty. Over 70 per cent lived at or below minimum benefit level by the end of the 1980s (Millar 1992: 151). The new welfare settlement operates in an increasingly unequal society, in which the contrast between the vulnerability of some groups and the security of others is a central concern of policy analysis. Many of the current changes appear likely to exacerbate such inequalities.

By the end of the 1980s, after a decade in office, the Conservative government had not succeeded in reducing state spending substantially. The impetus towards policy innovation grew stronger. In this context, the new state managerialism has emerged as a dominant theme in policy. The particular orientation of Conservatism has led to the re-casting of some of the key themes. Central government has taken the opportunity of decentralization of day-to-day administration to extend its power over budgets and the scope and quality of services. Efficiency is reinterpreted as cost-efficiency, at its crudest, as spending cuts. Severe limits are imposed on the range of consumer choice. Resources are heavily constrained and the inequalities between individuals are growing wider. The pressures on service providers to move in the direction of two-tier provision are particularly intense.

The paradox of the current implementation of the new managerialism is that decentralization means greater central power, and diversity of provision diminishes choice for some consumers. These issues are explored in more detail in the rest of the book.

The structure of the book

The first chapter sets the scene by examining the new philosophy of management that is fostered in local and central government and the theories and values that underlie it. Andrew Gray and Bill Jenkins trace the development of the new managerialism in central government over the 1980s and early 1990s, and discuss briefly the changes in local government and the NHS. They point out that the central arguments for the reforms concern efficiency and responsiveness, and that the changes are often represented as applying value-free 'tools' to the solution of commonly acknowledged problems. In this sense, the new approaches offer to take public administration out of politics. However, efficiency is to do with the meeting of goals with the expenditure of the fewest resources, and responsiveness begs the question 'to whom?' The detail of how goals are defined for the various services and how success in attaining them is to be measured is discussed in the various chapters. In general, financial pressures subvert the possibility of responding to consumer demands for high-quality services. In addition, the mechanisms for ensuring responsiveness are modelled on market systems, and the problem that demand from some groups is likely to have greater impact than demand from others, particularly at a time of resource constraint, is not adequately addressed. The argument indicates that it is as unrealistic to expect a purchaser/provider managerialism to be neutral as it is to expect the bureaucracy which it is designed to replace to prioritize responsiveness.

Chapter 2 focuses on the question of how far different European countries face corresponding problems and how far they are adopting similar solutions to them. In it, John Baldock shows how similar policies have emerged in a number of countries under a range of different titles (the mixed economy of welfare, the new consumerism, welfare pluralism, the third sector, the welfare triangle and, more recently, subsidiarity), but that it is essential to take the national institutional context into account in assessing their impact. Often systems which stress the kind of diversity of provision favoured by advocates of reform in this country operate in an institutional context where central control over spending and the general direction of policy is looser. Conversely, strong central control has often been linked to enthusiasm for state universalism. From this perspective, Britain is unusual in that recent changes combine greater centralization of power with the residualization of the Welfare State.

Chapters 3–8 consider the principal social services, each following a common pattern which covers the context of change, the policy debate, changes in the organization, management, funding and delivery of the service, the influence of developments overseas on UK policy and the impact of the new structure on service providers and users. The issues identified in Chapter 1 are examined in more detail. Policies designed to enhance efficiency in provision on the one hand and to develop greater consumer responsiveness and stronger opportunities for choice on the other may fail to achieve their objectives if efficiency is defined in terms of cost-saving and choice is subordinated to central control.

In Chapter 3, Ray Forrest examines the processes whereby the extension of owner-occupation, the increased emphasis on the role of housing associations and the cuts in public housing subsidy have led to greater divisions among home owners and the increasing residualization of council tenants. Chapter 4, by John Butler, deals with the new NHS settlement. Since the NHS has traditionally been the most popular welfare state service, and since controversy about the impact of spending constraint had been a major issue in the 1987 and 1992 election campaigns, the introduction of the new policies presented difficult problems for the government. The new settlement imposed a managerial system that divided the purchase of services from provision, so that the range of choice would be enhanced, and allowed hospitals to opt out of the NHS management structure and assume a quasi-independent 'trust status'. However, since professional groups in the NHS are influential, it was decided that doctors and health authorities should make decisions about access to hospital treatment on behalf of patients. At the same time, two mutually exclusive solutions to the problem of who should act as purchaser were adopted: some general practitioners (GPs) were permitted to become 'fund-holders', purchasing services on behalf of their patients. For other service users, the health authority is the purchaser. This gives rise to confusion in the service, which is likely to be resolved in favour of the GPs. So far, the radical impact of competition in the internal market in closing down the more expensive NHS hospital facilities has been mitigated by government, but there are indications that hospital closures will be allowed to take place in the near future.

Chapter 5 discusses the new technology of management in the personal social services as enshrined in the 1989 white paper on community care. Robyn Lawson describes the main vehicles for change: curbing local authority expenditure through central financial controls; the separation of the purchase of services from provision and the construction of quasi-markets; the recasting of local authorities in an enabling rather than a providing role; and the process of turning individual clients into consumers in the marketplace, facilitated by budget-holding care managers. She identifies the fundamental problem encountered by Conservative governments in implementing the reforms as reconciling needs and resources while maintaining their policy of reducing the power of local government. They have resolved the dilemma by giving local authorities responsibility for planning services yet retaining control over resource allocation at the centre. Many social service departments fear they face massive underfunding after the implementation of the new scheme in April 1993, and will be blamed for the consequent failure of the community care reforms.

Chapter 6 discusses social security reform. Here government has been concerned to develop private alternatives to state provision in areas like pensions (the most costly social service of all) and sick pay (which as been effectively transferred to employers). These shifts have only been achieved with the help of large subsidies to encourage people to move from state to non-state services. In the area of provision for unemployed and low-paid people and single parents, private alternatives are simply not available. The new approach has been evident in the establishment of an arms-length agency, the Benefit Agency, which has the role of delivering benefits to those entitled to them. Hartley Dean points out that much of the potential of new technology to enable the system to operate proactively, attempting to meet needs of the client other than those immediately presented to the agency, has been lost in the desire to save money in the development of the new benefits computer system.

In Chapter 7, Peter Taylor-Gooby deals with the new educational settlement. In this area as in housing, local government has lost much of its power. Schools can simply opt out of the local education system and be funded directly from the centre. The new managerialism is evident in the establishment of an internal market in which schools compete for pupils, or rather for the resources that they bring under the new funding arrangements. Central government retains strong control over the curriculum and over testing. However, there are problems in planning provision and in allocating pupils to schools, with the result that the system retains large numbers of empty places, it is difficult to close unsuccessful schools, the most successful schools seem likely to reintroduce selection and there is no mechanism to prevent individuals holding on to multiple places at different schools. Legislation in 1993 appears likely to resolve these problems by an extension of central control, so that central government will increasingly take over the direct funding of schools, decisions about school closure and the regulation of admissions policies.

Many of the features of the new managerialism in welfare are pre-figured in the story of the rise and fall of the Manpower Services Commission (MSC). Pat Ainley, in Chapter 8, discusses the way in which this agency sought to solve the problem of Britain's weakness in vocational training through the contractual management of a system of training places offered by local education authorities and private agencies. The cost of the system, the difficulty in monitoring the quality of provision and the inadequacy of training as a solution to the employment problems of chronic recession led to the closure of the agency. Part of its legacy has been taken up by the Department for Education in the new emphasis on technical and vocational schooling. The new training system relies on regional Technical Educational Councils, staffed mainly by businesspeople, who will administer training vouchers. The vouchers can be used to buy places on vocational courses available from private agencies or educational institutions. The scheme is experiencing severe difficulty in getting off the ground due to problems in finding people willing to serve on the Councils, budgetary constraint and the difficulty in monitoring the quality of courses properly.

The final chapter analyses different accounts of the new welfare settlement and assesses likely future developments in the organization and delivery of services. The new managerial approach mirrors developments in the private sector. In many areas of business, progress in information technology and in production techniques has made it unnecessary for firms to seek to control the processes in which they are involved by incorporating as many aspects as possible (from acquisition of raw materials to marketing and after-sales service) in one monolithic hierarchical operation. It is simpler and involves less risk to the parent company to separate out different activities, and for the centre to retain the core functions – planning, budget, monitoring performance – while other roles are hived off to semi-independent peripheral organizations. This approach is now evident in the shift from state bureaucratic provision 'from the cradle to the grave' to the new managerialism in which government decides what is to be done and enables consumers to obtain the service from a multiplicity of providers.

The logic of the new welfare settlement is imperfectly executed. In some areas (as Chapters 4 and 5 point out), professionals acting on behalf of consumers confuse the distinction between state as purchaser and the plurality of independent providers, since they have a foot on both sides of the line. Other services, such as social security and social housing, are concerned with the regulation of poorer people. The choices available to customers here are strictly limited and are combined with mechanisms designed to modify and direct behaviour, e.g. penalizing a presumed 'dependency culture'. However, tendencies within the system undermine the commitment of policy-makers to choice and diversity. Two issues are of particular importance.

First, the balance between consumerism and central power in many areas of policy is increasingly resolved in favour of the centre. This is particularly clear in the arrangements for setting up a national funding council to regulate grant-maintained schools, but also emerges in the strict budgetary regulation of NHS fund-holders and of social housing. Despite diversity in the detail of welfare administration, the centre will call the tune. Second, the balance of power in market transactions between provider and consumer is unresolved. In some areas, it seems likely that particular service users will be more attractive to providers – young and healthy patients, high-achieving pupils, tenants who can guarantee to pay the rent. These groups will get the most choice and the best service, so that there is an inherent tendency towards a two-tier system. Thus the new managerialism in welfare, as implemented by Conservative government, adds up to a strengthening of central control and greater inequality in outcomes for consumers – choice within limits, diversity between social groups.

1

Markets, managers and the public service: The changing of a culture

Andrew Gray and Bill Jenkins

John Major's election victory in April 1992 gave him a mandate for reform. One of his first appointments was that of William Waldegrave as Minister to oversee the development of the Citizens' Charter and the drive for civil service efficiency. Interviewed shortly after his appointment (BBC, 12 May), Mr Waldegrave described his task as ensuring that new forms of accountable management were diffused rapidly through the public sector while clients, citizens and consumers were treated as owners of the public service.

The European traveller newly arrived at Dover will undoubtedly be impressed by the public face of all this: Her Majesty's Customs and Excise will announce its Charter for Standards of Service while the bags are searched and then British Rail will advertise its Customers' Charter as the train limps across the Kent countryside towards its terminus in London which has become a shopping plaza. All this is the product of a set of events that have changed not only the way the public service is structured, but also how it operates and how it relates to citizens or 'customers'. In central government, for example, the dusty corridors are staffed by civil servants known as managers. They have budgets to account for, targets to be met and indicators to assess their performance (Flynn *et al.* 1990). Yet Whitehall itself is shrinking as much of its work is conducted by Next Steps executive agencies headed by chief executives and staffed by individuals exhorted to emphasize resource efficiency and customer care.

How have these changes come about and what is their effect likely to be? This chapter explores these questions by describing the background to changing conceptions of public administration and management that took place in the 1960s and 1970s. It then examines how new conceptions of public management emerged in central, local and health service administration. Finally, these changes are assessed in terms of their strengths and weaknesses and with regard to their consequences for the development and delivery of services.

Challenges to a culture: Management and rational planning

Any historical account of the development of the UK civil service or local government demonstrates that the traditional arrangements of twentieth-century British government developed as a deliberate effort to replace corrupt, inefficient and unreliable organizations by structures dedicated to a professional public service. The administrative class of the UK civil service, built on the foundations of the Northcote-Trevelyan reforms of the nineteenth century, was created to provide ministers and government with an elite corps of generalist administrators committed to the service rather than to any set of policies (Hennessy 1989; Drewry and Butcher 1991). In a different way, local government and the health service forged organizations based on professions and professionalism, in which technical expertise and responsibility towards clients, patients and citizens were encouraged. In both central and local government, however, the administrative machine also functioned to serve its political masters and to assist in the implementation (and possibly design) of their policies.

For most of this century, the public service has reflected such values as incorruptibility, equity and administrative professionalism. By the early 1960s, many critics believed that such a system was outdated. Among others, the Fulton Committee (1968) argued that the generalist ethos in central administration had limited relevance to the management of a modern state. During the same period, similar criticisms of local government, by the Royal Commission on Local Government in England (Maud 1969) and earlier Maud reports (1967), pointed to its inefficiency and structural weaknesses.

By the late 1960s and early 1970s, a consensus on the faults of central and local government had re-emerged. A particular problem was the absence of a rational strategy for planning and resource allocation and the lack of structures to facilitate this. This diagnosis, much of which developed out of ideas of what was best practice in the private sector (Gray and Jenkins 1982), can be found in the reform efforts of the Heath government in the period 1970–74, attempts to instal and develop corporate management in local authorities, and efforts to improve planning and resource management in the NHS.

In central government there had been concerted efforts during the 1960s to rationalize the allocation of public spending through the development and refinement of the Public Expenditure Survey (PES) (Heclo and Wildavsky 1981). The Heath reforms sought to provide a cutting edge to the PES through regular policy evaluations of spending programmes, a process known as Programme Analysis and Review (PAR). At the same time, efforts were made to improve the strategic capacity of the cabinet through the development of a

small 'think tank', the Central Policy Review Staff (CPRS). This would provide the centre of government with strategic analysis, assist with the co-
ordination of policy (for example, in the social welfare field) and perhaps nudge
ministers towards exposing their prejudices and thinking the unthinkable.

The stories of PAR and the CPRS are told in detail elsewhere (Gray and
Jenkins 1982; Blackstone and Plowden 1988). Here it is necessary to note only
that while they did not fail they never matched the aspirations of those who
designed them. Over a period of time, they slipped as political and administrative priorities and were eventually dispatched with few tears or mourners (PAR
in 1979, the CPRS in 1983). A similar fate befell corporate planning in local
government, while planning in the NHS remained mainly nominal with existing geographical and service inequalities relatively untouched by these fading
reforms (Ham 1982; Butler and Vaile 1984).

A failure of reforms in the early 1970s

The reasons for these failures of rational planning, policy evaluation and policy
analysis are often peculiar to individual cases. However, there are also common
strands, not least that many reform efforts failed to meet technical, organizational and political preconditions essential for their survival. In *technical* terms,
organizations could not satisfy the high information and skill demands of the
reforms. In *organizational* terms, the public service only rarely had in place the
structures and processes to link the changes to existing practices and sustain
the reforms. *Political* difficulties arose both within organizations (changes were
resisted by sections or groups whose activities were threatened) and from a lack
of political interest in sustaining reforms that were seen to provide little immediate (or often long-term) political advantage. In the face of such difficulties,
these reforms withered on the branch, leaving behind a sense that they had
been over-ambitious and had not addressed the fundamental problems of the
public service. These problems were a neglect of the basic skills of resource
management, an indifference to costs, and a failure to question whether many
of the activities undertaken by government and administered by the public
service in fact needed to be done at all.

Hood (1991) and Pollitt (1990) are among several writers who have
pointed out that while these reforms were under way, a number of factors were
combining to question both the form and function of British government and
its administration. These included the weakness of macro-economic management, the size of the public sector and its effect on private enterprise, the
inefficiency of the public service, and a recognition of the disadvantages of a
lack of competition in centralized state delivery systems.

Awareness of these factors can be linked to the collapse of consensus and
the polarization of party politics in the UK (Kavanagh 1987; Gamble 1988). As
Hood (1991) notes, these arguments also reflect the development of two different intellectual critiques of government organization and operation. The first
of these schools, that of the public choice economists, has questioned the ability

of governments to deliver services efficiently and of bureaucracies to act other than in their own interests (Dunleavy and O'Leary 1987; Dunleavy 1991). The second school is that of management theorists convinced that there is indeed a better way to organize and that the private sector has lessons that public sector organizations badly need to learn. Such lessons include strategies for organization, control, resource management and a concern with operational costs (Pollitt 1990). For those of the latter faith, management had for too long been a dirty word in the public sector vocabulary used to separate the artisan from the professional. What was required was a new public management.

By the end of the 1970s, the winds of administrative reform were blowing in a different direction from those at the beginning of the decade. Within public administration there was a common view that earlier initiatives had been too ambitious and wrongly targeted. Externally, the state was regarded as too large, too monolithic and too unresponsive to its public. Both perspectives combined to instal a new culture of management in government. In part evangelism, in part a pragmatic call for better quality in service delivery, this new public management (NPM) was intended to deal with both new and old problems. The greater part of the 1980s was to be taken up with developing and refining it.

The emergence of the new public management: Developments in British central government

To use the term 'new public management' may imply an unrealistic coherence in the developments described. It is questionable whether such a movement has clear values and embodies an identifiable culture. However, an identifiable movement towards an international redefinition of the way public services operate occurred in the 1980s. Hence Schick (1990), looking back over experiences in the 1980s in the OECD countries of Australia, Canada, Denmark, Sweden and the UK with regard to central government budgeting and departmental management, argues that the recent emphasis has been 'on fostering a managerial environment which is attentive to performance when funds are parcelled out' (p. 26). He goes on to note that in such a world the intention is to turn *spenders* into *managers* and to forge a tight relationship between *resources* and *results*. Structures are characterized by *administrative decentralization*, which is seen as 'a precondition for holding managers to account for what they spend and do' (p. 32). Finally, administrators are made to manage 'by nailing them down to the performance levels to which they will be held' (p. 33). Schick's review of contrasting but similar national experiences provides an empirical basis to the identifying characteristics of the new public management, namely an emphasis on *accountability, results, competition* and *efficiency*. This list can and has been extended (see, for example, Pollitt 1990; Hood 1991). However, it embodies the central tenets in a moral crusade to change the traditional orthodoxy of the public service. Thus the new public management is as much a doctrine or ideology as a simple neutral technique for improving performance and service delivery.

This account, however, is in danger of running ahead of itself. Changes occurred gradually and their effects were variable within and between the different sectors of government. The Thatcher administration in 1979 was, however, a watershed. The Conservatives were determined to hold down public spending, reduce the size of the bureaucracy (pursuing staff cuts as a policy in its own right), and held the notion, encouraged by sympathetic think tanks such as the Institute of Economic Affairs (IEA), the Centre for Policy Studies (founded by Sir Keith Joseph) and the Adam Smith Institute, that the public sector was inherently inefficient. What was needed was reorganization along the lines of successful private sector business.

Internal forces also pressed for similar changes. Within the civil service, the failure of PAR and the demise of many of the ideas of Fulton had been carefully considered. There was also a conviction (advocated by certain parts of the Treasury) that departmental spending needed tighter control and that a distinct management ethos must be created and sustained within both the central departments and their outposts (Gray and Jenkins 1991).

Efficiency scrutinies

These pressures for change gave rise to a number of separate but mutually consistent initiatives that were launched in central government after 1979. These included the creation of the Rayner programme of efficiency scrutinies. This took its name from Sir Derek Rayner, chief executive to Marks and Spencer plc, who after a couple of previous spells in Whitehall was appointed as the Prime Minister's personal Efficiency Adviser with a mission to seek out and cut back waste in central departmental operations. He headed a small team (the Efficiency Unit) located in the Cabinet Office and initiated a series of investigations (the scrutinies) that set out to identify inefficiencies in departments and present implementable proposals for savings. These scrutinies were carried out by the departments themselves under the broad supervision of the Efficiency Unit. The scrutinies were completed quickly (90 working days) and tightly focused. They were also supported by considerable political drive to produce results.

The scrutiny programme was more effective as a change agent than PAR had been (see above), not least because it was more coherent, more tightly focused, better organized and had a powerful political impetus behind it. However, the programme was not just about saving money. It was also about initiating what Rayner himself termed a 'cultural change' in Whitehall. Thus, one objective was to change the organizational culture to encompass a concern with resources and results.

Management information systems for ministers

The Treasury had been concerned for some time with the control of departmental running costs. Hence ideas, including those arising from efficiency scrutinies for delegating running cost budgets to departmental managers and improving departmental information systems, were sympathetically received. It was argued that public managers were habitual spenders knowing (or caring) little about resource costs. Few departments had developed information systems to aid management or cost control. There was also a concern that ministers or those at the top of any department often only had a hazy idea what those below them did and why. It was this type of problem that Michael Heseltine's Management Information System for Ministers (MINIS) in the Department of the Environment was designed to tackle, namely to provide an information base to strengthen top-down control within the department.

These developments reflected the belief that the culture of central administration needed to change, specifically that public management should emphasize the management of resources and the control of public expenditure. Such points were highlighted by the House of Commons Treasury and Civil Service Select Committee (1982). The committee praised Rayner and MINIS and sought to have the latter implanted in all departments. They also lamented the absence of a process equivalent to PAR and expressed concern that in the search for improved management in government, measurements of programme efficiency and policy reviews were being neglected (Treasury and Civil Service Committee 1982).

The Financial Management Initiative

The government's reply to the committee (House of Commons, Treasury and Civil Service Select Committee 1982) welcomed the enthusiasm for the strategies to improve management in government, but resisted proposals to reintroduce programme reviews. Rather it sought to proceed through the Financial Management Initiative (FMI). This would seek to promote the good management of the civil service as a policy in its own right through the development of management information systems and the processes of accountable management. It wold also serve to promote a new culture of public administration in which resource management was to be the cornerstone.

The FMI was seen and promoted as a major initiative. In the mode of Rayner, a small unit – the Financial Management Unit (FMU) – was created at the centre to facilitate its progress, although the actual development of the initiative was left to the departments. Throughout, the FMI sought to promote *accountable management* within and across departments in three major ways: the development of top management systems, decentralized budgetary control and performance appraisal. Here accountable management can be defined as 'a system in which authority and responsibility are delegated as far as possible to middle and junior managers who are made aware of and accountable for meeting their costs and other performance targets' (Gray et al. 1991: 47). It is this system more than anything else that represents the attempt to change the Whitehall culture.

We have written elsewhere on the development and implementation of the FMI, arguing that its application was shaped by the differentiation of government tasks, activities and traditions and by its political implications within departments (Gray and Jenkins 1985; Gray *et al*. 1991). For this discussion, these issues are of less importance than the fact that the FMI became the model for wider change initiatives outside central departments (e.g. in the police, probation, education and social services). The FMI represents a number of approaches not all of which are complementary. For some it is first and foremost a system for controlling *costs*, for others a more comprehensive system for planning, allocating and controlling *resources*, while for a few it is a more general philosophy and regime of *management* (Gray *et al*. 1991: 49).

Throughout the 1980s, the disciplines of the FMI were driven forward, most notably by the Treasury. Departments were pressurized to strengthen their financial management regimes, to develop performance indicators and where possible to advance top management systems. At lower levels, a generation of civil servants were drawn into an environment where they had to manage budgets and account for resources used. Failure to do this efficiently would probably lead to a loss of funds in the following public expenditure round. Thus the new Whitehall culture placed primary emphasis on the *management of resources* within a structure of *delegated responsibility*. As such, the focus was mainly on *finance*, with discussions of strategic objectives, priorities and effectiveness taking a back seat (Gray *et al*. 1991: 56).

Executive agencies

At the time of writing, the FMI has become almost institutionalized in government and its primacy supplanted by a further initiative in central government, the creation of executive agencies. These emerged in the wake of an Efficiency Unit (1988) study which concluded that the FMI had run out of steam and that further changes in the efficiency of central government organization could only be achieved by a radical restructuring of departmental organization. The study, known colloquially after its title as the 'Next Steps' Report, argued that departments were too big, ministers seriously overloaded, management neglected and that there were few positive incentives for civil servants to pursue quality of service and value for money. As a consequence, the report advocated the separation of executive operations from policy work and the hiving off of the former to departmental agencies that would remain under arms-length ministerial supervision but be free to manage their own day-to-day businesses. These agencies would be headed by chief executives and operate under a framework agreement negotiated between agency, department and Treasury that set targets and established performance indicators. They were to be given greater *freedoms* in their financial regimes and arrangements for personnel management.

The government accepted the proposals of the Next Steps Report in 1989. It established a small unit, the Next Steps Unit, under a senior civil servant Peter Kemp to advance the programme. Progress has been rapid, even spectacular by traditional government standards. At the time of writing, over fifty agencies have been created with another twenty or more candidates designated to achieve agency status in the near future. These agencies range from the Central Office of Information (700 staff), through the Meteorological Office (2250 staff) to the Social Security Benefits Agency (68,000 staff). They cover a very wide range of government operations and the objective remains to have over 80 per cent of the civil service in agencies before the end of the decade.

The development of agencies has been closely examined by a series of official enquiries (Treasury and Civil Service Select Committee 1990, 1991; Efficiency Unit 1991) as well by academic commentators (e.g. Flynn *et al.* 1990; Davies and Willman 1991). The official verdict from the Select Committee is that agencies are, by and large, a success. Questions have been raised about their accountability to Parliament and how far they have effective freedom from Treasury and ministerial interference, but overall, the agencies have been credited with significant improvements in the efficiency and responsiveness of services. Further, they are not seen as representing any political ideological stance, but rather as a transferable technology able to serve the policies of any political party (Smith 1991a).

Executive agencies represent a considerable change in the way government delivers its services. They also raise central issues in governance, some of which remain to be fully resolved. These include their relationship with their departments, the freedoms they can or should expect and their accountability to Parliament. Moreover, it is not yet clear how far framework regimes and their performance indicators and other targets will promote a new management culture. One fundamental tenet of Next Steps philosophy, for example, is that agencies will be better able to serve their clients or customers. This assumption is based on the argument that smaller, more clearly identifiable organizational units will attract a more motivated and committed staff who will take a greater interest in the recipients of their services. It also assumes that clients can identify more clearly with such an organization. However, establishing both who *is* the client of any public service and how far in a time of resource squeeze customer care can be given priority are both difficult and novel management problems for public service agencies. This point is made not to damn Next Steps but to demonstrate one of several tensions that underlay its operation, not least in the apparently competing concepts of efficiency and accountability (Flynn *et al.* 1990).

The ideas of Next Steps, therefore, draw together some of the major strands in the new public management as well as demonstrate some of its difficulties. At the macro-level, the move is from large homogeneous bureaucracies towards smaller, more tightly focused and responsive organizations. Next Steps involves a shift from a unitary civil service to a more federal system characterized by a diversity of working conditions, reward systems and career mobility. Agency administrators are first and foremost managers working under set budgets with their eyes on efficiency and customer satisfaction targets by which they will also be rewarded. How far they can be successful in all this remains to be seen, but there have been significant changes, the implications of which have not been lost on other parts of the public service as well.

Spreading the gospel: Local government and the National Health Service

So far, our discussion has concentrated on the emergence of the new public management within central government. However, the worlds of local authorities and health services have also been subject to headlong reform.

Local government

It would be difficult to overstate the changes in local government. Some now question whether there is anything substantive left of a providing model of local government in a climate of 'enabling' authorities, and 'empowering' parents, clients and citizens. Moreover, at the time of writing, there are governmental proposals to subject such bastions of professional local government activity as financial and legal services to compulsory competitive tendering (CCT). In addition, a Local Government Commission is undertaking a consultative examination of the merits of an English local government structure comprising unitary authorities (i.e. a system of single-tier authorities).

Local government has traditionally been a major service provider. Its historical logic is based in part on the idea that services are best delivered by elected bodies operating at a local level. Such a thesis rests on ideas of efficiency, responsiveness and accountability. While it is admitted that the UK is a unitary state and that central government has a responsibility for the determination of economic policy and ensuring equitable distribution of services, supporters of local government would argue that local politics are different from national politics and that centrally delivered services systems are generally neither efficient nor accountable in any local sense.

The case for local government within a liberal democratic state such as the UK is both strong and complex (Gray and Jenkins 1991; Stoker 1991). Supporters of local autonomy feel this case has been overlooked in a political vendetta against elected local councils carried out by politicians committed to extending central government powers. Thus the emphasis of public housing policy has moved from local authority departments to housing associations and other bodies, with much talk of efficiency, tenants' choice and the break-up of municipal empires. Similarly in education the talk is of 'empowering' parents and giving individual schools greater autonomy to run their own affairs, while the action has comprised the dismantling of the Inner London Education Authority (ILEA) and proposals to transform local education authorities (LEAs) into *enabling* rather than providing agencies. In the area of community care, local authority personal social service departments are to be designated as 'lead agencies', but even here they will operate by co-ordinating voluntary, informal and statutory services rather than offering comprehensive provision themselves.

These and other developments are examined in later chapters of this book, but they reveal common doctrinal and managerial assumptions about service provision, not least that there are managerial solutions to what may be essentially political problems.

The National Health Service

Changes in the NHS have proceeded down associated but in some ways different paths. Insulated from direct local political control (but not local political influence), the management of the health services in the UK has sought to deal with the problems of an inelastic resource base, rising expectations and drug and technological cost inflation. It has also attempted to grapple (generally unsuccessfully) with inequitable resource distribution, the priorities of service delivery and service development, and the influence and activities of powerful professional groups. Again the details and dynamics of this story are given later in this book (see Chapter 4). However, at this stage, it is worth noting that the solutions recently engineered to deal with these difficulties come straight from the new public management stable: emphases on general management and hierarchical control (Griffiths 1983), attempts to develop resource management and instal budgetary controls, and the development of internal markets and quasi-autonomous units (hospital trusts and general practice fund-holders) with their own budgets and enhanced freedoms over pay and the management of their own affairs. Like the civil service under the Next Steps, the new public management is taking the NHS towards a federated system of *semi-autonomous, self-managed* organizational units.

Politics and management in public services

The experiences of local government and the NHS reveal both the external and internal influences for change in public sector management and the public service even more sharply than the developments in central government. In particular, they demonstrate the *political* as well as the *managerial* forces for change and they highlight how particular strands of these have been caught up in a wider ideological battle.

The provision of local government services such as housing, education and welfare offer clear illustrations of this. For many public choice economists and new right thinkers, the traditional provision of services is subject to many if not most of the criticisms originally ranged against the nationalized industries: local authorities are monopoly suppliers of services, shielded from competition, subject often to union pressure that sustains restrictive practices, and uninterested in customers who are essentially powerless to 'exit' or exert sufficient 'voice' to change matters. The solutions are clear: monopolies should be broken up, systems deregulated to allow competition, and consumers should be empowered to move to other suppliers if they wish. Markets or quasi-markets will enhance the efficiency of service provision.

Such an analysis has an apolitical slant that is not accidental. To purists of this persuasion, local government should at best be minimal, perhaps meeting on an annual basis to award and assess contracts. Such analysts also deny any essential difference between *public* and *private* services that would invalidate the universal application of market-driven solutions. Indeed, such changes are seen to be neutral devices in the search for efficiency that politics and self-interest obstruct. However, local government is by definition a political body and, as such, is part of a pluralistic system of government. In the UK, central–local government relations by definition politicize the delivery of policies, which are themselves the product of choices among competing groups. In such a world, neutral management cannot be realized and terms such as 'efficiency' and 'effectiveness' become subject to political manipulation.

The foregoing is not intended to deflect criticism of the management of public services. Have many tenants mourned the passing of their housing departments or parents protested to save their LEAs? Where is the pressure group to rescue the county councils from extinction and what patient is concerned with the structure and accountability of the local district health authority let alone the region? The indifference these questions imply suggests that too often the structure and practices of public authorities and those who work in them have failed those they were intended to serve (Stewart and Clarke 1987). Thus the call for a *public service orientation* in which citizens and consumers are given a greater priority and political role, and the experiments with the decentralization of services and structures even within local authorities (Hambleton 1988).

Many of the developments described above, including central–local relations and government–health professional relations, have been driven first and foremost by the dictates of finance. In the case of local authorities, it was taken as fact from the mid-1970s on that local spending was out of control. Mrs Thatcher's successive Secretaries of State for the Environment were not the first to try (and fail) to devise a financial regime to control local authority spending. However, their policies have exacerbated the development of political differences between the Conservative central government and the urban Labour authorities over what local 'need' actually was, what represented a proper level or standard of service and how it should be managed.

The government's case in much of this debate was that many local authorities were badly managed and inefficient in their use of resources. Overspending was therefore a management problem driven forward by misplaced ideology. Inner-city authorities such as Liverpool, Hackney and Lambeth were castigated as villains, whereas frugal authorities, inevitably Conservative, such as Westminster and Wandsworth who sought market-driven solutions and held down spending and the community charge, were held up as exemplars. In turn, the victims blamed the grant system which they saw as loaded against them and their poor economic conditions exacerbated by national economic policy.

This debate *is* important because it throws up a number of issues often neglected in the discussion of the merits or otherwise of recent managerial developments. It is helpful first to recall the Layfield Committee (1976), which in the mid-1970s investigated the state of local government finance. Although most of Layfield's recommendations were neglected, the basis of its analysis remains valid, i.e. *the reform of finance and structure have to be considered together.* To fail to do so would only lead to chaos and muddle. With hindsight, experience in housing, education, personal social services and health, seems to have vindicated this analysis.

It is not necessarily true that all local authority, welfare and health services are well managed. Indeed, the question remains as to what 'good' management in this context is? One of the Conservative government's early reforms was the Audit Commission, an independent body whose task was to preach the message of good management in local government (and now within the NHS). This it has done over the years through specific work for individual local authorities and thorough comparative studies of services in a variety of authorities. Its work often reveals dramatic differences in spending on particular services or in running costs. The Audit Commission has been itself as an advocate of the new management – urging authorities to develop management systems, business plans and performance assessment systems. It is now helping them to cope with the 'enabling' role. Here, too, politics are often seen as an obstruction to efficiency, as in the case of school closures where local opposition may prevent the efficient use of resources or the optimal strategic management of schools (Audit Commission 1990).

The Audit Commission has a vision of what constitutes 'good management' and also of 'success' in running services, but not all local authorities agree with its definitions and judgements. In reality, it is not easy to determine objectively what good management is. Management is a means to an end rather than an end in itself and to define 'good' management requires some knowledge of what ends that management is intended to serve. Thus before making such judgements, it is first necessary to decide what the objectives of'local government and health authorities are and what structures and processes can serve them.

For the specific details of recent changes in service areas, the reader can turn to the chapters that follow. What we wish to stress here is that to understand these changes and the political and administrative structures that are emerging, one first needs to appreciate the changing political environment and the changing nature of central–local relations. These relations have been driven first and foremost by an economic ideology that has sought (though often failed) to restrain public spending and has been ideologically hostile to state provision. The failures have led the believers of the ideology to take out their frustrations on service communities by publicly castigating them and then tampering with service structures and financing.

Initiatives have therefore been resource-driven and assumed organizational inefficiencies. What the objectives of services should be, how they should be advanced and what structures are required are all neglected issues. As a consequence, policies have often been promulgated that contain multiple and conflicting objectives and are serviced by debatable theories. Such neglect has characterized the whole development of local government and health services since 1945. The complacency of the assumptive world of these services weakened their position in the face of the distinctive and focused attack of the late 1970s and 1980s. It helps to explain the lack of a public service culture, an issue which is now being raised as a by-product of a more incoherent debate about efficiency and resource management flavoured with a mild and sometimes confused concern for consumers. These are significant and important issues which, together with others, will be examined in the final section of this chapter.

Conclusion

Whether the new public management is a coherent concept or simply a collection of events, any account of its development must recognize that its momentum has been impressive. Its tenets have been seized on by a variety of governments in Europe, North America and Australasia. As a result, it is too easy to see it as simply a product of governments of right-wing free marketeers. In the Netherlands, New Zealand and Sweden, for example, many of its ideas have been pursued with almost missionary zeal by governments of the centre or left, while the countries of eastern Europe, aided by western government and western management consultants, are proceeding in a headlong rush to privatize state activities and train their administrators to appreciate the ways of markets and efficient management.

As Hood (1991) has noted, these developments might be explained by sceptics as yet another cycle of management fashions and fads, the latest version of the universal management solution, or what anthropologists would call a 'cargo cult' phenomenon, i.e. the idea that despite repeated failures the cargo of success will eventually be gained by performance of a ritual based on false interpretation of events long ago. These sceptical explanations do not account, however, for the rapid diffusion of the new public management in a variety of differing political contexts.

At least five factors have aided this diffusion. First, the legacy of past failures – foundered initiatives and lost (or never gained) controls – has conspired to give planning and rational management a bad name. Second, there have been the continuous economic crises through which governments have passed and which appear to demand drastic remedies. Third, there has been the disillusion with the performance of state services ranging from nationalized industries through to education and welfare systems, the causes of which are not always fully understood. Fourth, there is the break up of consensus politics into a polarization and in some cases now a fragmentation of government. Finally, shifts in socio-economic circumstances have been linked to rising public expectations and a general disillusion with politics, politicians and the state apparatus for which they are responsible. In such a world, the old values that underpinned public management may count for little, while those of efficiency, cost reductions and markets may serve the greater politics of self-interest that the new climate has fostered.

Has the new public management been a success? Its advocates claim that it has produced a number of benefits. First, it appears better geared to serve a market-driven system in which the role of the state is limited and, second, it replaces an old administrative model based on neutrality and professionalism that critics claim was either committed to nothing in particular (other than the *status quo*) or to advancing and preserving the interests of particular professional groups (for example, in health and education). These advantages are seen as reinforced by others specific first to public sector organizations themselves and second to those who work within them. It is also claimed that the new public management increases accountability, fosters efficiency and improves organizational performance. It does this by stressing the management of resources, providing better information on which decisions can be taken and hence leads to greater control. Over and above this it is based on a fragmented rather than a centralized organizational model in which the constituent parts have greater 'freedom', which in turn make them responsive and more sensitive to customer and client need.

There are also, it would be claimed, advantages for those who work in such an organization. They will have a closer identity with it since the unit will be smaller and more tightly focused and they will therefore 'own' the problems that they grapple with. This will strengthen motivation and foster awareness that faults and errors are an individual's or group's responsibility. A new organizational culture will be built embracing a loyalty both to the organization itself and to those it serves.

There is much that can be welcomed in the above model. Who could argue against efficiency and responsiveness in public sector management? Yet a closer examination of what is often prescribed as administrative reform might indicate that questions of values and identity are often discussed in general rather than specific terms. An organizational culture is first and foremost about values and identity, yet what are the values of the new public management and how do they compare with those of the old public or professional service? Examining this issue, Hood (1991) has argued that, depending on what values are emphasized, the design of administrative structures differs. A stress on honesty, fairness and equity leads to a different administrative structure than one on speed of response and cost minimization. It is therefore essential to determine what values administrative structures are attempting to serve. This leads to a questioning of the neutrality of the new public sector management, especially the argument that it is value-free.

The new public management represents elements of neo-Taylorism with all the problems that scientific management models of the past have displayed (Pollitt 1990). For example, it tends to argue that there is one best way to manage in all circumstances, that facts objectively measured speak for themselves, and that reward systems need to be linked to performance, however this is defined. All these claims are debatable not necessarily because they are *ipso facto* wrong, but because they conceal assumptions that need to be examined. Moreover, this argument can be taken further to question whether it can be assumed that good practice in private sector management is universally applicable in the public sector. Although it is often claimed that the private and public sectors are identical, the nature of relationships in private markets is often very different from that in public sector provision. In 'the private sector the basis of exchange is the contract between theoretically equal parties. In the public sector no such relationship can be assumed' (Walsh 1991: 14).

The new public management represents a political ideology of public service management and public service provision, using 'political' to refer not to a specific party, but to the advocacy of certain values, structures and procedures at the expense of others. This approach also determines in a particular way how issues are defined and dealt with and what is deemed 'good' practice and 'good' management in organizations. It is unquestioning rather than Socratic, it does not ask the 'why' questions of activities but rather assumes that an effectiveness of operation and service delivery will emerge from its procedures. This leaves many questions unasked. These include who represents the weak clients of many welfare markets (low in resources and incoherent in voice), and what will pull together in any strategic way the fragmented organizational systems that are often created. The new public management often denies the special characteristics of public sector markets and those who are affected by them, and assumes rather than demonstrates a link between results and reform.

Before results can be demonstrated, service performance must be defined and measured. Waiting list statistics may in the end tell us little about health care nor test results much about the education system. Parental choices may be rational in an individual sense but collectively disastrous for an effective education system in a particular area. These problems are political in that they depend on choices over values to be maximized rather than to be administered in a neutral and objective fashion.

Neutrality is a comfortable term. It was a hallmark of the Weberian bureaucracies that typified central government administrations of the past and, in a different way, of the professional services that dominate many welfare fields. The new public management has assumed a different mantle of neutrality, trading old values for new values and operationalizing these under a cloak of objectivity, cost minimization, accountability and the achievement of results. All of these claims can and should be questioned in specific service areas. In each it is important first to determine what type of policies are required and then to determine what organizations and mechanisms will serve them. Such an exercise may indicate that ideas of public service and public service management are fragmented but, as the following chapters will show, the problems that face governments in designing and providing public services at the current time may be too differentiated and complex to fit into a comfortable and universal dogma.

2

Patterns of change in the delivery of welfare in Europe

John Baldock

Introduction

For many of the public servants affected by the changes described in this book, it must seem that the last five or so years have brought a whirlwind of administrative reform. They have had to deal with the very real consequences – for them – of a government determined to shift the welfare role of the state from public provider to market manager. Local government managers are required to separate the purchase and delivery of services and frequently to contract-out provision; health service staff are forced to compete against other parts of their system to retain their funding; civil servants find their functions floated off to independent agencies; headteachers and staff are faced with the choice of opting out and confronted by a host of changes to their working practices. All these people might well ask whether similar, traumatic shifts are being experienced by their counterparts in other European countries or whether theirs is the singular outcome of a radical Conservative government. Are there more fundamental causes of what is happening to the administration of social services that lie beyond national politics?

It is the promise of answers to questions like these that make comparative social policy a tempting but extraordinarily difficult art. It is tempting because the differences and similarities between countries would seem to present a rich, natural source of data which it is foolish to ignore. It is difficult because of that very richness of information. Conclusions can only be reached by excluding most of the variety and complexity. Perhaps for these reasons the record of comparative social research is patchy. Witness the large literature that emerged in the 1950s and 1960s pointing to social and political convergence between

East and West, or the large body of work describing common patterns of 'modernization' in many nations. These have not turned out to be reliable indicators of the direction of social and political change. Observers tended to find order and pattern where time has proved diversity to be more important. This is the greatest weakness of comparative work and why it should always be treated with caution. Like most tempting activities, comparative social research should carry a health warning.

Nonetheless, comparative social policy is enjoying a boom. In particular, there has been much work recently that seeks to classify welfare states into different types. When it is done well, this writing can shed what appears to be a clear light on the complex variety of welfare systems (e.g. Flora 1986; Esping-Andersen 1990; Mishra 1990; Pfaller *et al.* 1991; Ginsburg 1992). Such extended comparisons and detailed classifications will not be attempted in the limited space available here, but they form the background to what must be a rather eclectic selection of information from a huge territory.

Three related issues are pursued. First, are the particular trends in British social policy with which this book is concerned part of a wider pattern of social policy change in Europe and, if so, how can the pattern be explained? Second, to what extent do European countries already have experience of the sort of changes being made in Britain? Third, what are the likely longer-term outcomes and, in particular, are state welfare systems being substantially weakened?

Patterns of change

A feature of the comparative social policy literature is that it attempts to show how similarities and differences at the level of the political are reflected in how welfare systems are organized and in the outcomes they produce. Arguments are usually advanced about the relationships between these three levels:

Politics $\Rightarrow$ organizational forms $\Rightarrow$ welfare outcomes

This book is largely concerned with the middle level, organizational forms. The comparative literature tends to give this level relatively less attention, despite the fact that organization is the mechanism by which political commitments and intentions are turned into welfare outcomes. This lack of emphasis on administrative matters is understandable, since they are often complicated and tedious, but to be regretted because this is the area in which many of the difficulties of comparative social policy lie. A central problem is that it is hard to find consistent relationships between organizational form and the other two levels which it inevitably links.

It is clear that the sort of reforms described in this book are by no means confined to Britain. The Thatcher administrations may have been the most noted advocates of market mechanisms in welfare, but their welfare reforms reflect a pattern of change that can be seen, to some degree or another, almost everywhere in Europe. In Britain, there was by the end of the 1970s a fairly widespread but inchoate concern across the whole political spectrum about the performance of the Welfare State, particularly about its spiralling costs but limited effect. Similar worries were to be found in all industrial societies (Flora 1986). The 'super-shock' of the oil price rises and the consequent worldwide recession had brought all industrial societies into an abrupt and unusual synchronization of their economic cycles. They all faced the same problems and constraints at more or less the same time. In Europe, the dominant welfare problems concerned the rapidly rising costs of social security and of health care in the face of higher levels of unemployment, an ageing population and worsening dependency ratios. The British response – 'Thatcherism' – was, however, distinctive. In most European countries, for example West Germany, Sweden and the Netherlands, the fact that government was to alternate between Christian and Social Democrats, governing only in alliance with smaller parties, meant that the debate about welfare had to be conducted in broader, more consensual terms. In Britain, on the other hand, effective political choice has been confined to a very limited range of solutions, partly because the simple majority electoral system has excluded opposition parties from significant influence on policy, and partly because the Conservative Party had been taken over by, what was for it, an unusually ideological leadership.

The central idea was to impose on state welfare what were believed to be the commercial disciplines of the market: income must determine expenditure; borrowing should be tightly controlled; people's wants are best measured by their response to price; expenditure decisions should be informed by knowledge about the costs of resources; those who could afford their own welfare should be permitted to purchase it directly rather than through taxes (Young 1990). The practical consequences of these ideological assumptions were attempts to return as much of welfare as possible to the market. In the end, pure privatization was only feasible in more marginal areas of welfare provision (Papadakis and Taylor-Gooby 1987). What remained in the state sector was to have 'pseudo-market' disciplines imposed upon it: cash-limited budgets, purchaser–provider splits, contracting out and the use of independent agencies to deliver services, the devolution of budgets to the lowest possible level, as near to the recipient as possible and often combined with the use of charges. This whole process of reform was given an extra special character by the Thatcherite dislike of local authorities. The amounts of resources available to them and the manner in which they used them were to be tightly controlled. Thus centralization of resource decisions was to be combined, paradoxically, with the devolution of responsibility for service provision.

However, the particularly sharp profile of Thatcherism has tended to hide, at least from the British point of view, the degree to which broadly similar decisions about changes in the operation of welfare systems have been reached across Europe. The terminology used to describe these changes is of almost infinite variety: privatization, contractualism, segmentation, shifting boundaries between public and private, commodification, re-mixing the formal and informal, social policy fragmentation, changing the welfare-mix (an excellent overview of this explanatory variety is provided by Evers et al. 1987).

Despite the range of concepts used to describe them, the practical changes in the delivery of social services show similar trends from country to country. In all the major European countries, governments have set up inquiries into the costs of social insurance and attempted to limit future commitments, particularly pensions. National health insurance arrangements have similarly been widely reviewed and where possible entitlements have been more tightly drawn with some items, such as home nursing, hospital 'hotel' costs, medicines and consultations with GPs, either excluded or charged for.

Some areas of welfare have been more vulnerable to reform than others. It has been more difficult for governments to curtail those social entitlements which are financed by some kind of insurance mechanism. Under these the state has usually, in effect, made certain specific commitments to individuals who have contributed premiums. It has been much easier to change those more marginal social services where people do not have insured, individual rights. Often these are areas of service provided by local and municipal government. Consequently, administrative reform which devolves more responsibility to local authorities has been a very common feature in recent years. It has often been justified in terms of greater co-ordination of services but, because local government is everywhere dependent to a large degree on central government funds, this frequently amounts to a 'contracting-down' of service responsibility without concomitant financial power. In particular, the provision of social care services, especially those for the rapidly growing number of frail elderly people, has been the site of much devolution and innovation in the organization of service delivery.

Frail elderly people are the fastest growing source of demands on European welfare states and, somewhat unusually for such a vulnerable group, they have often found themselves at the cutting edge of social welfare experimentation and reform (Baldock and Evers 1992). As in Britain, so too in Sweden, Norway, Denmark, France and the Netherlands, increasing responsibility for their personal care needs has been transferred from the health services to local authorities or municipalities. Forms of financial transfer have frequently been built into the relationships between health and social services to encourage the substitution of cheaper for more expensive services (Kraan et al. 1991). The need to provide domiciliary services within fixed cash budgets has become common in Norway, Sweden, Denmark and Germany. As a result, all of these countries have experienced reductions in the levels of home care services relative to population during the 1980s (Bertelsen and Platz 1991; Evers and Olk 1991; Thorslund 1991; Waerness 1992). In at least Britain, Austria, Finland and the Netherlands, there is experimentation with payments for care to dependent people or their carers to enable them to purchase the care they need (Evers and Svetlik 1992). Case management experiments, in which social workers 'buy' care from both public and private sources, have received considerable attention in Britain, the Netherlands and France (Kraan et al. 1991; Guillemard and Frossard 1992). Even in Sweden and Norway, there are the beginnings of a private home care service to tap these resources (Thorslund and

Parker 1992; Waerness 1992). In Germany, Sweden, the Netherlands and Britain, there has been a substantial publically subsidized growth in privately owned sheltered housing as a way of providing care (Kraan *et al.* 1991).

Overall, the pressure of demand for social care for the elderly has justified strikingly similar changes in the financing and management of services across European welfare systems. The key features are: the devolution of responsibility to the lowest levels of government; financial arrangements whereby local authorities and municipalities are effectively contracted to deliver services in return for cash-limited funds paid by the health sector or central government; the increased purchase with public funds of private and voluntary support services; growing efforts to stimulate or even buy and manage informal care; and a much greater emphasis on targeting and charging for social services. The effect of these changes is to emphasize financial and contractual relationships between various parts of the care system, to expand greatly the range of possible care sources and to make explicit the need for a managerialist rather than a welfare approach to service allocation.

What is less clear is the effect that these changes will have on the level of services provided. Do these reforms amount to tighter forms of rationing in the face of growing needs, or will they create the conditions under which needs can be more effectively translated into demands on the public purse? There is at least the possibility that sometimes the latter might turn out to be the case. For example, the community care reforms introduced in Britain from April 1993 (see Chapters 5 and 6) may serve not to control expansion but stimulate it. A genuine mixed economy of care, in which all the various actors are forced to negotiate continuously and to bargain with each other, may in the long run expose needs, provide more platforms from which to articulate it, raise public awareness and make social care issues more politically significant.

Anne-Marie Guillemard has suggested just such processes following the devolution of much social service responsibility in France:

> A 1986 circular made it obligatory for local authorities in France's departments to draw up a gerontological plan, which would adjust supply to demand. The 1986 Decentralization Act reinforced this requirement and called for such plans for other groups, in particular children and the handicapped . . . Policies are no longer governed by rules and standards adopted at the top level of the state. Social services are being 'dehierarchized'. This has set up a framework wherein actors adopt decentralized strategies adapted to local factors. These innovations create a local dynamic but with the risk of greater inequality. Standards and rules are negotiated and drawn up locally, and compromises slowly worked out. A consensus indispensable for collective action is worked out as actors adjust their responses. Since this consensus and these rules are perpetually reworked, the solutions adopted will be flexible – better suited for dealing with problems in the field and for the handling of fluctuating demand. (Guillemard and Frossard 1992)

This suggests that substantial social policy reform has its risks for government. Administrative reorganization rarely works out as predicted and attempts to control expenditures may sometimes backfire and produce the opposite results.

Explaining cross-national trends: Shifts in the welfare-mix

As has already been pointed out, there have been a very large number of attempts to explain common developments among welfare systems and some of these involve the construction of quite complex models and classifications. Any selection from them must, to an extent, be quite arbitrary. Here we will focus on arguments concerning what have been called 'shifts in the welfare-mix'. This is a fairly elaborate, managerialist set of ideas about how welfare systems are organized and change. Its main feature for our purposes is that it attributes much of the reform in modern welfare states not to the ideologies of particular governments but to more fundamental social and economic changes. If this argument is correct, then 'Thatcherism' was not an exception but rather an extreme example of the rule.

There is now an extended body of writing that explains the introduction of market mechanisms and consumerism into welfare as the particular manifestations of a wider shift towards a greater 'welfare-mix' in all European countries. The term 'welfare-mix' was first coined by Richard Rose (1985) and refers to the observation that people satisfy their welfare needs in three distinct arenas of production and consumption: the market, the state and the household. The production of welfare services by the state is often of less significance in people's lives than the role of household and market arrangements. Yet social policy after 1945 tended to be constructed either without much reference to the non-state sectors, or around unfounded, ideological images of them. This has changed. Governments are deliberately seeking a more explicit integration and balance between the sectors: a more explicit welfare-mix. In particular, governments everywhere are seeking to reduce the role of the state in both the funding and the production of welfare services.

Peter Abrahamson (1991), among others, has represented the welfare-mix of European welfare in terms of the 'welfare triangle' (Fig. 2.1). In the market sector, welfare is obtained through private purchases of goods and services and their allocation depends on money and the ability to pay. In the state sector, allocation is a reflection of political power. In the civil society sector, allocation is the product of forms of solidarity, the most important of which is the family, but other bases for mutual support are possible such as work, religion, ethnicity, gender and shared disability.

The triangle can also be used to characterize movement from one form of welfare to another. The movement to the west becomes *debureaucratization* as public welfare is reordered according to market mechanisms. Movement to the north is *commodification*, as support which was previously allocated as a part of personal relationships comes to be delivered in terms of welfare rules or ability to pay.

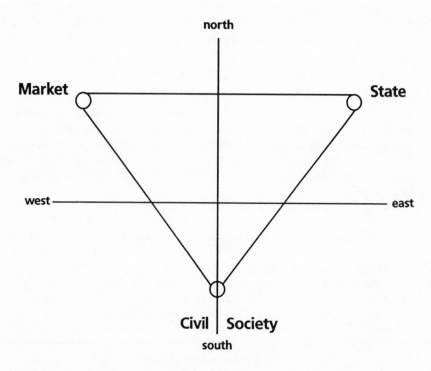

Figure 2.1 The 'welfare triangle' (after Abrahamson 1991).

Traditionally, Western Europe has emphasized market solutions, while Eastern Europe has favoured state solutions. In both the East and the West, the Southern countries – the Mediterranean region – have emphasized family, household and community assistance over both market and state programs, while such community forces have diminished in the North. (Abrahamson 1991: 239)

Abrahamson's broad thesis is that there is a European tendency to convergence towards the centre. Northern states seek greater integration of, and emphasis on, family and community sources of welfare. Eastern countries are increasing the role of the market. The southern European societies are modernizing and constructing both state and market forms of welfare production. Where the model fails is that it suggests that western nations are moving in the opposite direction, towards a greater role for state solutions, whereas the evidence is to the contrary. They, too, are increasingly emphasizing market mechanisms. Welfare systems everywhere appear to be shifting into the left-hand half of the triangle. However, this does not undermine the usefulness of the 'welfare triangle'. Reality will rarely conform to the idealized purity of a simple model. The diagram still serves as a useful summary of the potential variety of welfare-mix arrangements and a framework for describing and explaining the direction of change.

The reasons advanced for these Europe-wide policy shifts can only be summarized here. The common thread is that they focus on the constraints all governments face rather than the choices some make. First, governments perceive a political need to constrain public welfare expenditure, largely because of public resistance to higher taxes. At the same time, the rising dependency ratios produced by Europe's ageing population and greater unemployment mean that needs are growing relatively faster than the existing tax base. It therefore becomes necessary to find other ways of paying for welfare and market mechanisms provide these. Second, some public welfare services appear to have reached real limits in the availability of suitable staff to carry them out. This is a particular concern in the Scandinavian countries (Lagergren 1982; Thorslund 1991). Additional labour is sought, largely by finding ways to stimulate voluntary and informal care, sometimes through financial inducement. An example of this is the growing interest in 'payments for care' (Leat 1990) and 'paid volunteers' (Ungerson and Baldock 1991). Third, public services are perceived to be too monolithic and inflexible to respond adequately to people's needs: a greater variety of provision and more choice are required. Most welfare systems were designed for economic and demographic structures that have now changed dramatically. The post-war welfare states served relatively youthful, full-employment societies and their welfare needs could be catered for by mass, universal services. As social forms become more diverse and a much larger section of society has needs other than those generated by employment, so a greater range and flexibility in the provision of services is necessary.

The effect of a model of welfare change such as the welfare-mix triangle is that it tends to downplay purely political factors, such as the presence of a neo-liberal reforming government in Britain during the 1980s, and it emphasizes economic, demographic and social pressures shared by many European countries. For example, it can be used to explain why there is in almost every country, irrespective of political complexion, an increased use of charges and selectivity, and greater emphasis on the separation of provider and funding roles, on care-packaging and the tailoring of services to users. The relative impact of these pressures varies from country to country, but the direction of change is everywhere the same as governments are forced to adjust the burden between state, market and household.

The European experience of purchaser–provider splits

Much of European social provision is organized through compulsory, state-subsidized systems of social insurance. One of their principal features is that they have always separated the functions of paying for social services from their provision. The relationship between the funds and service providers are contractual ones built around agreements on costs and service provision. These are just the sort of relationships that are expected to appear within the British health service and between local authorities and service suppliers.

From the point of view of comparison with changes in the organization of the British Welfare State, the Netherlands presents a particularly interesting and challenging example. To put the issue in its crudest form, many of the methods now adopted in Britain to control and diversify the welfare system would to a degree appear to have long existed in the Netherlands and to have had quite the opposite effects to those intended by the British reformers. This is particularly true of purchaser–provider splits and the use of the voluntary sector.

The Dutch welfare system is an extreme example of the problematic relationships between politics, organizational forms and outcomes. It does not fit at all neatly into the classifications of welfare systems so beloved of students of comparative social policy. It has been variously classified as social democratic in terms of levels of expenditure and coverage and as conservative-corporatist in terms of political support and organization (Knipscheer 1992). On the face of it, the Dutch would appear to have gone far down the road to a pluralist, delegated and contracted-out system of social provision that the British government now advocates. In the Netherlands, much of the operation of social security (unemployment, sickness and retirement benefits) is delegated to independent funds run jointly by employers and unions, the employers characteristically paying 50 per cent of these pay-as-you-go schemes. In health care, the provision is largely by private and voluntary organizations funded by over seventy independent insurance funds. The provision of domiciliary and social work services is carried out by a large number of independent organizations that have their roots in the vertical, denominational divisions or 'pillared' nature of Dutch society. The role of central government is largely to regulate this system, whereas the role of local government is mainly to reach contractual agreements with independent organizations to provide services.

However, the consequences of this pattern of provision have been to create one of the most generous welfare systems in Europe. Sickness pay, for example, is generally equal to 100 per cent of lost wages, although the relevant legislation requires only about 70 per cent. Agreements between the union and employers responsible for the administration of the funds have tended to raise the minimum. In health care, by the mid-1980s, the Netherlands had the highest percentage of GDP expenditure and of hospital beds per head of population in Western Europe excepting Luxembourg (Chambers 1988). The health care system, less than 5 per cent of whose costs are provided directly by the state – the remainder coming from the compulsory sickness funds and private health insurance schemes – grew by 70 per cent in raw expenditure terms between 1976 and 1983 (de Kok 1987). In the provision of social care, the country has an exceptionally high level of institutionalization of the elderly – 13 per cent compared with 5 per cent in England and Wales – as well as a system of home care some three times as generously funded as that in the UK (Kraan et al. 1991).

It would, of course, be rash to jump to ready conclusions about the reasons for these relatively generous levels of provision in key social services. Any attempt to isolate the organizational causes from political and economic factors would be immensely complex and contestable. All that is being suggested here is what might be called circumstantial evidence that there is a prima facie case that a system that typically separates funding from provision and which nominally has many competitors in the provision of social services may be less than ideal as a way of controlling welfare spending.

There is some consensus in the Dutch literature as to the reasons why expenditure on the welfare system had 'got out of hand' by the mid-1980s (de Kok 1987: 126). Principal among these are the tendency of service providers to form what are effectively cartels, and of professionals to dominate the processes of price and task setting:

> Local organizations were part of national umbrella organizations, whose main tasks were policy-making, development work and lobbying. The élites of the national organizations had close ties with political leaders and good contacts with administrators. There was a good deal of consensus between all those involved: the growth of the social sector was their common concern. (Pijl 1991: 111)

In 1986, the Netherlands government appointed an independent committee to advise on a revision of the structure and finance of the health care system. The 'Dekker Report' was published in 1987 and argued that the core problem was the lack of instruments available to government to control costs in a 'complex, pluralistic health care system, with its highly institutionalised balance of power between government and private institutions' (Ministry of Welfare, Health and Cultural Affairs 1988: 13–14). The publication of the report precipitated a sustained debate in the Netherlands about alternative methods of organizing the health care system. Some have even argued for a British-style national health service:

> An efficient health service is so essential that nationalisation as well as socialisation of demand, is justified. If health care were provided by state institutions, then all decisions concerning investment could be integrated into a nationally agreed framework which could avoid things like over-capacity, undercapacity, imperfect regional distribution and imbalanced functional structures. (de Kok 1987: 130)

Other countries where social provision is organized through systems which depend on market-like relationships have exhibited similar tendencies to expansion rather than contraction. In Germany, much of social security and health and social care is organized through social insurance. Income insurance is compulsory but organized by employers and unions through a range of regional and national funds. On the whole, they have found it easier to agree on the expansion of benefits than on their limitation. Similarly, the health insurance funds are tending to expand their coverage to include social service functions. These slow but definite trends to more generous interpretations of entitlement appear to owe a lot to the institutionalized compromises that emerge over time between the different parties who in theory are bargaining with each other: employers, unions and government.

This is particularly true of the relationships that develop between, on one side, the health and social assistance funds, which pay for medical and care services, and, on the other, the independent organizations that provide them. Health and social care provision is dominated by large non-profit organizations. These have a specially privileged position under the German constitution, which effectively requires that government and the insurance funds should prefer them to both state and fully private provision. They have been able to establish a commanding market position, setting costs high enough for their own survival but too low to permit private competitors to enter the market easily. (Dieck 1989)

> These relationships have created a system of well-established co-operation between non-profit welfare organizations and public authorities, including parliaments at all state levels and social affairs administration at all levels too. All over the West, these non-profit welfare agencies are defined as inter-mediary agencies, standing between the public authorities on the one hand and the individual citizen or client on the other. (Dieck 1992)

These semi-monopoly relationships between purchasers and providers take a long time to develop. In both the Netherlands and Germany, they have grown over half a century and are now clearly seen as in need of reform. Might not a similar inbuilt tendency to expansion develop in Britain between government contractors and welfare providers? The limited evidence available so far suggests it might. A recent survey of 109 local authorities found only 23 having contracts with independent suppliers for the provision of domiciliary services (Booth 1990). Thirty-six contracts were involved, seventeen with private organizations (of which sixteen were for meals-on-wheels) and nineteen with voluntary bodies (of which thirteen were for day services). Only a third of the contracts had in fact been put out to a competitive tender (all of them meals-on-wheels). In no case had a voluntary agency actually had to tender, the arrangement was 'simply formalising a relationship previously based on grant-aid'. The researchers conclude, 'there is as yet no sign of a competitive market developing'.

The consequences of organizational change

Looked at from a British point of view, the recent reforms of social services in the direction of competitive pluralism would appear to be the particular result of governments with an explicit preference for market mechanisms. The sharp profile of 'Thatcherism' has tended to obscure the fact that similar changes are taking place across Europe, often in welfare systems which have hitherto been driven by rather different ideologies. This paradox is the product of two factors. First, as this chapter has tried to show, European welfare states from Scandinavia to the Mediterranean have faced similar combinations of budget constraint and demand growth. Some observers may question whether these pressures are inevitable or necessary – they have been called a 'demographic and moral panic' (Means 1986: 102) – but there is no doubt they have had their effect. Once those responsible for social services are faced with the need to achieve more within existing resources, it becomes almost inevitable that they will attempt to introduce greater competition within public services and search for resources beyond them. Current trends are in this sense almost a technical consequence of budget pressures.

Second, it is important to notice that even the ideological arguments used to support market-like innovations can cut across established divisions between the political left and right and between those who support state welfare and those who tend to oppose it. Again, this is a factor that has been obscured by 'Thatcherism'. Many European social democrats, for example, see competition between government-funded providers as a way of defending the Welfare State rather than of undermining it. This blurring of the traditional divisions over social policy has begun to happen in Britain too, where, for example, a Conservative government is making much of its 'Citizens' Charter', a policy area which might have been seen as more appropriate to the Labour Party. On the other hand, Labour has become more vigorous in its championing of the current community reforms than the Tory government which enacted them.

These are all examples of a problem pointed out earlier in the chapter – the difficulty of finding regular relationships between the three social policy levels of the political, the administrative and outcomes. European comparison would appear to show that very similar changes in the delivery of services are associated with different political rationales and with a variety of consequences from the contraction of welfare to its expansion. There are a number of ways of explaining these irregularities. One, which cannot be pursued here, is to be more discriminating in comparing and defining what may at first sight appear to be similar administrative and organizational changes. Saltman and von Otter distinguish between types of what they call 'planned markets'. On the one hand, 'public competition' can be a method by which governments that largely support state welfare seek to strengthen state social services by making different parts of them compete for funds and consumers. On the other hand, 'mixed-market' solutions force the state sector to compete with voluntary and private providers and are more clearly a potential way of weakening state welfare (Saltman 1991; Saltman and von Otter 1992).

The remainder of this chapter pursues a third and related resolution to the problem by suggesting that changes in the delivery of social services are in a sense 'policy neutral'. That is to say whether particular kinds of organizational change – the use of internal markets, for example – turn out to strengthen or weaken state welfare, depends very much on the ideological and political contexts in which they are used. In the Scandinavian countries, the consequences of planned competition will be limited by the continuing, strong commitments to universalism. In those countries such as Germany and the Netherlands, where welfare ideologies are more contested, the fact that control over social policy is less centralized will tend to protect it. Where Britain differs from many of its continental partners is that it is building a marketized, mixed economy of welfare on the foundations, or possibly ruins, of a universalist welfare state. The recent reforms to the welfare system have been able to combine the decentralization of delivery with the continued and even increased centralization of financial control. Central government in Britain has much greater control over the total size of welfare budgets than many continental governments enjoy, and therefore its ideological preferences are likely to be more potent.

In contrast, in those European countries where social insurance is the main instrument of allocation, centralized power is limited. The levels of both contributions and benefits are usually a matter for negotiation within management boards on which government is only one of the parties. In these societies, the very reason for the creation of insurance-based schemes in the first place was the absence of a broad political commitment to collective provision. As a result, the insurance funds were able to retain a degree of autonomy from government. In Britain, the limited range of benefits that are funded through social insurance are set by government alone, as is the level of contributions. For most of the rest of the welfare system, the size of expenditure is cash-limited and is decided entirely at cabinet level. This considerable, centralized power to control the volume of the public welfare is both the product of the British electoral system and the inheritance of a brief post-war period when there was widespread support for centrally funded universalism.

In Germany, the more diffuse control over welfare spending is reflected both at the level of political ideology and in the way welfare reform evolves:

> The German welfare state is neither a Bismarkian conservative one nor a pure product of the labour movement, but rather a mixture of both these streams of thought with more market liberal elements gaining importance over the last twenty years . . . Although we can find in Germany not only a 'mixed economy' of care but also a mix of different ideological elements, it is, nevertheless, interesting to see that a relatively stable ideological compromise has been achieved over a long period. (Evers and Olk 1991: 78)

These policy compromises are now under pressure as demand for social services grows at a time of economic stringency. However, the nature of the German political system, where governments rule only in coalitions and where the autonomy of the regional states (Länder) is considerable, means that reform has to incorporate concessions to all shades of opinion about welfare: liberal, conservative and social-democratic. This political framework of itself tends to generate a diversity of solutions and to extend public welfare responsibilities rather than constrict them.

In the Scandinavian countries, on the other hand, until recently government has been almost monopolized by social-democratic parties and their welfare systems have 'been constructed on a needs-based command-and-control model' in which planners evaluate demographic and epidemiological patterns and then allocate money and personnel accordingly (Saltman 1991: 615). One consequence of this centralization of decision making about resources has been that the Scandinavian states have been relatively more successful in restraining the growth of public spending in recent years than have the more corporatist states like Germany and the Netherlands. For example, in Sweden, the social-democratic hegemony has allowed not only 'socialist ideology and rhetoric to remain the rationale for the party's existence and a benchmark for ideological renewal, but populist pragmatism and political realism to shape much of the party's policies in government' (Ginsburg 1992: 31). There is evidence of this combination in the recent changes to the organization of Swedish health services:

> Confronted by increasing pressures during the 1980s from an ageing population, intensive new medical technology, and tightly constrained public sector budgets, Nordic health systems have begun to search for new models of health service delivery that incorporate at least some elements of market-oriented systems. The current situation can be viewed as a search for 'planned markets' that combine market-style incentives with certain residual planning mechanisms. The objective of this effort is to overcome the traditional planning model's problems of inefficiency, rigidity and insularity and to respond to the new challenges faced by publically operated systems, while avoiding the adoption of the neoclassical market model with its own clear set of liabilities. (Saltman 1991: 615–16)

Similar changes are taking place in other areas of Swedish provision such as community care (Kraan *et al.* 1991). Yet this search for market-model solutions takes place with a widely shared consensus as to the extent of public responsibility. There is no sign that even the new centre-right government that won power from the social-democrats in 1992 will attempt to substantially dilute a public commitment to, for example, a health system that seeks to provide 'care on equal terms for the entire population, guaranteed regardless of age, sex, nationality, residential locality, financial resources and powers of initiative, ethnic identity and cultural differences' (Diderichsen and Lindberg 1989: 223).

Conclusion

While it is true that experiments with internal markets and the delegation and contracting-out of service provision are remarkably widespread in western European welfare systems, the consequences are often limited: in the Scandinavian countries by the continued ideological primacy of universalism; in the more liberal and conservative societies examined here by the fact that a pluralism in service organization is subject to a greater decentralization of political control. In Britain, by contrast, the centralized power of a universalist welfare state has fallen into the hands of a government committed to a residualization of state welfare.

3

Contracting housing provision: Competition and privatization in the housing sector

Ray Forrest

The context

State housing provision in Britain has for most of this century been associated with the management and ownership of council housing by local authorities. Council housing as we know it today has its principal origins in the housing conditions and legislation of the 1920s. The context was one of substantial housing shortage, the decline of the private landlord and the necessary but negative consequences of rent controls, rampant urbanization and the social dislocations occasioned by the 1914–18 war (Merrett 1979; Malpass and Murie 1990). Since that period, its history has been one of continuing if uneven growth. In 1938, roughly one in ten dwellings were in the council sector. By 1971, almost one in five households were renting from local authorities. At its peak, in 1980, a third of the British housing stock was in the public sector (Department of the Environment 1977; Central Statistical Office 1991b). These national statistics conceal substantial regional variations. For example, in 1981, 52 per cent of households in Scotland were council tenants, compared with 23 per cent in the South-East (excluding Greater London).

These statistics emphasize the enormous importance of direct state provision of housing in Britain and paint a contrast with the patterns of provision for working-class households which evolved in most other western European countries. More typically, social housing was provided by a range of institutions such as employers, religious and quasi-religious organizations and charities or through conditional subsidies to private landlords. In the Netherlands, for example, social housing has a more pluralistic base in the voluntary housing association sector, while local government has a relatively limited role in housing provision. In Germany, the chosen vehicle for low-cost rented housing has been the provision of state loans to private landlords with attendant obligations to house low-income tenants until the loan expires (see, for example, Ball *et al.* 1988; Leutner and Jensen 1988). In some respects, therefore, the virtual monopoly of social housing by local authorities and the size of the sector by the end of the 1970s locates the tenure structure of Britain more comfortably in the context of some former state socialist societies than in western capitalist ones. The recognition of the peculiarities of British council housing also guards against drawing unwarranted parallels with apparently similar policy trends in other capitalist nation-states. Different institutional and housing tenure structures offer different policy conditions and possibilities. To put it bluntly, the state cannot sell what it does not own. The kinds of privatization policies pursued in Britain throughout the 1980s would simply not be feasible in countries with small public housing sectors.

The growth of the council housing sector in Britain has been paralleled by the expansion of individual home ownership. In 1938, a third of households in England and Wales owned their own homes. By the early 1980s, the figure was close to 60 per cent. Again there are strong regional variations with home ownership more dominant in southern Britain outside London. The development of a large, mature owner-occupied sector with relatively youthful entry also sets British housing apart from many other countries in western Europe. The private landlord has been squeezed by direct state provision on one side and mortgaged home ownership fuelled by tax reliefs on the other. Until the early 1980s, both main housing tenures grew independently of one another through new building and transfers from private renting.

The growing dominance of council housing in the rented sector and its monopolistic position should not conceal the very real differences that exist between housing and other areas of social provision. Unlike health or education, it has always represented minority provision for sections of the working class. The eclipse of the private landlord was largely through the development of a new form of private provision, owner-occupation. Middle-class interests were largely tied to that sector. For this reason, the 'sharp elbows' of the middle class have played little part in the defence of council housing and public housing is one of the few areas of the Welfare State which have unambiguously benefited the poor rather than the better off. As Raynsford (1991) has observed, no government minister has thought it necessary to claim that 'council housing is safe in their hands'.

Housing is also different by its very nature. It has a fixed location and is consumed on an individual basis. Council housing has also always involved the payment of fees (rents) and was in the main built by private developers and financed through borrowing on the private money markets. It is important to recognize the particular social role of council housing, its limited decommodification and its position in what has always been a predominantly private housing market. While the attack on council housing was very much in the vanguard of the broader privatization strategies of the Thatcher governments, it could be argued that the state in housing (at least in terms of direct provision) was rather less pervasive than in other areas. Municipal landlordism dominated the rented sectors, but in most localities it was the private sector which was the dominant provider either through mortgaged owner-occupation or private renting.

The policy debate

With the election of the first Thatcher government in 1979, the decline of council housing and the growth of home ownership became clearly inter-twined. The Right to Buy scheme for local authority tenants was attractive to the Conservative Party for a number of reasons. It circumvented recalcitrant (usually Labour) local authorities, reduced the size of the council housing sector, promoted the further growth of home ownership and delivered sub-stantial and increasing fiscal benefits in the form of capital receipts (for a detailed account, see Forrest and Murie 1991). In policy debates on privatiza-tion, however, housing differs again from other areas of social policy. The broad shape of privatization policies in housing was established well before the late 1970s and 1980s and is not the product of the New Right thinking of that period. Council dwellings had been sold in relatively large numbers in the 1960s and 1970s and it had been possible to sell dwellings to tenants almost since the inception of council housing. Indeed, the Right to Buy was one of the few fully worked out privatization policies in the 1979 Conservative Mani-festo. According to Bell and Cloke (1989: 1–2):

> At the outset of the Thatcher government there was little indication that the New Right predilection for privatisation would become so domi-nant . . . The emphasis quickly changed, however, as some tenets of monetarism were gradually eased into the background and privatisation initiatives were brought to the fore.

Local enthusiasm for selling state-owned dwellings, therefore, predated the radicalization of the Conservative Party in the 1970s or the more apparent anti-municipal stance of the 1980s. Leading members of the Conservative Party had published proposals to sell council houses in the 1960s (Corfield and Rippon 1965; Howe 1965). Current proposals to convert rents into mortgages have their origins in suggestions made by Peter Walker in 1977.

Given this history, it is not surprising that the justifications for transform-ing council housing were not initially about introducing competition or in-creasing efficiency. They were expressed principally in terms of widening ownership, enhancing freedom and contributing towards the realization of a property-owning democracy. Pirie (1985) refers to council house sales as a process which involves the creation of new groups with vested interests and emphasizes the strong antagonism among Conservatives to the perceived use of council housing as a source of power and electoral influence. In a similar vein, Bulpitt (1983) refers to the perception within the Conservative government of an increasingly corporatist alliance in local affairs between trades unions and councils. From this perspective, the Housing Act 1980 sits with other legislation such as the Transport Act 1980 and the Education Act 1980 as an attempt to open up local government to ordinary citizens – a strong central state creating political space for individual choice and expression. The Right to Buy could be represented as a purer form of decentralization than was on offer from the Left.

The evolving policy debate in housing throughout the 1980s had its origins therefore in a long-standing political polarization along housing tenure lines and in initiatives which had been developed well before the election of the Thatcher administrations. There was nothing new about selling council houses. What was new was the statutory right given to tenants, the removal of discretion from local authorities and the changing structural relationship between home ownership and council housing. By the early 1980s, private renting had been reduced to a residual rump and the scope for further transfers from private renting to home ownership was severely limited. The relationship between the state housing sector and owner-occupation was therefore increasingly oppositional. If home ownership was to continue to expand, then tenure transfers would have to come from the public rather than the private rented sector.

The point is that the policies towards state provision in housing in Britain were being shaped in the context of an already highly developed private market with a range of specialist agencies and institutions. This is in contrast to many other countries and to earlier periods in Britain and may be part of the explanation for the relatively rapid progress of privatization in this country. Maintaining the growth of home ownership was important to a variety of interests and was generally regarded as a popular political platform. In contrast to some accounts which represent housing privatization as primarily demand-led (Saunders 1990) or as a reaction to dissatisfaction among tenants, it may be more appropriately seen as sustaining the growth of home ownership and extending political promises.

Policy and legislation in the housing field in the early 1980s can be understood as an acceleration and accentuation of previously developed ideas. A different emphasis did however begin to emerge in legislation and debate from 1986 onwards. What could be seen as previously paternalistic concerns to extend individual home ownership to sections of the working class gave way to more broadly based attempts to privatize the housing service and erode local government involvement. In 1985, a publication of the Adam Smith Institute argued that 'There is scope . . . for taking the whole problem of housing out of the local political arena, and contriving a situation in which both ownership and rent are regulated not by political whim but by demand for them and the supply which can be generated to meet it' (Butler *et al.* 1985: 43). This shift of emphasis from encouraging home ownership as the principal element in the policy package towards the full-scale dismantling of council housing finds political expression in a Ministerial statement by William Waldegrave, then

Minister of Housing, in 1987. He stated that, 'It is an oddity confined largely to Britain among European countries that the state goes landlording on this scale. The next great push after the Right to Buy should be to get rid of the state as a big landlord and bring housing back to the community.'

By the mid-1980s, there was little to choose between the two main political parties on the issue of council house sales. Whether for reasons of principle or political pragmatism, the Labour Party had accepted selling council houses to sitting tenants as a desirable policy. The Party differences revolved mainly around new building programmes. The Labour Party was in favour of council house sales in the context of replacement through new building. For the Conservatives, if there was a need for more rented housing it should be provided by the private or voluntary sector.

The policies pursued towards council housing until the late 1980s (and the progressive breakdown of any resistance to tenure transfer) were buttressed by evidence of the overwhelming preference for home ownership in the population as a whole and among council tenants. A procession of surveys showed that home ownership was increasingly favoured and that public tenants approved of council house sales as a route into that tenure (for a review of this evidence, see Forrest and Murie 1990a). However, the shift from promoting home ownership to advocating a more pluralistic landlord structure and a greater market orientation in the delivery of services to tenants raised quite different issues. Here there was no popular mandate as evidenced by opinion surveys. The same surveys which showed the popularity of home ownership also showed that private landlordism was the least preferred option. They also showed that while satisfaction among owners was higher than among public sector tenants, it was by no means the case that council housing could be said to be unpopular. It must be acknowledged that the interpretation of data on satisfaction is fraught with difficulties. Nevertheless, surveys of satisfaction among council tenants on whatever basis show an overwhelming majority giving a favourable response. A survey in 1989 by the British Market Research Bureau found only 10 per cent of council tenants expressing dissatisfaction with their housing. The latest British Social Attitudes Survey found rather more at 19 per cent – still however a clear minority (Jowell et al. 1991).

All this is not to suggest a complacent attitude towards state housing but to set current policy developments in a proper context. The delivery of housing welfare through the council system has, on balance, been a success rather than a failure. It is not possible to 'read off' from the evident support for council house sales some measure of disenchantment with the management and delivery of state housing. Tenants may desire substantial improvements in the quality of service they receive from a local authority but they do not necessarily believe that the solution lies in the privately rented sector or through transferring from a large municipal landlord to a housing association. From this perspective, it is those tenants who had benefited most from the periods of relatively high-quality new building in the state sector who derived most benefit from sitting tenant purchase. There is substantial evidence that many council house purchasers could have bought a property elsewhere in the private sector (Forrest and Murie 1991). They bought through the Right to Buy because they got a well-maintained valuable asset at a discount, not because they were dissatisfied with council housing. Government has had less success with other policies for reducing the number of council tenants and for dealing with those tenants unable or unwilling to purchase their properties. State tenants, it seems, do not want to exit from the council sector regardless of the destination.

Policy changes

Housing policy throughout most of the 1980s can be summarized as measures to extend and promote home ownership either through the maintenance of tax relief on mortgages or through various low-cost schemes with the Right to Buy being by far the most prominent and important. In parallel, investment in new building for council housing was consistently reduced so that the public sector was squeezed in terms of both disposals and reduced new build. As the decade progressed, it became evident that there was a growing lack of rented accommodation, since private renting was also continuing to decline. And it was clear that while council house sales would continue to provide a route into home ownership and a stream of capital receipts to the Treasury, they would not of themselves comprehensively reduce the council housing sector.

The Housing and Planning Act 1986 continued the trend to extend discounts for sitting tenant purchase and tighten up sales procedures. However, it also facilitated the sale of whole blocks of dwellings by councils and the possibility of delegating housing management functions. It was made easier to dispose of empty blocks of dwellings to developers for refurbishment and resale or to sell off tenanted estates to private trusts or developers. Usher (1987: 16) observed that the legislation 'was offering an avenue for local authorities starved of capital and prevented from renovating their own stock to dispose of it to the private sector'. The Act also made it possible for the local authority to appoint an agent to undertake housing management functions. Agents could include tenant cooperatives, private sector management companies, building societies or indeed any organization approved by the Secretary of State. From a tenant's point of view, the important aspect was the lack of consultation with tenants should a local authority wish to pursue these options. The possibility of substantial, large-scale sales of local authority estates to developers (as opposed to such disposals which had previously occurred on a *laissez-faire* basis) provoked some tenant resistance and the formation of a Campaign Against the Sale of Estates. It would be wrong to exaggerate the scale of this reaction, but it was nevertheless indicative of greater circumspection among public sector tenants towards the emerging policy agenda.

The shift towards a stronger market ethos in the management and delivery of public housing, market value rents and a more pervasive reliance on market processes in the delivery of rented housing generally, and away from a narrower concern with home ownership through asset sales, was more explicit in the main provisions of the Housing Act 1988 (Murie *et al.* 1989). Here the emphasis was on the revival of the private rented sector through rent deregulation (further assisted by extension of the Business Expansion Scheme in the 1988 budget to cover new investment in private rented accommodation), procedures to enable tenants to opt out of local authority control, the creation of Housing Action Trusts (HATs) and a new financial regime for housing associations. Local authorities were envisaged as performing a much reduced role in the supply or management of housing in the future. In their new strategic or enabling role, local authorities would be expected to encourage innovations by other housing institutions and organizations and to maximize the use of private finance.

The proposals giving tenants a right to choose their landlord were particularly controversial. Tenants could approach alternative landlords or be approached by them. Tenants could form cooperatives and be responsible for the management and budget of their estate. There were suspicions, however, that this was a measure to open up the more desirable and profitable parts of the council sector to predatory housing associations and private landlords. Furthermore, the balloting procedures to ascertain tenants' views of such proposals seemed to confirm a built-in bias against the local authority. Those eligible to vote but not doing so were taken to be in favour of a transfer proceeding. This was close to 'inertia selling', a practice frowned upon by consumer organizations.

The establishment of HATs provoked equal suspicion. The trusts were intended to tackle the problems of run-down estates. Areas of public housing would be removed from local authority control, renovated and repaired through public and private partnership and after a limited period passed on to other forms of ownership and management. Initially, there were proposals to set up HATs in six inner-city areas. They were either abandoned or delayed because of tenant resistance. Woodward (1991) provides an account of tenant resistance to a proposed HAT in Tower Hamlets. This resistance centred on fears over reduced security of tenure, rising rents and the uncertain future role of the estate. Although the estate itself was run-down and of low quality, the land was valuable with potential for gentrifying redevelopment.

Originally, there were no procedures to ballot tenants on proposed HATs. When this was conceded by government, it effectively undermined the policy. 'Originally the Government budgeted for £125 million to be spent on HATs between 1988/9 and 1990/1. In the event all that may end up being spent is less than £2 million – all on fees to consultants looking into the viability of HATs which were ultimately rejected by tenants' (Hills 1991: 27). HATs have subsequently emerged in a different form – albeit in a small number of cases – as partnerships between local authorities and the private sector. The context and the probable consequences in terms of ownership and control are, however, rather different from the initial intentions. These new-style HATs are at the initiative of the local authorities and after a period may well revert to local authority ownership. They are in effect a way for local councils to qualify for the earmarked resources which have not been used as they were originally intended.

Tenants' choice has also met a similar fate. After the legislation emerged, government talk of private landlords soon gave way to an emphasis on socially responsible social landlords – principally housing associations. By May 1990, only one formal application had been made; on the Walterton and Elgin estate in Westminster by tenants who had formed their own housing association (*Hansard*, 10 May 1990, cols 188–189). One of the primary motivations was to protect the stock of dwellings from the privatizing tendencies of the local authority.

It is voluntary transfers rather than enforced or predatory transfers which have taken off and which are likely to accelerate. These are transfers initiated by the local authorities themselves to newly established housing associations. By mid-1991, some 100,000 properties involving seventeen local authorities had been, or were in the process of being, transferred (Kleinmann 1993). Such transfers are possible under sections 32 and 43 of the Housing Act 1985. As with HATs, the initial intention of such transfers has effectively been subverted. While the effect of voluntary transfers is inevitably to reduce the size of the stock labelled as council and provide a significant boost to the housing association sector, it may involve the exchange of one monopoly landlord for another. Moreover, it often involves the same personnel with the new landlord taking over most of the existing staff of the local authority housing department. While the motives vary from one authority to another, in many cases it is connected with escaping from central government constraints on local authority finances and thus allowing more scope for new building and redevelopment, and to protect the stock more effectively from the Right to Buy. Kleinmann (1993) refers to the effect of stock transfers on gearing ratios, that is the ability to borrow against the asset value of the stock, which is increased when dwellings are in the housing association rather than the council sector. Councils and housing managers have therefore been making increasingly creative use of legislation originally designed for other purposes. Whereas stock transfers were devised as part of a consumer/tenant-led strategy to reduce the dominance of council housing, they may in practice have become a management-led strategy.

There are three aspects of stock transfers which are of particular interest. First, there is an erosion of tenants' rights. Tenants have to balance an uncertain future that could be an improvement on remaining as council tenants against becoming *assured* rather than *secure* tenants. They retain the Right to Buy as existing tenants, although this right is lost to new tenants – one of the attractions of transferring from the point of view of managers. Second, the Right to Buy, which has been so important to Conservative government strategies, generates problems in stock transfers. It is difficult to value a stock which could disappear at an uncertain rate and affect rented income and capital receipts in varying ways depending on the vagaries of the economy and property market (see Gardiner *et al.* 1991). Privatization measures devised for one purpose can become therefore a problem for subsequent phases. Third, the transfer of stock from the public to the independent or private sector on any scale could absorb substantial amounts of investment from the Housing Corporation and the private sector. At the moment, 150 councils are said to be contemplating voluntary transfer at an estimated total cost of £10.5 billion (Roberts 1992). This represents around 40 per cent of all local authorities in England and Wales. So far, however, it is mainly councils with small public sector stocks which have shown serious interest in voluntary transfer. Any transfers of large metropolitan stocks would involve enormous capital sums.

The legislative and policy changes discussed above must be linked to a long-standing tug of war between central and local government as regards the financial regime for council housing and the relative autonomy in this sphere for local administrations. For the purposes of this chapter, it is inappropriate to go into a detailed account of what is a relatively complex area (see, for example, Malpass and Murie 1990; Malpass 1991). However, it is necessary to outline the main changes which have occurred following the Local Government and Housing Act 1989. The legislation had two particular features. First, the Housing Revenue Account (HRA) becomes a self-standing account which is effectively ring-fenced to prevent transfers to and from the General Fund of a local authority. The intention is to create a clearly defined account for the provision of council housing in which the net cost of services not met from subsidy would have to be covered by rents. The effect is to force a thorough assessment of what precisely is involved in the provision of the service. This task is not without its difficulties, but is essential if purchaser/provider functions are to be increasingly separated through subcontracting and compulsory competitive tendering (CCT). A second related feature is a redefinition of housing subsidy which conflates housing cost subsidies for tenants and subsidies provided to cover the gap between the costs of providing a service and revenue. Malpass (1991: 172) sums up the general effects of these changes as follows.

> The most important point here is that together these two elements give central government much greater control over HRA income and, there-fore, rents. Under the 1980 system, at least as it was operated after 1982–3, central government had little real control over rate fund contributions or rent rebate subsidy, the former being a matter for local decision, the latter being determined by tenants' incomes and unrelated to the state of the HRA.

This concern by central government to enmesh income maintenance sub-sidies within the new financial regime for local authorities was understandable given the high proportion of tenants on state benefits – some two-thirds by 1986–87. The problem from the point of view of central government was that there was a progressive weakening of the link between tenants' ability to pay and locally determined rent increases. Central government, through housing benefit, was picking up an ever higher proportion of the bill. In simple terms, therefore, the idea was to include the housing benefit element in the overall assessment of local subsidy. Through this move, nearly all local authorities are brought back into subsidy and central government achieves greater leverage on council rents. Prior to the new financial regime, in 1988–89, aggregate subsidy amounted to less than £500 million. Under the new regime, the redefined aggregate subsidy is over £3000 million (Malpass 1991: 175).

In focusing on changes in management structures and styles, we should not be mesmerized into forgetting the strong grip which is imposed by central government on local housing finance. This is nothing new, but it is important to set discussions of decentralization, the separation of purchaser and provider, the enabling council, management sensitivity and responsiveness within a context which recognizes the constraints within which local authorities have to operate. There is a legitimate concern that the underlying motivation is one of cost-cutting and the further erosion of local autonomy – of providing housing services on the cheap and at the same time removing much of the responsibility from elected local councils.

The need for changes in the management of state housing is widely recognized and certainly precedes the election of the first Thatcher administration. A concern with user-interests and decentralization was evident in the 1970s. What remains unclear is whether the acceleration of organizational and other changes – from the Right to Buy through voluntary transfers to compulsory competitive tendering – is in the ultimate interests of those who remain (or wish to be) in public housing. Managers may have very different interests from elected members and users of the service. For those in senior positions, a more market-oriented approach and streamlined bureaucracy may involve greater freedom to innovate, less political interference and the ability to use funds more creatively. As has already been intimated, new organizational forms may often involve the same personnel in a new relationship with the local authority. There is growing pressure for councils to make such changes in order to cope with financial pressures.

For Conservative governments, the model of the future is of the local authority as arms-length enabler, as co-ordinator of a range of agencies, taking a strategic overview of local housing needs and circumstances (Cabinet Office 1991b: 19). In this model, the local authority is regulator rather than provider in the delivery of housing welfare. Direct landlording functions give way to issues of contract compliance, the setting and monitoring of housing and environmental standards and the meeting of annual targets on various criteria.

A model of the local authority as direct provider of housing on a substantial scale or as minimal safety net for emergency cases does not, however, neatly correspond to political party differences or state/market distinctions. There are a variety of permutations. A high degree of state intervention in housing provision could combine with weak local government and direct provision of housing by state agencies. Equally, local government could act as a strong and comprehensive regulator of housing mainly provided through market or quasi-market processes (Warburton 1991). Contracting out and the general ethos of the market which has permeated various aspects of local government has eroded restrictive practices, clarified the division of responsibilities and forced a

specification and costing of services. Many defenders of old-style local government now acknowledge that there have been some benefits, particularly in
relation to cost-awareness. However, even some of the local authorities most
sympathetic to central government objectives acknowledge a very mixed experience of contracting out housing services. Wandsworth, for example, has
made substantial cost savings from contracting out its caretaking services but
sees the promotion of a more competitive edge in its in-house services as being
more desirable than the blanket application of CCT (*Housing* 1990). There are
also concerns that working conditions may suffer and that cost-cutting may
involve reduced quality and increased uncertainty in the delivery of services.

It may be true that provided a good-quality service is delivered efficiently, the customer could not care less whether it comes directly through the
council or is subcontracted to a private agency. However, it may matter to
some employees whether they are working primarily to make a profit or
primarily to provide a public service within cost constraints. These are important issues which remain relatively unexplored in contemporary debates on
contracting out and new forms of service provision. They raise the questions of
how far a public service ethos pervades housing management, and whether a
change in the organizational culture is required when purchaser–provider functions become separated. This may matter more if we are referring to key
functions in the provision of social rented housing rather than more peripheral
items such as laundry or canteen services.

The consequences of policy changes

There is often a long time lag between policy change and policy consequence
and this is particularly true of many aspects of housing provision. Moreover,
cause and effect can prove difficult to establish given the way policy changes
and external factors combine to produce evident effects. For example, it is
often argued that the rise of homelessness and the increasing use of bed and
breakfast and other temporary measures as a response to pressing housing needs
can be attributed to the corrosive impact of the Right to Buy. However, the
decline of housing opportunities for lower income households is more appropriately connected to the lack of new building for low-cost rent. The impact of
recession and economic restructuring on certain sectors and jobs, affordability
problems within the owner-occupied sector and the squeeze on state benefits
are other important factors.

Over time, the sale of a substantial segment of public housing has inevitably reduced rental opportunities for those in need of such accommodation.
Sitting council tenants who bought their dwellings would not, in the main,
have moved had they remained as public sector tenants. Therefore, the loss of
potential relets is much less than the actual number of sales. However, some
would have moved and there is inevitably a cumulative effect. A reasonable
estimate of the loss of relets from sales (including those taking place before the
Right to Buy) is around 36,000 per year (Forrest and Murie 1991). These

cumulative effects mean that managers of public sector housing have less flexibility in what they can allocate to those on the waiting list and those in emergency need. While the precise numbers involved are uncertain, it is clear that council house sales and reduced public sector capital investment have not increased housing opportunities for those in greatest housing need.

The impacts of the post-1988 policy and legislative changes are only now beginning to emerge. Some of these initiatives have been transformed as the policies have evolved and as the housing and economic context has changed. Housing Action Trusts have, for example, been of marginal importance and their further development is likely to be more in the form of partnerships between local authorities and other agencies rather than as central government takeovers of local authority functions. The result of the 1992 general election will ensure the acceleration of voluntary transfers, albeit more often led by management than by consumers. The scope of the housing functions of local authorities will be further diminished and the voluntary or independent sector will continue to grow through new building and property transfers.

The context for these changes in terms of the population most directly and immediately affected is one of increasing impoverishment and marginality. The public tenant population, through the selective nature of movement from the sector, the pattern of new allocations and the uneven impact of recession and economic restructuring on different social groups, increasingly consists of households on low incomes and state benefits. This process is generally referred to as residualization and various statistics can be mobilized to show the connection between council housing and disadvantage. In summary, council housing is now more correctly referred to as the housing of the non-working classes. Rather than being housing for working-class families, it accommodates a tenant population which is increasingly elderly; contains large numbers of the sick, disabled and unemployed; increasing numbers of female lone parents; and a majority of households on state benefits (for a recent review, see Forrest and Murie 1990b). Throughout the 1980s, the income profile of council tenants became more heavily skewed towards the bottom two income deciles. A number of factors have been at work to produce this situation, many of which are extraneous to the housing market and housing policy. Nevertheless, the continuing decline of the private rented sector, affordability problems in home ownership, the selective movement out of better-off tenants and the virtual cessation of new building in the public sector have been important elements.

The traditional left-wing critique of council housing argued that the poorest group were excluded, whereas commentators on the Right to Buy claimed that relatively affluent tenants received subsidized housing. In these terms, recent policy changes may be justified as better targeting of social housing on those in greatest need. However, targeting can also be seen as a recipe for segregation and ghettoization, particularly when more limited resources are being directed at a tenant population which in some areas comprises an increasing proportion of ethnic minorities. New tenants are more likely to be black, homeless and to be allocated a flat (rather than a house) in a less popular estate. For those managing social housing, this means that the social distance between the managers and the managed is likely to grow greater and management functions increasingly take on elements of social work and social control. At a time when housing management is aspiring to greater profession-alization, there is understandable resistance to what could appear to be a down-grading of the function in terms of both scope and content. Reference to residualization is often met with considerable antagonism from housing man-agers as it is seen to imply a residualization of their status as much as a descrip-tion of the changing social role of council housing. It may also explain the apparent enthusiasm among many housing professionals for voluntary transfers and a more business-oriented approach to social housing.

Perhaps the critical issue to recognize is that the attempt to transform tenants from clients into consumers and to promote empowerment and parti-cipation is trying to inject the vocabulary and practices of the market into a situation where many of those in this target group are casualties of market processes and generally have weak market positions as both producers and consumers. This is not to deny the possibility of real improvement in the quality of services which can be delivered by more responsive housing agencies or of more active and meaningful participation by tenants. However, it does underline the fact that talk of consumerism or charters in this context cannot be a substitute for adequate resources, and that the delivery of better welfare in housing is not just about better management. It may be that many of the changes now envisaged would have had a greater chance of success when council housing (or its evolving variants) contained a more mixed population. Effective tenant participation in other countries tends to be associated with large, socially diverse rented sectors as in Sweden. It is difficult to find examples of smaller-scale housing sectors serving poor minorities which are not charac-terized by stigmatization and exclusion.

Towards a new agenda in the delivery of housing welfare

The last decade has seen a major reshaping of housing provision in the UK. The key developments have been a substantial increase in the level of home ownership and a parallel decrease in the size of the council housing sector. The dominant discourse has been one of privatization, public–private partnerships and competition. As we progress into the 1990s, we will see a further erosion of the municipal role in housing provision, a greater diversity of social landlords and a blurring of the distinctions between the public and the private sectors. What is less certain is whether home ownership will continue to expand or whether the collapse of property prices in the late 1980s and the prolonged recession marks a watershed in the development of that tenure. The weakening of old certainties about how to provide social housing may be joined by a new caution among both consumers and producers with regard to house purchase. For housing analysts, housing managers and politicians, life was simpler when tenure divisions and the distinctions between the state and private sector appeared less ambiguous. The state sector was council housing and housing problems were limited to the rented sectors.

We are now moving into very different territory. Questions arise in relation to the organization of housing provision (who are the providers?) as well as what is being provided for different social groups (where are the housing problems?). These questions are tied into a much broader reshaping of the role of local government and the dynamics of the owner-occupied market.

From the point of view of the reshaping of local government, compulsory competitive tendering will be a major force in service provision. In housing there are a number of unresolved issues. These include how much interest there will be from private sector organizations in tendering for housing services; which elements will be put out to tender; whether the split is geographical or functional (for example, all functions on an estate or a single function across the whole authority); and the role of tenant consultation in the process. It is likely that central government will introduce new measures to make it more difficult for in-house bids to win tenders. There are also legitimate concerns about the impact of CCT on the working conditions of those providing the service. If the emphasis is on reducing costs rather than enhancing or maintaining quality, then the consequences may be cuts in wages, fringe benefits, statutory rights and job security rather than the delivering of a better service for the consumers (for a useful discussion, see Dwelly 1991; Richards 1992; *Welsh Housing Quarterly* 1992).

All these changes begin to transform local authorities from direct providers to monitoring, regulating and contract-enforcing agencies, so new management issues will arise. In this context, Alexander (1991: 69) has referred to the difficulties of 'managing fragmentation' as service delivery is transformed from 'a vertically integrated hierarchy to . . . a series of more or less autonomous agencies loosely linked in a local network of service provision'. Alexander observes that in the traditional local authority the organizational form was relatively simple and hierarchical, decision making and service delivery relied on the exercise of power and authority, and decisions flowed vertically through the organization. In a situation where service delivery is a network rather than a hierarchy, organizational forms become more complex, negotiating skills become more important, there is more emphasis on performance monitoring and contractual specification, and services emerge from a series of separate and largely independent bilateral relationships (ibid.: 70). The implication is that in housing, as in other areas, the reorganization of service delivery involves the learning of new management skills to cope with more complex organizational settings. This is particularly important if housing managers are not to become immersed in technical issues to the neglect of broader questions of democratic accountability in the meeting of local needs and demands.

A consideration of changing welfare needs in housing must, however, move beyond a concern with the reorganization of the social rented sector and embrace the housing market as a whole. This chapter has concentrated on the forces which have reshaped the council housing sector over the last decade and the specific organizational changes occasioned by the policy and legislative measures of the late 1980s. As these factors have begun to impact on the public and independent sectors, in combination with the continuing significance of the Right to Buy, so transformations have also occurred in the owner-occupied sector. In general, housing policy and assessments of housing problems have assumed a one-way traffic between the rented and owner-occupied sectors. People achieved home ownership status and escaped the problems associated with private landlordism, public landlordism and more acute welfare problems such as homelessness. As home ownership has expanded, however, problems supposedly confined to the rented sectors have surfaced within owner-occupation. It is no longer valid – if it ever was – to assume that home owners share a common set of privileges and are immune from the problems of unemployment, underemployment, relationship breakdown and debt. A period of falling property values, high real interest rates and rising unemployment has accentuated these difficulties among home owners. Rising mortgage arrears, repossessions, the demand for rented accommodation from the casualties of owner-occupation and the introduction of mortgage rescue schemes indicate some of the new demands on local housing agencies and the more varied problems which will be faced by housing managers in the future.

The expansion of home ownership towards 70 per cent of households and its encompassing of a much wider section of the social structure makes such developments inevitable. Even without a major recession, the increasing variety of household circumstances within home ownership means that the focus of housing welfare cannot be limited to those unable to gain access to that tenure. A growing number of lower income owners are likely to remain vulnerable to the vagaries of the residential property market. The policies that were assumed to deliver housing welfare in the past will not necessarily do so in the future. There are particular issues associated with the growing number of elderly owner-occupiers. They are a diverse group with a diverse range of needs and resources (Mackintosh et al. 1990). Some are equity-rich, living in valuable, spacious dwellings; others have limited resources and are in poor housing conditions. There is going to be an increase in the very elderly in all tenure groups, which raises a range of new welfare issues for housing agencies.

All of these issues should also be set in a context which recognizes the growing internationalization of housing debates and policy influences. There is a common vocabulary in housing policy of privatization, competition, deregulation and partnership. It is always difficult to ascertain the direction of influence. However, UK policies towards the selling of state-owned housing assets, particularly the Right to Buy, have undoubtedly helped shape the housing policies of other countries in various parts of the world. This has arisen for the simple reason that there were substantial assets to sell in the UK. Other countries had much smaller state housing sectors or a plurality of social landlords which limited the scope and influence of central government. More recent policy initiatives associated with deregulation, competitive tendering and contracting out have, however, more clearly drawn on the experience of the USA in a variety of policy areas (Forrest 1991).

The future shape of British housing will be more clearly influenced by pan-European debates and processes. British housing managers are unlikely to be faced by substantial cross-border migration and any attempt at a comprehensive European housing policy is probably neither viable nor desirable. However, housing is creeping up the European policy agenda, particularly in relation to homelessness and social exclusion. Issues of discrimination and equal opportunities in housing are likely to become more prominent. Deregulation and competition in housing finance will have an impact on the cost of borrowing. There is greater awareness at European level that family assets and resources are part of the housing welfare equation and that issues of housing provision cannot simply be located on a state/market continuum. In principle, there is nothing to prevent the cross-national transfer of ownership of housing assets or management functions. This is not an adequate basis for a crude convergence theory in housing policy. There are elements of similarity in the direction of policy change across a range of countries, particularly in relation to fiscal retrenchment, the promotion of individual home ownership and a greater pluralism in forms of renting. Equally, there are major differences in the role of local government, patterns of decentralization and broad institutional structures. A common preoccupation is, however, the management of housing provision in the context of more dominant but more volatile private markets and the apparent divergence between the housing opportunities of majorities and minorities.

4

A case study in the National Health Service: *Working for Patients*

John Butler

The legacy of 1948

When Mrs Thatcher became Prime Minister in May 1979, the National Health Service (NHS) was almost 31 years old. The Report of the Royal Commission on the NHS, the most thorough review of the service yet undertaken, was still two months from publication (Royal Commission 1979). A major structural reorganization of the service, aimed at producing a more efficient and better co-ordinated system of care, had been undertaken in 1974 (Levitt 1976), and a new and fairer formula for allocating revenue and capital resources to the regional and area health authorities had been introduced in 1976 (Department of Health and Social Security 1976); but many problems and issues still remained. Political conflict over the availability of pay beds in NHS hospitals was threatening to escalate (Klein 1989: 117–24). Concern was growing about the long-term prospects for funding the service in the wake of the country's poor economic performance through the 1970s (Bacon and Eltis 1978). Questions were being asked with new intensity about the effectiveness of medical treatments and the efficiency of the service structures through which they were delivered (Cochrane 1972). All was far from sweetness and light.

Yet the essential fabric of the NHS on that spring day in 1979 had changed little since its birth in 1948. The largest single component of the Welfare State, it employed some 700,000 people in that year and consumed about one-fifth of all government expenditure. About 4.5 million spells of hospital treatment were given; over 600,000 deliveries were made; about 150 million consultations were held with general practitioners (GPs); more than 300 million prescriptions were dispensed; and some 30 million courses of dental treatment were undertaken (Department of Health and Social Security 1982b). In principle, the NHS was still committed in 1979 to the provision of a comprehensive range of health and medical services to the people of the UK, largely without charge at the time they were used and broadly comparable in scope and quality across different parts of the country. It was, in intent if not always in reality, a genuinely national service, constituting the sole source of care for nine out of every ten UK citizens. About 90 per cent of the cost of the service was met by the Treasury, and revenue and capital resources were allocated to the regional and area health authorities through a formula agreed by the government (Butler and Vaile 1984). Though locally administered, therefore, the NHS was heavily controlled by central government, the accountability of the local health authorities lying directly with the Secretary of State. The employees of the NHS were contracted on national terms and conditions of employment. The clinicians in the service retained a good deal of local power through their control over resources, and they had the support of the incoming Conservative government in 1979 which made great political capital from the supposed over-burdening of the public services with unproductive managers and administrators. The concept of general management in the NHS was explicitly rejected by the new Secretary of State (Department of Health and Social Security 1979: 7). Competitive markets in health care were confined to the small world of private hospitals, the barrier between public and private sectors of health care being all but impermeable. In its fundamentals and in many of its details, the NHS would still have been recognizable to the founding fathers of the Welfare State as the egalitarian machine they had struggled so hard to create.

The NHS under Mrs Thatcher

This settled view of the NHS in 1979 was plainly evident in the conclusions of the Royal Commission, published two months into Mrs Thatcher's premiership (Royal Commission 1979). The commissioners felt that, while the NHS was by no means the envy of the world, neither was it suffering from a terminal disease susceptible only to heroic surgery. Their report explicitly endorsed the view of a former Treasury official that 'it would be difficult to argue that there is widespread inadequacy in the NHS, or that there are significant improvements which could readily be made' (ibid.: 356). To enhance the performance of the service would be a 'long slogging job' at the margins of change. It soon became apparent, however, that if this was to be the text for the 1980s, the government had failed to be informed. Because of its size and cost, its dominance by authoritarian professions, its lack of clear lines of accountability, its sharply demarcated separation from the private sector, and its overwhelming reliance on Treasury funding, the NHS was almost bound to be a key target for the reforming zeal of a government bent on rolling back the frontiers of the state. Early in the decade (in 1981) the government had seriously examined the feasibility of a shift from funding by the Treasury towards a social insurance scheme (Timmins 1988a), and, as the decade progressed, the ideas that gave it its reforming zeal and energy found increasing application in the NHS. They culminated in the government's White paper *Working for Patients*, published in 1989, which finally marked the break with the service structures erected by Bevan and Beveridge (Secretaries of State 1989). Among the more important ideas providing the platform for the great reforms mandated by the National Health Service and Community Care Act 1990, designed to implement the major recommendations of *Working for Patients* were those of managerialism, income generation, contracting out and internal markets.

The growth of managerialism in the NHS, though initially spurned by the incoming government as a requisite for the 1980s, was evidence of the critical role that managers soon came to be seen to play in sharpening the accountability of doctors, opening up the service to the bracing breezes of competition, and enforcing the various value-for-money initiatives mandated by the government for enhancing the efficiency of the system. The introduction of the philosophy and structures of general management in the middle years of the decade, following the publication of the Griffiths Report in October 1983, became important for various reasons (Department of Health and Social Security 1983b). It demonstrated the fallacy of the belief that the management of health care could be separated from its politics. It laid down the foundations of a management culture of command and obedience that increased the responsiveness of the NHS to political direction. And it created a climate of opinion and practice that finally enabled the government to implement its plans for the internal market in the NHS in the face of unremitting opposition from all the professional groups in the service.

The introduction of schemes for the generation of extra income for the health authorities was also of great symbolic significance, signalling the gradual retreat by government from the existing regulations preventing health authorities from selling their services for profit. The passage of the Health and Medicines Act in 1988 effectively gave the health authorities the power to buy and sell goods, services, land, ideas and anything else at commercially appropriate rates; and in the following year the Department of Health issued guidelines to the authorities on how to run their local schemes of income generation (Department of Health 1989b). The promise was held out of a future replete with commercial potential: among the things that might be considered suitable for sale were clinical services, expertise, amenity beds, laboratory services, catering services, advertising space, car parking slots and conference facilities (Moore 1988). Shopping arcades could be built in unfilled corridors and health clubs opened in unused basements. Mail order services were created to sell everything from bandages to stretchers, and fees were charged for measuring the bodies of those who died in hospital. Commercial enterprises of this sort were never likely to raise huge sums of money, and in the early years they fell far short of the expectations that ministers held out for them. In 1988–89, £20 million was expected and only £10 million realized (Leathley 1989); and in 1989–90, a target of £35 million was set but less than £20 million attained (Little 1990). Of greater significance than their yields, however, were the signals that the income-generation schemes were sending throughout the NHS about the changing climate of expectation. The long years of isolation from, and indifference towards, the world of business and profit, were giving way to a new era of entrepreneurialism. Marketing perspectives were permeating through to the soul of the Welfare State (Sheaff 1991).

   If the income-generation schemes of the 1980s gave managers the experience of selling in a market, the introduction in the early part of the decade of schemes for the contracting out of certain services equally enhanced their skills as buyers. The principle of inviting competing contractors to tender for the supply of ancillary services in the NHS was one that, for obvious reasons, was greatly favoured by the incoming Conservative government in 1979: it would subject what had hitherto been largely in-house services to an efficacious dose of competition, and it would begin to open up the public sector to commercial companies. In September 1983, a Departmental circular required health authorities to set up programmes of open tendering for their cleaning, catering and laundry requirements, and financial steps were taken to ensure that private contractors could compete on equal terms with existing in-house services (Department of Health and Social Security 1983a). By the end of 1986, 274 out of a total of 1281 contracts (21 per cent) for domestic services had been awarded to private firms, and from 1987 onwards the process of competitive tendering spread steadily beyond the restricted areas of cleaning, catering and laundry (Key 1988). At first, the spread was confined to other non-clinical services (such as portering, transport and computing), but it quickly spread to quasi-clinical services (such as sterile supplies) and then to clinical services (such as pathology). By the end of 1990, a directory of business opportunities in the NHS was reportedly in circulation, detailing commercial possibilities in such areas as pathology, blood transfusion services, information technology, property development and retailing (Dean 1991).

   As with the income-generation schemes, the importance of the contracting out of domestic and other services lay less with the financial gains that were achieved, or even with the problems that were experienced in setting and monitoring the quality standards that the contractors were obliged to follow, than with the establishment of the principle upon which it was based: that the ultimate responsibility of health authorities was not to provide and manage these services themselves, but rather to ensure that they were available when and where they were required at no direct cost to the patients using them. Authorities were responsible for determining service needs and for using their resources to ensure that such needs were met efficiently and to a specified standard; but they were not necessarily responsible for the actual processes of producing and managing the services. They could fulfil their obligations just as well by commissioning services that had been produced elsewhere (whether in the private sector or by other public sector bodies) and making them available to NHS patients through local service structures.

The internal market

The growing expertise and confidence of NHS managers in buying and selling services created a prototype market within the NHS that was eventually to find its full expression in the 1989 White Paper *Working for Patients* (Secretaries of State 1989). The experiences of the London teaching hospitals provided an early example of how it could work. Worried for a long time that they were being asked to treat large numbers of patients living beyond the boundaries of their own districts and for which they were therefore not adequately recompensed, many teaching hospitals in the capital were, by 1987, accepting referrals from other districts only if the referring authorities were willing to pay an agreed price reflective of the real cost of the treatment given (Timmins 1987). Cross-boundary charging had begun and the rudiments of an internal market established. It lacked any competitive edge and it diminished the traditional freedom of GPs to refer their patients to the consultant of their choice; but London managers saw it as a foretaste of things to come. 'At the moment', one was reported as saying, 'we are just nibbling away at an internal market, but I believe it has got to come' (Timmins 1987).

If the London experiments amounted to a nibble, a veritable banquet was being prepared in East Anglia. Anticipating the eventual introduction of some form of market throughout the NHS, the East Anglian Regional Health Authority offered itself to the Department of Health in 1988 as an experimental region (Moore 1990). The scheme proposed by the regional health authority envisaged the allocation of an annual revenue budget to the region's eight districts, from which each district health authority would purchase the services it required through contracts with its own hospitals, with hospitals in other districts, or with private hospitals. The scheme was intended to be a competitive one, the most efficient hospitals attracting the greatest share of the business. The region's offer was refused by the Department, but the project still proceeded. By May 1989, all the districts in the region were negotiating contracts with their own hospitals and units for the provision of care, and in October 1990 the market began in earnest, with real money exchanging hands under the contracts negotiated between the providers and the district health authorities.

In parallel with these assorted experiences and initiatives within the NHS, academics were attempting throughout the 1980s to develop models of how the widespread introduction of market competition into the NHS might actually work. These models divided into two main types (Brazier et al. 1990). Some envisaged the GPs as the principal buyers in the market, receiving annual cash-limited budgets from which to purchase, from among a range of competing sellers, whatever hospital services were required by the patients registered with them. Such a market, it was argued, would control the indiscriminate referral of patients for specialist attention (since the GPs would bear the opportunity costs of unnecessary referrals) as well as enhancing the efficiency of the hospitals (by pitching them in competition with each other for the custom of the budget-holding GPs) (Marinker 1984).

Other models of an NHS market, however, envisaged the district health authorities as the buyers, using their annual revenue allocations to purchase packages of care from their own directly managed hospitals, or from hospitals managed by other district health authorities, or from the private sector. As with the first type of market, the hospitals would be in a competitive relationship with each other, thereby enhancing their productive efficiency. Hospitals that could not compete effectively in terms of the price and the quality of their services would suffer a loss of custom, even (*in extremis*) going out of business. The most celebrated exponent of this type of market, the American Professor Enthoven (1985: 38–42) was later acknowledged by ministers to have had a decisive effect upon the course of government thinking.

The context of the government's review

The scope for market trading within the NHS was therefore well worked out in theory, and to some extent in practice, long before Mrs Thatcher announced, in January 1988, the existence of a government working party to review the National Health Service in the UK. Politically, the announcement was a surprise: the Conservative manifesto for the 1987 general election had promised nothing more specific for the NHS than stronger management and greater efficiency, and the legislative agenda was already full of contentious issues. Less than a week before the Prime Minister's announcement, the Secretary of State for Social Services (Mr Moore) had strongly defended the government's record on health care in a parliamentary debate and had outlined his plans for the future of the NHS (Parliamentary Debates 1988b). No hint was given of an imminent review of the service. That a major review was instigated at that particular time was an explicitly political response to the intense concern that had arisen about the supposedly low level at which the NHS was funded.

The storm of professional and public concern about the funding of the NHS that finally broke in the winter months of 1987–88 had been gathering for some time. Throughout most of the 1980s, the government had been rather more committed than its predecessors to reining back the growth in public spending, including the NHS. While there is no single or simple method of measuring year-to-year changes in spending on the NHS, much less relating them to a generally recognized benchmark of adequacy, it was widely believed that the years between 1980 and 1988 were ones of particular financial difficulty. Between the financial years 1980–81 and 1986–87, for example, the purchasing power of the district health authorities in England had grown by a little under 10 per cent (Robinson and Judge 1987), and the gap between aspirations and resources had become ever more apparent. In 1986, the Commons Social Services Committee calculated that, between 1980–81 and 1986–87, the hospital and community health services in England had been underfunded by £1.325 billion (Social Services Committee 1986), and in an updating exercise carried out in 1988, the Committee found that the amount of underfunding between 1981–82 and 1987–88 was £1.896 billion (Social Services Committee 1988).

By the middle of 1987, the funding of the NHS had become a major theme in the general election campaign then under way, and reports from all over the country were revealing the dire financial circumstances in which local health authorities were finding themselves (McKie 1987). Piecemeal attempts by the government to supplement the financial allocations to health authorities to pay for increases in the wages and salaries of health service staff failed to stem the tide of political disquiet. In the first six months of the 1987–88 parliamentary session, twenty-six early day motions were tabled about the service cuts being imposed by health authorities and nine debates were held in the House of Commons, six of which were adjournment debates about local problems in members' constituencies (Social Services Committee 1988). By December 1987, as a survey conducted by *The Independent* revealed, well over 3000 hospital beds in England had been closed through the lack of money or manpower (Timmins 1988b), and later that month the Presidents of the Royal Colleges of Physicians, Surgeons and Obstetricians directed an almost unprecedented lament at Mr Moore (Hoffenberg *et al.* 1987: 1505):

> Each day we learn of new problems in the NHS – beds are shut, operating rooms are not available, emergency wards are closed, essential services are shut down in order to make financial savings. In spite of the efforts of doctors, nurses and other hospital staff, patient care is deteriorating. Acute hospital services have almost reached breaking point. Morale is depressingly low . . . An immediate overall review of acute hospital services is mandatory. Additional and alternative funding must be found. We call on the government to do something now to save our Health Service, once the envy of the world.

In response, the Minister of State for Health (Mr Newton) announced the allocation of an extra £90 million to the NHS to 'meet the immediate problem' (Parliamentary Debates 1988a). By the turn of the year, the government appeared to have weathered the worst of the storm. Then, in January 1988, some night nurses in Manchester went on strike; others followed suit, and the issue of nurses' pay erupted afresh as the government refused to commit itself in advance to funding whatever increases might be recommended by the Review body later that year. The *British Medical Journal*, in a gloomy editorial, declared that the NHS was moving towards terminal decline, and called for the appointment of a commission of enquiry into the financing of health care (Smith 1988). The pressure could finally be contained no longer, and in the course of an interview on BBC television on 25 January, the Prime Minister revealed that just such a review was already underway.

The government's review of the NHS

The review, which began in January 1988 and took exactly a year to complete, was conducted in private by a small group of cabinet ministers chaired by Mrs Thatcher herself. The group's deliberations focused at first upon alternative ways of funding the NHS, in the hope that additional or alternative sources of funds might serve to allay the widespread and politically damaging belief about the financial neglect into which the service had been allowed to fall. Among the ideas considered and rejected was one from the Conservative Political Centre involving a switch in funding from the exchequer to a social insurance scheme, including the right of people with private health insurance to opt out of the national scheme (Brittan 1988).

By the summer of 1988, little apparent progress was being made in these directions, partly perhaps because of the realization among the review group that for all its drawbacks, a tax-funded service with cash-limited budgets is very good at controlling the overall level of spending. Instead, attention began to deflect away from the volume and sources of money going into the NHS towards the ways in which it is used. If the root concern of the public was an insufficiency of services rather than of money, it could be addressed just as well by expanding the output of services as by increasing the input of resources. The real problem from this perspective was not primarily a shortage of public money, but rather the inefficient and unresponsive way in which it was used. By the latter part of 1988, therefore, the principal issue for the review group was no longer that of funding but of the efficient use of the resources available to the NHS, especially the resources allocated for the hospital care of acutely ill patients.

It was one thing, however, to aspire towards the diffuse goal of greater efficiency; it was quite another matter to identify the changes required in the NHS to create the climate in which the quest for enhanced efficiency might prosper. A large part of the history of the NHS has been the history of a continuing search for the more productive use of resources, and most of the major changes that have occurred in the structure and management of the service have been justified on these grounds. Indeed, Conservative governments since 1979 had already made many such changes, most notably the abolition of the area health authorities in 1982, the implementation of the principles of general management following the Griffiths Report in 1983, the introduction of performance indicators and performance reviews, the greater accountability of clinicians for the financial implications of their work, and the investment in better information systems. What more could the review group do that had not already been tried? And how could it give embodiment to the Prime Minister's apparent view that, since change was now on the agenda, it might as well be radical in form?

The answer that finally emerged reflected a particular (and subsequently disputed) view of the springs of the supposed inefficiencies that stubbornly remained. Managers and clinicians were insufficiently motivated to make the best use of the resources under their control because neither the rewards of success nor the penalties of failure were woven into the fabric of the service. The beneficial stimulus of competition among the providers of care was largely absent from the bureaucratically controlled machinery of the NHS. If ways could be found of introducing real competition into the service without incurring the political hazard of challenging its basic principles, then several objectives might simultaneously be achieved: the output and quality of services might rise without a commensurate increase in the input of money; clinicians might be forced to pay greater heed to the costs of their activities; business principles would become more prominent and an important step would be taken towards the privatization of the NHS should that become politically expedient; substantial inroads would be made into the heartlands of bureaucratic control in the Welfare State; and political disquiet with the state of the NHS could more easily be deflected away from government towards the performance of local managers. An enticing prospect indeed!

Working for Patients

The White Paper that gave expression to the ideals of the review group, *Working for Patients*, was published in January 1989 (Secretaries of State 1989). Building upon the general theory of markets in their application to health care, and taking account of the experiences accumulated throughout the 1980s of the buying and selling of services in the NHS, *Working for Patients* set out a visionary plan for the creation of an internal market in the NHS in which multiple suppliers (or, as they came to be called, providers) of services would compete against each other in the market for the custom of buyers (or, as they came to be called, commissioners) who would be entirely separate agents. Commissioning and providing, which had hitherto been a unified responsibility of the district health authorities, would be split and divided between agents located on either side of the market divide. At its simplest, the vision could be understood as an extension of the well-established principle of contracting out beyond the familiar territory of the domestic services to include (eventually) the full spectrum of clinical care offered through the NHS. The key questions addressed by the White Paper were, therefore, those of the identity of the buyers, the identity of the sellers and the nature of the relationship between them.

Buyers in the internal market

The models of an NHS market that had developed throughout the 1980s identified two possible buyers: the GPs (Marinker 1984) and the district health authorities (Enthoven 1985). In the event, the White Paper settled for a hybrid version, with both GPs and district health authorities as purchasers. General practices that met certain criteria and that elected to do so could apply for budgets, which the doctors would use to buy out-patient care, diagnostic testing and a range of in-patient and day case treatments for their patients. In addition, each practice's budget would also cover the reimbursements that it had hitherto received directly for part of the staff costs of other members of the practice team, any improvements that were made to the practice premises, and the cost of the drugs prescribed by the GPs in the practice. It would not include the doctors' own remuneration, which would be unaffected by the budget. Budget-holding would be voluntary, and the budgets would be negotiated individually between each practice and its regional health authority. They would be monitored by the Family Practitioner Committee (later renamed the Family Health Services Authority). Practices would be free to switch their expenditure between budgeting headings, and they could retain and re-invest any end-of-year savings. Overspending by up to 5 per cent of the budget in each year would be carried over to the next year's allocation; persistent over-spending in excess of this could result in the loss of budget-holding status. The White Paper envisaged that, initially, about 1000 practices in the UK would be eligible to apply for budgets, covering about a quarter of the population.

Practices that elected not to apply for a budget, or that were ineligible, would not be unaffected by the forced division between commissioning and contracting, but they would not be direct players in the game. Instead, the commissioning of the hospital services required by patients registered with these practices would be done by the district health authorities; and, as foreseen by Professor Enthoven (1985), the GPs would normally be able to refer patients only to those hospitals with which their authorities had negotiated contracts. The district health authorities (and their equivalent boards in Scotland and Northern Ireland) were therefore to be the second category of commissioners, along with the budget-holding general practices. Initially, and possibly for some time, the district health authorities would account for much the larger share of the com-missions that were placed; but their responsibility would steadily diminish as the number of budget-holding practices grew, for the element of each practice budget that covered the purchase of hospital services would be deducted from the district allocations. The total volume of resources available for the commis-sioning of hospital services in each district would thus remain the same, but, with the passage of time, more of it would be channelled through the budget-holding GPs and less through the district health authorities.

Sellers in the internal market

So much for the White Paper's proposals for the commissioning side of the market. On the provider side, *Working for Patients* envisaged three types of hospitals competing against each other for the custom of the district health authorities and the budget-holding practices: independent hospitals, self-governing hospitals and hospitals remaining under the management control of the district health authorities. The inclusion of independent hospitals, though seemingly radical in enabling public money to be spent on the treatment of NHS patients in private facilities, was no more than the logical extension of a trend that had been developing throughout the 1980s. The Health and Medicines Act 1988, formalizing the growing experiences of NHS managers in trading with the private sector, had given the health authorities wide powers to buy and sell their services; and the White Paper was merely building upon this: 'The Government believes that there is scope for much wider use of competitive tendering, beyond the non-clinical support services which have formed the bulk of tendering so far. This can extend as far as the wholesale "buying in" of treatments for patients from private sector hospitals and clinics . . .' (p. 70).

Much more innovative than the buying in of services from the independent sector was the White Paper's proposal for the creation of self-governing hospitals. Any large hospital, but particularly the major acute hospitals, could apply to opt out of management control by their district health authorities and become NHS Hospital Trusts, governed by boards of directors comprising both executive and non-executive members. Trusts would be able to employ their own staff, buy and sell goods and services, and raise capital by borrowing either from the government or in the financial markets. They could compete for both NHS and private patients, and their revenue would derive exclusively from the sale of their services. They would be accountable not to the district health authorities but to the Secretary of State, who might delegate his responsibilities in this respect to the regional health authorities.

The concept of the self-governing hospital trust had its historical model in the pre-NHS voluntary hospitals and its contemporary model in the chronologically more advanced policy of allowing schools to opt out of control by their local education authority. There was, however, curiously little public discussion of the concept until just before the White Paper's appearance. Professor Enthoven's (1985) vision of the internal market, which had exerted a considerable influence over government thinking, contained no trace of a self-governing hospital, nor did the discussion of the internal market in the 1988 report of the Commons Social Services Committee on the future of the National Health Service (Social Services Committee 1988). Yet stories were appearing by December of that year of the government's attempts to interest some London teaching hospitals in the idea, albeit a modified version in which the hospital's fixed overhead costs would be funded directly by the Department of Health and only the variable costs covered by contracts with the district health authorities (Pike 1989). By January 1989, with the publication of the White Paper still three weeks away, local managers were talking openly to the press about the prospects for self-government of their local hospitals. Those in districts containing large teaching hospitals such as Guy's and St Thomas' in London and St James' in Leeds, with the capacity to do more work than they were funded for, saw nothing but hope in the prospect of self-government; others were more cautious. 'I can see no advantage in opting out', a London manager was reported as saying, 'and I would not like to break the links we have with the local community.' 'Opting out may work for a single specialty hospital with a large patient remit', said another, 'but it is total madness for the average district general hospital' (Millar 1989).

The third category of providers, along with the independent hospitals and the self-governing trusts, were those that – for reasons either of choice or size – would not be destined for self-governing status. Though not specifically identified in the White Paper as direct competitors against the other two, the logic of the market assigned them just such a role. The budget-holding general practices would be hampered in their dealings in the market if they had no rights of purchase from the directly managed hospitals, and the hospitals in turn would lose revenue if they were not permitted to compete for the GPs' custom. Although, therefore, much was made in the White Paper of the distinction between self-governing and directly managed hospitals, with the promise that the former might enjoy privileged access to new sources of funds, it soon became apparent that the distinction was largely illusory: all NHS hospitals, however they were managed, would be in competition with each other and with the independent hospitals for the cash-limited crock of gold, and all could be winners or losers in the market.

Relating the buyers and the sellers

The White Paper's proposals for relating the commissioners and the providers embodied the commercial principles upon which the edifice was built: they would behave towards each other as buyers and sellers, the relationship being a contractual one. The contracts governing the trade in services would be agreed between the parties and would stipulate the amount and quality of services to be provided and the basis for the calculation of their costs. Contracts entered into with the private sector would be legally binding; those between district health authorities and their own directly managed hospitals would be enforced through the normal management process; and those with the new self-governing hospitals would be governed by arbitration procedures aimed at avoiding the need for recourse to the law.

Buttressing the internal market

Around these central features of the internal market a number of buttresses were proposed in the White Paper to hold it all in place and make it work. A clear and effective chain of management command would be created, running from the Secretary of State to the districts and units, to ensure that managers at all levels of the service were accepting of the new commercial principles and responsive to the political pressures that were driving the change. The method for allocating revenue resources to the district health authorities would be changed, reflecting the size of their resident populations for which they would be purchasing care rather than the numbers of patients they treated. Capital resources in the NHS would be taxed to ensure that the trust and directly managed hospitals did not have an unfair financial advantage in competing against the independent hospitals. Information systems would be improved to enable the market to operate properly. Systematic methods would be introduced for auditing the medical care delivered both in hospitals and in the community to ensure that the market did not emphasize cost at the expense of quality. And the contracts of the hospital consultants would be changed to align their clinical freedoms more closely with the business plans of the hospitals in which they worked.

Propaganda and counter-propaganda

The aims of all these changes were the stimulation of increased efficiency in the production of services through the creation of a competitive market in the NHS in which the successful providers would expand and flourish, the boundaries between the public and private sectors of health care would blur, and the health authorities would be free to measure and plan for the needs of their resident populations unhampered by the dominance of self-interested providers. The key phrase reiterated by enthusiastic ministers was that henceforth 'money would follow the patients' to the most efficient providers. No longer would the district health authorities be obliged to 'spend' their money in their 'own' hospitals which they themselves managed: in future they (and the budget-holding general practices) would be free to contract with other and diverse suppliers to ensure the best value in services for the money they expended.

Laudable though such aims undoubtedly were, the creation of an internal market as the chosen method of their attainment met with almost universal opposition. The publication of *Working for Patients* sparked off a battle of propaganda and counter-propaganda that was remarkable for its scale and cost, for the furious intensity and acrimony of its conduct, and for the levels of personal vilification to which it sometimes descended (Butler 1992). Rarely can a social policy initiative by a British government have evoked such costly and widespread condemnation, ultimately to such little effect. Prominent among the hostile voices were those of the doctors, individually to the extent that their contracts permitted them to do so and collectively through their professional organizations; but they were by no means lone voices. Other professions within the NHS, the trades unions, patients' organizations, charities, churches, think tanks, health authorities and political groupings within parliament and outside were all caught up at one time or another in the persistent whirlwind of critical opinion that raged around the White Paper. It would be almost impossible to over-emphasize the breadth and depth of the anxiety and concern that was evoked, and that seemed likely at one stage to deal a mortal blow to the government's aspirations for the NHS if not to the government itself.

The grounds of concern were many and varied. Some of them high-lighted the White Paper's sins of omission: that it failed to address the problem of funding the NHS, that it had nothing to say about community care, and that it ignored the risks to teaching and research that would be posed by the internal market. Yet if a storm was raised by what the White Paper omitted, a hurricane was provoked by what it included. For at the heart of the protest was a deep-seated fear about the long-term impact of the internal market: that market competition would be bad in principle, that it would be unworkable in the particular form mandated by the White Paper, that it would be structured in a way that would frustrate the achievement of its own objectives, and that it would damage or even destroy many of the best features of the NHS (Butler 1992). Curiously, the battle was both lost and won by the opponents of *Working for Patients*. It was lost in the sense that, for all the expense and ingenuity of the campaigns against the government's proposals, all of the key elements were enacted in the National Health Service and Community Care Act that received royal assent in June 1990 and that came into legislative force in April 1991. Nowhere was the sense of defeat more keenly felt than by the British Medical Association (BMA), which had taken a costly and imaginative lead at the head of the assorted band of fellow-travellers in protest. By the summer of 1991, having failed in its primary purpose of persuading the government to think again about the reforms, the BMA was left suddenly bereft of purpose and direction, being likened in an editorial in the *British Medical Journal* to a bull that had charged the toreador, missed, and now did not know what to do (Smith 1991b).

Yet although all the key structures of the internal market were in place and operational by April 1991, the influence of the protestors did not finally go unheeded, in the short term at least. For behind the outwardly confident assertions of the government and its supporters about the beneficial effects of market competition in enhancing efficiency and generating greater value for money, steps were progressively being taken throughout 1991 to ensure that the new internal market of the NHS would actually generate very little competition, and almost none at all in its early days. The shifting use of language was perhaps the clearest public signal of the attitudinal transformations that were taking place (Sheldon 1990). What were 'buyers' in the White Paper became, with the passage of time, purchasers and then commissioners; 'sellers' became providers; 'general practice budgets' became general practice funds; 'indicative drug budgets' became indicative amounts; 'contracts' became service agreements; 'self-governing hospitals' became trusts; 'marketing' became needs assessment; 'pilot studies' became demonstration sites and then locality projects. Most telling of all, the initial introduction of the market, destined originally to bring about the most fundamental changes ever engineered in the NHS, came to be depicted as a time of 'steady state', implying a smoothly progressive continuity with the past rather than a sharp divergence from it.

Nor was the sea-change merely one of style: as the appointed day in 1991 approached, the management of the market became increasingly heavy, ensuring that, for a while at least, it would produce no alarming or embarrassing outcomes that could give political capital to the government's opponents. Freedoms that had earlier been proclaimed as vital to the effective functioning of the market failed to materialize in ways expected, and the much-vaunted vision of a service offering greater choice was rapidly becoming a mirage. The explicit promise to the NHS trusts of employing their staff on locally negotiated terms and conditions, and the veiled promise to them of favoured access to funds for capital development, began to fade as the realities of life for the first-wave trusts became apparent (Glasman 1991). Fund-holding general practices were restricted in the terms of their contracts with the provider hospitals to minimize any residual disadvantage to patients registered with other practices (Jones 1991). The assurances given to the non fund-holding practices of the continuation of their favoured referral patterns began to weaken as the capacity of the district health authorities to finance the extra-contractual referrals came into doubt (O'Sullivan 1991a). Most telling of all, perhaps, the outworkings of the internal market were explicitly abandoned (at least in the short term) as a means of solving the long-standing over-supply of hospital beds in London in favour of an administrative review of the capital's needs and resources (O'Sullivan 1991b).

The outcome of the 1992 general election ensured the continued building of the infrastructure of the internal market. The second wave of trust hospitals and fund-holding general practices came into being in April 1992, and the third wave began to form. Purchasing authorities merged into larger agencies or consortia to increase their purchasing power in the market. Outposts of the NHS Management Executive were set up to oversee the workings of the NHS trusts (in the process raising long-term doubts about the future of the regional health authorities). Managers who succeeded in retaining their jobs in the tense political climate enjoyed a field-day of unprecedented freedom to review their alliances, extend their fiefdoms and generally rewrite the rules of the game to their own advantage. A new White Paper, *The Health of the Nation* (Department of Health 1991), gave fresh impetus to health promotion and disease prevention. Gradually, as the foundations of the internal market became established and the superstructures began to rise, opposition to the changes started to moderate to resignation and even acceptance.

Yet it was rather unclear, in the immediate aftermath of the election, what kind of beast the NHS had become. To the casual observer, little had changed. The periodic closure of beds continued; claims and counter-claims about trends in waiting lists reverberated around the media; the flows of patients through the hospitals increased at the customary rate; the chorus of complaint about the underfunding of the NHS continued its rehearsals; and the government maintained its output of smoothly reassuring messages. Patients continued to be treated efficiently and well within the available resources. Yet Bevan's NHS had been fundamentally (and probably irrevocably) destabilized. The new market structures contained the capacity for fiercely competitive behaviour among the providers of care, and the signs were beginning to appear that they would be used in this way. The first- and second-wave fund-holding practices were flexing their muscles in the market; the trusts were dipping at least a toe into the enticing pool of advertising; and senior managers were throwing their weight around as only those with purchasing power can do. The changes appeared to be driven as much by pragmatic opportunism as by ideological vision.

By the end of 1992, then, the critical question was not whether the NHS would be allowed to function as a market, but the extent to which the free play of the forces of the market would (and perhaps even could) be constrained. The competitive capacity of the new NHS had, for obvious reasons of electoral strategy, been minimized in the run-up to the general election. With the prospect of a further five years of Conservative government, the hands that were grasping (or grasping for) the levers of economic power had the capacity to throw off the last vestiges of 1948, and to recast the NHS in ways that would have been unimaginable (as well as unthinkable) to its founding fathers.

5

The new technology of management in the personal social services

Robyn Lawson

Introduction

The past decade has witnessed a series of dramatic policy changes for the Personal Social Services (PSS), introducing new management techniques, a new role for local authorities as 'enablers' of a more pluralistic system, and a new role for service users as consumers in the marketplace. However, implementation of the policy reforms has been far from smooth. This chapter describes the context of these changes and their development during the 1980s and early 1990s in relation to community care, and discusses their impact.

Context

The PSS are concerned with a range of services for children, for elderly people and for those with physical disabilities, mental health problems and learning difficulties. Local authority social services departments (SSDs) are the principal providers of these services, which include social work, domiciliary and day care, and residential care. SSDs were created following the Report of the Seebohm Committee (1968), whose task was 'to review the organisation and responsibilities of local authority PSS in England and Wales, and to consider what changes are desirable to secure an effective family service'. The Committee recommended the unification into a single department of local authority welfare and children's departments, together with parts of their health departments, and a structure based on area offices giving a single geographic focus. Many of the services now drawn into the new SSDs had their roots in the much hated Poor Law, so the Seebohm reorganization split welfare from financial assistance; elsewhere in Europe, welfare services tended to develop within financial assistance services. The Seebohm reorganization redefined the users of the services as clients rather than paupers, and the new services were to be available to everyone and not just targeted on the poor, although most recipients would be poor (Rees 1985).

This system continued more or less unchanged until the latter part of the 1980s, when major legislation was introduced. In 1986, the Secretary of State for Health and Social Security asked Sir Roy Griffiths, chairman of a leading British supermarket chain, to 'review the way in which public funds are used to support community care policy and to advise me on the options for action that would improve the use of these funds as a contribution to more effective community care'. The review was to be about value for money, not the level of funding.

Griffiths (1988) identified the problems of the PSS as a lack of assessment, the excessive use of residential care, a lack of community-based alternatives to residential care, high costs and low value for money, and the fostering of dependence. Successive attempts to shift the balance of provision towards community-based care had failed, and a new approach was needed. The answers suggested and later picked up in the Community Care White Paper (CCWP), entitled *Caring for People* (Department of Health 1989), reflected the ideology and mechanics of the marketplace and new management techniques. The key areas of change are shown in Table 5.1. Measures were to be introduced to match services to need, to promote choice, flexibility and innovation, and to promote value for money, efficiency, accountability and quality. In structural and managerial terms, a new form of management can be seen emerging, with a core purchasing function, decentralization of service provision, and the latter increasingly contracted out to voluntary and private providers. What gave rise to these fundamental changes?

Table 5.1   Key areas of change introduced by *Caring for People*

Measures to match services to needs:
A clearer picture of demand, need and supply
Budgets and managerial responsibility devolved downwards
Assessment and case management for targeting and individual care packaging

Measures to promote choice, flexibility and innovation:
Stimulation and use of a flourishing independent sector, and floating off in-house services
A greater range of day and domiciliary services

Measures to promote value for money, efficiency, accountability and quality
Competition between providers
New role for SSD as purchaser, setter and monitor of standards, with only residual providing function
Distinction between, and possibly separation of, purchasing and providing functions

First, government policy over the last 30 years has promoted community rather than residential care, but with little success. Despite the institutional image of residential homes, the residential sector has continued to grow over the years, albeit with smaller homes emerging as the norm. Since 1980, when the Department of Health and Social Security (DHSS) started to meet costs of private residential and nursing home care through social security benefits, expenditure rose from £10 million in 1979 to over £1000 million in 1989 (Department of Health 1989). In the meantime, there has also been substantial growth in community services (e.g. day hospitals, day centres, meals on wheels, home helps), often arising from voluntary initiatives. Kelly (1989) has shown that prolonged economic constraint has lead to non-incremental changes in the balance of resource allocation in favour of community care for elderly people and children. However, demand has continued to outstrip supply in community services, and there is the unfortunate tendency for local authorities to use home care services and other services such as aids and adaptations as 'expenditure taps' in the process of budgetary 'fine-tuning', since they are easy to trim (e.g. Rees 1985; Webb and Wistow 1986: 128). Furthermore, despite the unification of the PSS, the continuing division of responsibilities between the PSS and health services has proved over the years to be a major barrier to improved community care.

Second, a growing awareness of demographic trends towards an ageing population together with social trends reducing the number of available carers, heightened concern about the provision of care. As these issues came to the forefront of debate, the economic retrenchment arising from the mid-1970s oil crisis resulted in financial constraint. Although there was an injection of resources into the PSS following the Seebohm Report (1968), which achieved a faster growth rate between 1969–70 and 1975–76 than that experienced by any other category of social service spending (Rees 1985), financial stringency has prevailed ever since 1976 when cash limits were introduced. In fact, the PSS continued to grow in real terms because they were protected by local authorities who have persistently devoted more resources to this area of expenditure than Whitehall thought appropriate (Rees 1985). Although the first public expenditure white paper of the Conservative reign in 1979 cut back PSS, subsequent policy has allowed a small margin of growth in the belief that community care is cheaper than residential care and should eventually yield savings. The government budgeted for most of the 1980s for a 2 per cent growth in PSS expenditure which, while insufficient for maintaining a constant level of outputs (Webb and Wistow 1983), has helped the PSS to weather some bad times. Nevertheless, local government expenditure as a whole has been progressively squeezed, with serious implications for the PSS in the 1990s.

Third, the change of policy represented by the CCWP reflected the development of 'New Right' thinking within the Conservative Party. One of the important early advocates of the New Right was Sir Keith Joseph. He believed that collective democratic politics leads to centralization, uniformity and the tendency to excessive public spending, bureaucracy and the growth of state intervention. In particular, he believed that the Welfare State, made up as it was of large bureaucracies, was wasteful, inefficient, over-resourced and under-managed. Progress would only be achieved through monetarist economics, entrepreneurship and the limitation of democratic power (Bosanquet 1981). In 1979, when the Conservatives came to power, economic recession and mounting welfare expenditure provided fertile ground for such ideas.

Policy debate and changes

The key policy goals of the PSS in the late 1980s and early 1990s – the emphasis on community care and the tightening of the arrangements governing child care – would probably have been the two major objectives of any political leadership. The distinctive features of the Conservative administration since 1979 involved new methods of achieving change and a shift in underlying values. This is neatly described by Evandrou et al. (1990: 213):

> Throughout the period [1974–87] there has been a steady shift away from a position where the policy focus was on centrally-defined need and equality, with an emphasis on priority groups, targets and planning, to one where the main concern is with public expenditure restraint and a shift in the balance of care provision between the state and the non-statutory sector. This change in emphasis has been both explicit, enshrined in certain policy changes, and implicit within the mechanisms used to achieve such aims.

The following sections discuss the main vehicles for change and the obstacles they encountered. First, new techniques of management have been imported into the PSS from the commercial sector in answer to the perceived failure of bureaucratic control strategies to achieve change. Second, the opening up of social care provision to market forces has given rise to a new role for SSDs as 'enablers'. Third, the clients of the PSS have been seen more as consumers in the marketplace. Fourth, the major stumbling block to implementation of the community care reforms in the late 1980s and early 1990s has been the difficulty encountered by the Conservatives in reconciling needs and resources.

Changes in the technology of management

During the 1980s, central government abandoned attempts to control the PSS directly – always problematic since they are part of local government – and adopted indirect control strategies, through stringent expenditure restraint, and the promotion of 'new management', which would thrive under conditions of resource pressure (Kelly 1991).

Curbing local authority spending through central financial controls
The mechanisms used by central government to exert financial control began with cash-limited budgets introduced in the mid-1970s during the oil crisis,

followed by a formula for the rate support grant allocated by central government to local authorities which penalized high-spending authorities. The formula included a grant-related expenditure figure, which was in effect a target figure for social service spending for each authority. The round of Standard Spending Assessments (SSAs) in 1992 (on which the rate support grants are based) was widely criticized by local authorities and local government commentators as being arbitrary, and bearing little relation either to the standard of care provided or to local needs. Finally, a rate-cap (now 'charge-cap') was introduced, preventing high-spending authorities from setting their local rates higher than a limit imposed centrally, in order to finance services (Evandrou *et al.* 1990).

The financial restraints imposed by government have created problems for the expansion of community care in many authorities in which total expenditure is being cut through the SSA and charge-cap mechanisms. Central government assumes that SSDs will make efficiency savings to finance service developments (Audit Commission 1984), but it is unclear where these savings can be made. Although private residential care financed by the social security system expanded in the 1980s, there was no corresponding 'new money' for community services, either in the state or independent sectors. The introduction of joint finance in 1976 provided local authorities with an incentive to develop community care, but has had limited impact for two important reasons. First, it requires local authorities to relieve the financial burdens on the NHS while adding to their own and, second, the joint finance contribution to individual schemes is temporary, tapering after a set period (Webb and Wistow 1986).

In 1986, the Audit Commission published *Making a Reality of Community Care*, which stated that the social security system had lead to a shift from hospital-based care to residential care, bypassing community services. It identified five fundamental underlying obstacles to the achievement of community care, three of which were to do with financing:

- A 'mismatch of resources', including the deterrent effect of the rate support grant.
- A lack of funding to bridge the transition to a community-based service.
- The perverse effects of social security policy, which encouraged admission to private residential care.

The other problems identified were organizational fragmentation and confusion, and inadequate staffing arrangements. This report was an important precursor to the Griffiths Report (1988) on community care, on which recent and more dramatic changes have been based.

Emergence of the 'new management'

The government gave only general guidance to local authorities on how to cope with expenditure restraint, handing them responsibility for determining local priorities. Instead, the government set up the Audit Commission as a quango to help them. Its job is to preach the message of good management in local government, and to ensure authorities make proper arrangements for securing efficiency, effectiveness and value for money in resource use. The Commission has operated by the exploitation of the crises generated by financial constraint, and influenced policy through the publication of major reports (Kelly 1991). The Social Services Inspectorate (SSI) (1987, 1988) also promoted the theme of better management. During the latter half of the 1980s, the term 'new management' began to be used, both in a descriptive and normative sense, for changes that were happening in local government. Phrases such as 'thinking total', 'the learning organization', 'strategic management', 'devolving responsibility' and 'reviewing performance' found their way into managers' language (Stewart 1986; LGTB 1988).

In fact, what was happening was what Hoggett (1990) calls the demise of bureaucratic control strategies, and their replacement with new forms of management, a change which was already well underway in the private sector in the 1970s and 1980s. Hoggett describes this as a fundamental transformation of the technology of control which will have a profound effect on the organization and management of the Welfare State. Management in the welfare sector has tended to follow the example of industry. Corporate management was introduced in the reorganizations of local government and the NHS in the early 1970s, characterized by integration and control from the top, in the belief that institutions could only have effective control over activities that occurred within their boundaries, and by exerting bureaucratic control through hierarchical and centralized command structures (Whittington and Bellaby 1979).

However, at the time of its adoption by local government, the bureaucratic model was already in crisis in the private sector. Hoggett (1990) contends that the crisis was brought about by the complexity of the work of large organizations requiring the division of labour into segmented, specialist areas, leading to the emergence of a 'pluralithic' organization, underpinned by groups of specialists, or professionals, each with their own interests and power base. The result was that central management began to take on a policing role, encroaching on professional activities through such techniques as cost-centre budgeting and performance indicators, witnessed in local government and the NHS in the 1980s. This meant, however, that central managers had negative power to prevent certain things happening but very little proactive power. 'As a result, radical change became virtually unimplementable within large, pluralithic bureaucracies' (Hoggett 1990).

The answer to this dilemma in the private sector is 'the decentralization of production and centralization of command' (Murray 1983), or 'tight/loose' systems of organization (Peters and Waterman 1982), otherwise known as the 'core–periphery model'. Such a model involves the centre tightening its grip on the essentials, such as values, culture and strategy, and devolving control over day-to-day management. This structure is made possible by developments in computerized management and financial information systems. The characteristics of such 'new management' forms include the shift from direct employment of workers to contracting out work, and a federal structure created through an internal market, with cost and profit centres relating to central management in a quasi-contract relationship; this structure combines the advantages of scale together with those of decentralization, by helping to deal with conflicts between the centre and the divisions (Handy 1984).

Having previously tackled organizational change through structure, there was an incremental process of experimentation with new forms of management in the welfare sector between 1979 and 1987, including the introduction of general management in the NHS, and government encouragement for recruiting managers from outside the public sector to establish a managerial culture. It was not until the Conservatives' third term of office that the pace and scale of change increased, and 'new management' changes became formal policy. It is no coincidence that the government commissioned a key private sector manager (Griffiths) to advise on community care, and that the solutions he came up with were based on private sector solutions.

The enabling authority

It is argued in the previous section that it is changes in the technology of management that have lead to the new structure advocated by the CCWP (1989), in which it is suggested that SSDs take on an 'enabling' role as purchasers, setters and monitors of standards, which is intended to foster accountability and quality, with only a residual providing function. They are to enable informal carers, voluntary and private providers, to support and expand their role in welfare provision.

An early indication of the concept of the 'enabling' local authority was to be found in *Growing Older* (Department of Health and Social Security 1981: para. 1.9):

> . . . the primary sources of support and care for elderly people are informal and voluntary . . . it is the role of public authorities to sustain, and where necessary, develop – but never to displace – such support and care. Care in the community must increasingly mean care *by* the community.

The concept of 'care *by* the community', while recognizing that the bulk of work is done by informal carers, has been criticized by many researchers, and especially by feminists, on the grounds that informal care is costly to carers, especially to women who do the bulk of the work largely unpaid and unsupported (e.g. Moroney 1976; Parker 1990). Indeed, Rees (1985) contends that the reason that the PSS have not become a 'fifth social service' as hoped for by Townsend and his fellow Fabians, similar in size of budget to social security and the NHS, is that 'we are dealing here with too much of a mixed economy, dependent on self- and family care'.

The term 'mixed economy' has now become more closely associated with the promotion and public purchase of voluntary and private provision. This idea was introduced in the speech made by Norman Fowler (then Secretary of State for Social Services) to the Conference of Directors of Social Services at Buxton in 1984, when he argued that local authorities should not seek to be monopolistic providers of care, but rather to 'enable' services to be provided from a variety of non-statutory as well as statutory agencies. This idea was later expanded by Griffiths (1988). In fact, the purchase of care from voluntary and private sources is not new; the Association of Directors of Social Services (ADSS), while supporting the Griffiths Report, emphasized that supply was already more diversified than was often appreciated, and that the enabling role should be seen as an extension of their current activities rather than as a complete break with the past (ADSS 1989).

What is new in Griffiths' (1988) and the CCWP's (1989) vision of a mixed economy, is that it incorporates both the informal and formal aspects of care. The importance of the contribution of informal carers is explicitly recognized. SSDs are pressed to make support for carers a high priority, and carers' needs are to be taken account of in assessing clients' needs. However, it is not clear how carers' needs will be met, especially since services are increasingly targeted on those most in need – often defined as those without carers. Most notably, the CCWP does not allow carers the ultimate choice of whether or not to become, or continue to be, a carer (Wistow and Henwood 1991). The CCWP also changes relationships with voluntary providers to a more market orientation. Grants to such organizations are increasingly being superseded by more formal contractual and service agreements, which may make them more accountable, although at the same time reducing their autonomy, capacity to pursue an advocacy role and flexibility, which are the very strengths sought by statutory agencies (e.g. Johnson 1990). In addition, private providers are now seen as more acceptable by some authorities. Local authorities are also encouraged to identify areas of their own work which are sufficiently independent to be 'floated-off'. The idea is that the SSD becomes a small core, purchasing from a periphery of providers.

The purpose of developing a mixed economy, as outlined in the CCWP, is to increase the variety of services available, and therefore the choice of services. It is believed that pluralism will give rise to greater flexibility and innovation, and that if competition is introduced, it will promote increased value for money and efficiency by driving down prices. Competition is also believed to generate variety of products and innovation. SSDs are expected to stimulate the development of independent supply, while reducing their own role as providers. However, the CCWP does not entirely commit the PSS to marketization: SSDs have the crucial role of planning to meet need and to ration demand by need assessment, and the market is not allowed to allocate resources – providers will compete, but users will not (Kelly 1991).

In fact, the expanded use of voluntary and private providers, except in relation to residential care, has been one of the slower elements of the CCWP to be implemented. There are a number of reasons for this. First of all, there is scepticism about the sufficiency of the voluntary sector, in terms of their numbers, distribution and capacity to take on a larger role (Johnson 1990;

Lawson 1991a; Wistow *et al.* 1992). It is also unclear that a private sector market will emerge in some services, the exception being the residential sector where private owners and companies are dependent on public finance from the Department of Social Security (DSS). A survey of 109 local authorities concluded that there was no sign of a competitive market developing in domiciliary services, and that the existing contribution of private domiciliary agencies is insignificant (Booth 1990). Furthermore, the relationship between an expansion in variety of providers on the one hand, and the range, flexibility and innovatory capacities of provision on the other is not a clear one (Wistow 1989; Pfeffer and Coote 1991; Wistow and Henwood 1991).

Other criticisms revolve around the introduction of competition. A competitive mixed economy is expensive and difficult to organize and regulate, leading to high 'transaction costs', which may cancel out or even exceed any efficiency savings (Bartlett 1991b). This may encourage reliance on one or two large providers, although the reluctance of SSDs to become dependent on a monopoly contractor, and fear that private contractors might 'pull the plug' if profits fell, contributed to the slow development of social care markets in 1990–91 (Wistow *et al.* 1992). There is also real concern that private providers, competing to survive, may cut quality and choice. For example, in the early 1990s, many private residential homes were struggling to survive the combined effects of economic recession, past high interest rates, and the freeze in income support levels for residents. An ADSS survey in 1992 revealed that the means by which many home owners were seeking to reduce their costs included shedding staff and reducing choice of food, leading to less flexibility and choice for residents, unless they or their families pay for 'extras' from their own pockets.

European experience of a mixed economy in social and health care also gives cause for concern. The Netherlands has a mixed economy of both provision and financing (through social insurance), and in many ways exhibits the features that the British government would like to see in its welfare services (see Chapter 2, this volume; Baldock and Evers 1991). The Dekker Committee was set up by the Dutch Government in 1986 with a remit to advise on 'strategies for volume and cost containment against the background of an ageing population'. The Committee found that it was the very pluralism of the Dutch system which was the source of rigidity and inflexibility, since the diversity of finance and supply meant there was little substitution between one part of the care system and another. Elderly people found it difficult to change provider, and there were particularly tough barriers to 'substitution down' towards cheaper forms of care. The Dekker Report indicates that there is no necessary relationship between competition and socially desirable outcomes, and it seeks to devise a regulatory environment that will make competition improve welfare rather than detract from it (Dekker 1987). Added to these cautionary indicators, the German experience, where there is also a mixed economy of supply and finance, is that five big voluntary organizations have come to dominate the provision of personal social services, controlling it in a corporatist manner without expanding choice. Baldock and Evers (1991) contend that they 'combine monolithic immobility with managerial nonprofit amateurism'.

Consumerism

Part of the purpose of a mixed economy is to provide a variety of services so that clients of PSS can be offered a choice, and so that individual client packages of care can be put together to meet their needs flexibly. The CCWP (1989) turns clients into consumers, emphasizing consumer choice, and reducing the allocative power of producers, an emphasis reflected in the government's *Citizens' Charter* (Cabinet Office 1991a).

The CCWP (1989) included a number of means of turning clients into consumers. First of all, local authorities are required to conduct what might be termed 'market research' to find out what their local population wants and needs by way of services, in order to ensure that this is made available in service planning and purchasing. They are also required to publish their community care plans based on the latter information for public perusal, and to make information available about what services are on offer, and how people can get hold of them. Case managers are crucial to empowering clients, since it is their job to assess a potential client's needs, and then to offer them a choice of services, and to construct an individual care package, which will be adjusted over time as the need arises. The fact that clients will only be able to gain access to state-supported services through a third party – the case manager – is one reason why the term 'quasi-market' is used to describe policy intentions for the PSS (Le Grand 1990). Other mechanisms to give clients a voice include the formal introduction of complaints procedures and an emphasis on quality assurance.

However, consumer choice is not always what it seems. First, choice involves trade-offs between interest groups. For example, the emphasis on the virtues of self-help, personal responsibility and individualism as counteracting a collectivist 'dependency culture' infused all areas of government policy after the Conservatives came to power in 1979 (Wistow and Henwood 1991). Baldock and Evers (1991: 125) argue that this facilitates a reduction in state spending on welfare:

> . . . the concept of the enabling state allows an apparent resolution between the conflicting need of a growing number of old people for care and the preference of the fit majority for as inexpensive a social welfare system as possible. This is done by arguing that the best interests of the old are served by maximising such citizenship rights as choice and autonomy rather than security and protection.

Furthermore, in purchasing services from independent providers, local authorities must balance the need of consumers for choice against their own and providers' needs for continuity and security of supply, and the benefits of economies of scale that would be achieved by purchasing from one or two large providers (Lawson 1991b).

Second, in some areas, the CCWP will not increase choice. For example, the mechanism by which elderly people were automatically entitled to social security benefits to pay for private and voluntary residential care gave people a choice which was taken away once local authorities assumed financial responsibility in April 1993; people are now entitled to an assessment, but not necessarily to a residential place, even if that is what they would like, unless the authority deems this appropriate. The pressure on local authorities to keep people out of residential care is especially strong, since the SSD budget, unlike the DSS system, is cash-limited. Since SSDs may lack a sufficient quantity and variety of community alternatives, the new financial mechanisms could remove choice, security and protection for elderly people.

The other policies which have a direct bearing on consumerism – the publication of community care plans and the setting up of complaints procedures – were achieved on schedule, in 1991 and 1992. However, aspects of implementation which will have a more indirect but nevertheless profound effect on consumers are developing more slowly. These include the decentralization of budgets and the establishment of care management. Flynn and Common (1990a) argue that the degree of choice and flexibility of provision is related to the degree to which purchasing responsibilities are decentralized. However, with a few notable exceptions, it is unclear when, if at all, local authorities are likely to decentralize purchasing budgets, and the lack of adequate information systems is likely to hold this up (Lawson 1991a). Meanwhile, care management is developing slowly and like the implementation of the mixed economy is to evolve over time (Social Services Inspectorate 1992).

Finally, there is evidence of a two-tier system developing in some PSS, so that those who can pay have access to choice, while those who cannot have access only to a basic minimum service or no service at all. This is particularly true in the private residential sector as some owners seek to cut costs in order to survive economic recession (ADSS 1992).

Reconciling needs and resources: The stumbling block to implementation

Clearly, there are practical difficulties in implementing the policy reforms as noted above, but the most fundamental problem is the difficulty the Conservatives have encountered in reconciling needs and resources, while following through their policy of reducing the power of local government. Wistow and Henwood (1991) note that the CCWP brought need, and the definition and measurement of outcomes, back to centre stage in the PSS through assessment and case management, which could have been enormously significant for welfare. However, needs must be identified and met 'within available resources'. Herein lies the crux of the problem. The arrangements for the planning and funding of community care have been the most criticized elements of *Caring for People*, which in other respects has been broadly welcomed (Wistow and Henwood 1991).

The CCWP has reintroduced the formal requirement for SSDs to plan services locally but in a different way to the old norm and guideline-based planning of the 1970s. The new form of planning is consistent with the new public management; it is oriented towards researching, managing and monitoring markets, and is less bureaucratic and centralized than previous planning. SSDs must now build up a population profile identifying demand, need and supply, must collaborate with the NHS over what services should be provided by whom, and must produce community care plans.

However, when the requirement to plan is examined more closely, the holes begin to appear: Griffiths (1988) recommended that local authorities should take the lead role in community care, to help solve the problem of co-ordinating with the NHS. He wished to eliminate the perverse incentive in the social security system favouring residential care and further encourage collaboration by creating a unified community care budget allocated through a specific grant with 40–50 per cent being provided by central government. The grant would be paid on condition that local authorities submitted plans which provided evidence of local needs, collaborative planning and the promotion of a mixed economy of care. This would have given central government explicit political accountability.

Government delayed its response to Griffiths' proposals for over a year because they conflicted with the Conservative commitment to controlling and restricting local government powers and finance. When it did respond, in the form of the 1989 CCWP, local authorities were given the lead role, but Griffiths' proposal of a specific grant was rejected in favour of incorporating the funding in the rate support grant allocation with no ring-fencing which would safeguard it for community care. By so doing, the CCWP abandoned the link between plans and resource allocation. Furthermore, the Department of Health committed only £2 million for 1990–91 to fund implementation, compared to the development investment made available for the NHS reforms (£85 million in 1989–90 and over £300 million in 1990–91: Wistow and Henwood 1991).

The new policy formalized in the National Health Service and Community Care Act 1990 was to have been implemented over one year, by April 1991, but the timetable has since been slowed down twice. In part, the delay is due to the sheer complexity of introducing such radical changes within large organizations. However, problems in reconciling needs and resources for community care are causing delays in implementation. Kenneth Clarke, the then Secretary of State, announced the first delay in implementation in 1990 because of fears that it would add £15 to the community charge bill in the run up to the next general election. This figure was based on local authority associations estimates; the government itself never attempted to put a figure to the cost of implementation. However, the delay in full implementation until April 1993 was announced in such a way as to suggest that it was to give authorities longer in which to discharge their duties efficiently and at a cost which the community charge payers could afford. In other words, local authorities, rather than government, were to be held responsible for reconciling needs and resources, despite tight central constraints on their spending (Wistow and Henwood 1991). Crucially, the transfer of funds for residential care for publicly funded residents from the DSS to SSDs, to help create a unified community care budget, was to be delayed until April 1993, and this is one reason why SSDs have been slow to develop a mixed economy (Wistow et al. 1992). The formula for the transfer proved a highly complex and contentious issue. When the eventual figure of £539 million (£399 million from the DSS and £140 million new money) was announced in October 1992, the funds were after all subject to a partial and temporary ring-fence. However, local authorities remain concerned that the figure will be insufficient either to support people in long-term care or to fund the expansion of community services.

A further delay was announced in March 1992 in a letter from the SSI and NHSME to local and health authorities in which the Department of Health admitted that some of the more 'difficult' aspects of the community care reforms would take much longer than the 1993 deadline to implement. In 1992–93, local authorities were to focus their attention on long-term care, with assessment of applicants for residential care and continuing care as the main issues, together with collaboration arrangements and the establishing of financial and other management systems to meet demands after April 1993. The development of care management, the purchase of services and the mixed economy of care are to continue, but it is asserted that 'the progress of SSDs towards becoming enabling authorities will be an evolutionary one'.

Policy impact

In general terms, the impact by the end of 1992 of the community care reforms was significantly less than originally intended. There are a number of reasons for this. First, the lack of investment funding together with the earlier refusal to ring-fence community care funding, delays in implementation, and uncertainty as to the adequacy of the resources to be transferred from the DSS call into question the government's commitment to the policy reforms and do not bode well for the future of community care or for the PSS as a whole. They suggest that the Conservatives continue to place a reduction in the power of local government and the restriction of public expenditure above the achievement of the community care policy. The uncertainty about future community care financing was compounded by political uncertainty up to the April 1992 general election, and the slow emergence of Department of Health guidance on different aspects of implementation.

Second, the effect of the uncertainty about future community care funding has been exacerbated by the continued fiscal squeeze upon local authorities through SSAs and charge-capping. It could be argued that this has forced many SSDs into a position of trying to maintain service levels and survive, rather than spending time and scarce resources on strategic change, although Kelly's (1989) findings indicate that prolonged economic constraint can lead to non-incremental behaviour on the part of local authorities. While there are some notable examples of SSDs introducing radical change along the lines of the CCWP, many believe that once funds are transferred to them from the DSS in 1993, they will face massive underfunding and will be blamed for the consequent failure of community care.

Kelly (1991) notes that the CCWP requires a high level of analytical capacity and managerial skill which local authorities currently lack. It is instructive to look at reports from the Audit Commission concerning the implementation of the CCWP and their interpretation of current problems. In *Managing the Cascade of Change* (1992a), the Audit Commission criticized poor financial management systems in SSDs, and the Department of Health promptly announced a £93,000 grant per SSD for developing new technology. Lawson (1991a), reporting on the experience of four local authorities after the first year of implementation, also noted that client-based information systems were at an early stage of development, and that this would be a major impediment to progress in a number of areas. It is worth noting Hoggett's (1990) contention that the new management revolution can only be made possible by computerized financial management and information systems. In another report, *The Community Revolution* (1992b), the Audit Commission argued that SSDs lacked management systems for bringing in care management and purchasing, saying that the traditional culture of social services management has an in-built resistance to 'destabilizing' changes such as the advent of the purchaser–provider split. One is lead to ask whether the Audit Commission has failed in its task of introducing new management to help local authorities cope with resource contraction. The ADSS denied the charge, however, stating that although SSDs were proceeding cautiously, most senior managers were strongly committed to carrying out the reforms. More broadly, the implementation difficulties reflect the problem of transferring new forms of management which have developed spontaneously over some years in the private sector into a complex state welfare system, which differs from commercial markets in a number of crucial ways, and which will be explored in the final chapter.

Reflecting upon specific aspects of implementation, what is the likely future impact, and what will endure into the Conservatives' fourth term in office and beyond? Starting with the structure and function of SSDs as a result of the CCWP, a 'core–periphery' model is emerging in local authorities in the 1990s, with decentralization of production to area offices, and the core tasks of strategic planning, design and control remaining at the centre. Hoggett (1990) notes that just as integrated forms of area service management were beginning to emerge as a result of the Barclay Report (1982), which advocated generic work based on patch or neighbourhood systems, the above changes threaten to disintegrate/fragment services by reintroducing the old division between community and child-care services, separating functions such as assessment, purchasing, provision and inspection, and introducing a plethora of alternative providers. This more complex organizational environment itself requires new techniques of management.

With regard to the local authorities' enabling role and the mixed economy, it is unclear that the voluntary and private sectors will be able or willing to fulfil the role expected of them by the government without sources of finance such as social security which boosted the private residential care sector. (The mixed economies of countries like The Netherlands and Germany have evolved partly because of the third-party payment system of social insurance which is absent in the UK.) The government is unlikely to try this experiment in other areas, since the growth in expenditure on private residential care appeared to be exponential, leading them to stop increasing supplementary benefit (now income support) in line with inflation. Furthermore, there is a growing awareness of the complexity and cost of regulating a mixed economy, particularly in competitive situations. It is significant that the government slowed down the introduction of competition in the NHS reforms, declaring 1991–92 a year of 'steady state', and that the mixed economy in relation to the community care reforms has been placed on the back-burner during 1992–93 (Social Services Inspectorate 1992). Commentators wait to see whether the Conservatives will have the courage of their convictions and introduce competition in the NHS in their fourth term of office; the PSS reforms have tended to follow developments in the health service. However, Kelly (1991) argues that the purchaser–provider split, needs assessment, planning and quality control, together with the role of a central quango to monitor change, seem to mark a return of non-market solutions to the problems of resource allocation, and to acknowledge a central role for the state in the management of welfare. But he also suggests that the delay in implementation may have been intended to provide breathing space for consideration of a more full-blown market solution. Local authorities may be keen to retain some aspects of the quasi-market whether or not government pursues its policy to full implementation. Such aspects might include the distinction between purchasers and providers, the clearer specification of standards and their inclusion in contracts.

Turning now to the impact of implementation on PSS staff, the clearest implications are for the role of social workers. After a number of changes in focus, social work since the Second World War has centred on therapeutic treatment (Rees 1985). The new role of social workers in the 1990s will be as 'care managers' who assess, refer and manage resources, without necessarily undertaking any therapeutic work themselves. A report in 1989 said that many social workers were concerned that the community care proposals would lead to de-skilling, partly because of the increased use of non-professional helpers, and partly because care packages would concentrate on practical help with a lower value being placed on other aspects of social work support (Hearn 1989). Devolved budgets and management, and the case management function, are an attempt to turn professionals into managers working within tight financial or resource controls (Hoggett 1990). While cost-centre budgeting helped make professionals more accountable, this step could be seen as further restricting their powers, while appearing to give them greater influence. Kelly contends that the purchaser–provider split and competition will also undermine professional power and resistance to change. Furthermore, there is concern that a competitive mixed economy will lead to poor employment conditions (Labour Party 1985), a fear which is borne out in some parts of the private residential sector (e.g. Hunt 1989).

Finally, and most importantly since they are the object of the PSS, the impact of the policy reforms on clients will vary. There is scope for increased choice and 'voice' for consumers, and for services which are designed to fulfil their individual needs, through care management, complaints procedures and so on, but ultimately choice is determined by income. For those with money, confidence and clout, the changes may give greater choice of services; for those who rely on state or family support, they may result in reduced choice, protection and security. Perhaps the people who will be most affected are those who are too well off to be eligible for most state benefits, but not well enough off to afford to pay for care, and whose families cannot or will not foot the bill. Baldock and Evers (1991) argue that the twin emphases on charging anyone above a minimum income and contracting-out a service wherever possible, mean that the principle (if not practice) of universal entitlement enshrined in the Welfare State since its creation will be replaced by selective state provision of social care for the minority of old people who are officially in poverty, and who will receive a basic minimum service. Others will have to fend for themselves. This will return the PSS to its pre-Seebohm days as a stigmatizing paupers' service and will promote inequalities (Johnson 1990).

Acknowledgement

I would like to thank Aidan Kelly and Peter Taylor-Gooby for their helpful comments and suggestions on earlier drafts of this chapter.

6

Social security: The income maintenance business

Hartley Dean

Social security is the UK government's largest expenditure programme, accounting for 31 per cent of planned public spending in 1992–93. Spending on social security increased in real terms by some 44 per cent between 1978–79 and 1991–92 and is officially projected to continue to rise by over 3 per cent per year for the next four years. The cost of administering the system accounts for approximately 5 per cent of total expenditure (DSS 1992a).

The relentless increase in the scale of the social security programme has been driven by demographic, social and economic factors: in particular, by population ageing, by changes in household/family composition and by high levels of unemployment. This chapter, however, is not about the accumulating demands upon the social security budget, but about issues of benefits delivery and how, during the 1980s and early 1990s, the government responded. In each section below, I shall focus on three aspects of that response: first, the attempts by Conservative governments to privatize aspects of income maintenance; second, their attempts to achieve the administrative simplification of benefits; and, third, their approach to the managerial reform of benefits delivery.

The policy debate: Ideas for change

In 1983, Norman Fowler, then Secretary of State for Social Services, announced a series of reviews that resulted in proposals for the reform of social security (DHSS 1985a), and subsequently in legislation, the main provisions of which were implemented in 1988. These and other reforms implemented

during the Thatcher years were ostensibly aimed at shifting the balance between state (i.e. collective) and individual (i.e. private) provision and at producing a state system which would be 'simpler to understand and easier to
administer' (ibid.: para. 1.12). However, with the advent of John Major's
premiership in 1990 and the launch of his *Citizens' Charter* (Cabinet Office
1991a), a further debate has begun, bearing upon the managerial reforms
required to produce the standard of 'service' which social security claimants as
'customers' should receive.

Privatization

The Fowler reviews were informed, in part at least, by an agenda set by right-
wing ideologues who wished to see a diminution of Welfare State activity
(Ward 1985). The 'basic principle' was that 'social security is not a function of
the state alone. It is a partnership between the individual and the state – a
system built on twin pillars' (DHSS 1985a: para. 1.5). This meant that the
government wished in particular to relieve itself of the burden of financing the
State Earnings Related Pension Scheme (SERPS) and to encourage people to
provide for the 'topping up' of their basic state retirement pensions by joining
personal or occupational pension schemes. At the same time, the government
eroded the real value of the basic retirement pension by uprating it in line with
price inflation, rather than average earnings.

The government claimed that private financial institutions could provide
future pensioners with greater choice and flexibility when planning for their
retirement. Commentators of the left, however, objected that strengthening
the private and occupational sectors while marginalizing state welfare would
shift the burden of the 'social costs' of capitalism to those who were most
disadvantaged in the marketplace (Walker 1984). Other critics of a free market
in pensions complained that the returns which pensioners might receive from
private schemes need not be guaranteed: SERPS, which had been introduced
in 1978, promised gradually to lift increasing numbers of pensioners out of
poverty, whereas dependency on private provision would result in greater
inequality in old age and in increased numbers of pensioners having to resort to
means-tested benefits (SSC 1987).

Other benefits were also considered for privatization. In 1980, the
government had proposed the introduction of statutory sick pay (SSP) in
place of national insurance sickness benefit (NISB) for employees during
short-term sickness absence. The government should 'disengage itself from
activities which firms and individuals can perform perfectly well for themselves' (DHSS 1980:2). Such a view was opposed by the welfare rights lobby,
which argued that 'income maintenance is a collective responsibility which is
best discharged by the state' (CPAG 1980), and by small employers' organizations who argued that such responsibility belonged neither to the state nor
employers, but to individual workers who should buy private sickness insurance (e.g. NFSESB 1980).

In the event, the SSP scheme, introduced in 1983, 'privatized' not the cost of sickness benefit, but its administration. Provision was made for employers to pay SSP during initial periods of sickness and to be reimbursed by the government. This, it was hoped, would indirectly encourage the development of occupational provision above the statutory minimum (Disney 1987). Having established this precedent, the government sought to introduce statutory maternity pay (SMP) upon a similar basis and even proposed that Family Credit (a means-tested benefit for low-paid families) should be administered by employers. The latter proposition met with opposition from the welfare rights lobby and employers, who both agreed that it would involve an unwanted intrusion into the personal circumstances of employees.

Administrative simplification

The social security system inherited by the Thatcher governments was highly complex. The basic structure established in the 1940s involved a tripartite division between a national insurance scheme (funded in principle through contributions), a means-tested social assistance scheme (originally national assistance and later supplementary benefit) and a family allowance scheme (now child benefit). However, various accretions to this structure had been introduced: new means-tested schemes, such as rent and rate rebates (now Housing Benefit) and family income supplement (for low-paid workers with children), and non-contributory contingent benefits for disabled people and their carers. What is more, the structure as originally envisaged by Beveridge had become distorted. National insurance benefits had been intended as the mainstay of a comprehensive system of income maintenance, while means-tested social assistance had been provided as a safety-net. In practice, by 1983, over 7 million people were dependent on supplementary benefit (DHSS 1985c), despite attempts to improve national insurance benefits through the addition of earnings-related components. In the meantime, as it struggled to adapt to its role as a mass benefit scheme addressing the needs of diverse groups within the population, supplementary benefit was becoming so complicated and unwieldy as to be unadministrable.

This was the background to the government's call for 'simplification'. Prior to the Fowler reviews, the government had already swept away the administratively complex earnings-related additions to short-term national insurance benefits and now sought to abolish SERPS. Taken as a whole, the reforms reduced the role of the national insurance scheme and embraced means-tested benefits, not as a safety-net, but as the mainstay of the income maintenance system and as the most efficient way of 'targeting' help.

In acknowledgement of the central role of existing means-tested benefits (supplementary benefit, family income supplement and Housing Benefit), the government proposed to rationalize them by making them all subject to the same basic criteria, and by altering such criteria from entitlement based upon individual needs to entitlement based upon broad 'client groups'. Supplementary benefit was to become Income Support, family income supplement was to become

Family Credit, Housing Benefit was to retain its name but conditions of entitlement under the Family Credit and the new Housing Benefit schemes were to be brought into line with those for Income Support. Those conditions would no longer rest upon the specific additional requirements of claimants (for heating, diet, etc.), but upon set 'premiums' according to claimant type (pensioner, family, lone parent, disabled, etc.). The complex system of single payments which had been available under the supplementary benefit scheme to meet exceptional needs was to be replaced by the controversial Social Fund. While no less complex than the previous scheme, the Social Fund was to be administratively distinct.

Critics of these proposals argued that simplification would lead to inflexibility and there was fierce debate about how many people would gain and how many would lose. The government claimed that the majority of supplementary benefit claimants would be better or no worse off after the reforms and acknowledged that 'only' 35 per cent would lose, but independent calculations suggested that as many as 60 per cent of claimants would be worse off (see Svenson and MacPherson 1988).

Managerial reform

During the 1980s, discussion of managerial reform was overshadowed by debate over administrative structure and as to the proper role of the state in income maintenance provision. It was not until the late 1980s that the language of consumerism began to be accepted into political and technical discourse relating to social security. Arguably, the Thatcher years had established the limits to which the state could withdraw from responsibility, so attention turned to the reconstruction of social security provision as a 'service'. In the language of the *Citizens' Charter* and the Benefit Agency's 'Business Plan' (DSS 1991), the social security claimant has been recast as a 'customer'.

However, the seeds for such managerial reform had been quietly sown at the beginning of the 1980s with the announcement of the 'Operational Strategy' (or OS) (DHSS 1982a). This was ostensibly a technical project for the computerization of the social security system, which it was claimed would be the largest civil computerization project in Europe. The introduction of information technology was seen by the authors of the OS to make attainable far-reaching managerial objectives:

[1] to improve operational efficiency, reduce administrative costs and increase the flexibility of the operational system to respond to changing requirements;
[2] to improve the quality of service to the public, e.g. by treating customers in a less compartmentalised benefit-by-benefit manner and more as 'whole persons' with a range of social security business: and by improving the provision of information to the public; and
[3] to modernise and improve the work of social security staff (ibid.: 1).

The OS portended a move away from 'Fordist' production principles, by which social security offices functioned as self-contained clerical 'factories', and towards 'post-Fordist' principles, by which the offices would constitute 'high-tech' components within a flexible decentralized network (Wyatt 1991). The OS also portended a new deal for claimants based upon the 'whole person concept'. In the event, while the OS proceeded in technical terms, neither of these radical justifications were subject to serious debate until quite recently. The potential of the OS as a vehicle for managerial reform began to be realized in the late 1980s with proposals (in a report characteristically entitled *The Business of Service*: DSS 1988a) for the reorganization of the local office network, and with the emergence of the so-called Next Steps Initiative (Efficiency Unit 1988).

This last development led in 1991 to the creation of the Benefit Agency, an 'arms length' executive limb of government. If the state was to retain extensive responsibilities for income maintenance, one way to make benefits administration more 'business-like' was to render it semi-autonomous and accountable for achieving targets set by government. To the extent that the OS was intended to make possible significant reductions in staff and greater flexibility in deployment, it now became the motor behind the Benefit Agency's drive to meet its targets (SSSC 1991: paras 235–359). However, the reforms were to be guided increasingly by business principles and by 'service framework agreements' between ministers and the Benefit Agency. The rhetoric of 'Next Steps' spoke in terms of giving managers the freedom to manage, although critics of the government feared this might make the system less not more accountable to users (see, for example, Islington 1991; Lynes 1991).

Meanwhile, the 'whole person concept', although widely endorsed, remained 'something of a skeletal idea' (Adler and Sainsbury 1991:1). It is unclear whether the idea is supposed to relate to the integrity of the administrative processes to which claimants are subjected or to the way in which claimants ought to be treated.

The policy changes: The process of implementation

While the pace of change in the social security system was considerable, there has been no single decisive break from the past.

Privatization

The government's original wish to abolish SERPS and usher in a free market in pensions was frustrated by 'highly complex and entrenched institutional arrangements and by the ambiguities of public opinion' (Papadakis and Taylor-Gooby 1987: 133). Nevertheless, SERPS was substantially modified so that the value of benefits to pensioners under the scheme was approximately halved (SSC 1987). The Social Security Act 1986 set out to promote alternatives to state provision by allowing employees to contract out of SERPS and to take out personal pension plans (PPPs). In parallel with this, employers were permitted to convert contracted out occupational pension schemes (which under the Social Security Act 1975 had been required to guarantee a proportion of final earnings for each year of service) into Contracted Out Money Purchase Schemes (COMPS), in which it was the level of contributions rather than the level of benefits which must be guaranteed. PPPs, COMPS and all new occupational pension schemes created after 1986 were promoted by the promise of 'special incentive' payments by the government equivalent to 2 per cent of reckonable earnings to supplement employees' contributions.

By October 1991, 4.6 million people had taken out PPPs and 18,500 COMPS and 6100 new salary-related occupational pension schemes had been established. The total cost of 'special incentive' payments had risen to £1.8 billion (DSS 1992a: 16), while the cost of revenue foregone by the national insurance fund had been estimated at £5.9 billion in 1990 (NAO 1991: 18).

Turning to the introduction of employer administered benefits, having conceded major revisions, the government managed in 1983 to introduce SSP. The scheme initially covered only the first eight weeks of sickness absence, though this was extended in 1986 to twenty-eight weeks, thus virtually abolishing NISB. Also in 1986, SMP was introduced: like SSP, it was fully funded by the government but was provided for up to eighteen weeks, thus replacing the national insurance maternity allowance for the majority of eligible employees. The government made negligible if any financial savings from the introduction of SSP, but under the administrative arrangements of the scheme employers – especially large employers already operating occupational sick pay (OSC) schemes – benefited from expenditure savings (see Dean and Taylor-Gooby 1990a).

Since 1991, however, employers have been made to meet 20 per cent of the cost of SSP and their exemption from national insurance contributions (NICs) on SSP payments to employees has also been withdrawn. The fears of those who foresaw that employer mandated benefits might represent the 'thin end of a wedge' (by which responsibility for costs as well as administration might be transferred from government to employers) have been vindicated. However, the government retreated completely from its proposal that Family Credit should be employer administered.

Administrative simplification

Reforms to the structure of benefits proceeded broadly in accordance with the government's plans. However, the government's claim that 'claimants will no longer need detailed knowledge of the system to claim their full rights' (DHSS 1985b: para. 1.29) proved unfounded for at least three reasons. First, the reforms amounted in a general sense to 'a shift in the centre of gravity of the benefits system away from benefits as of right towards benefits requiring a "test of income" ' (Bennett 1987: 125). The clearest example of this was the decision to freeze child benefit from 1988 in order to switch resources into the means-tested Family Credit scheme. Means-tested benefits are necessarily more complex to administer and to claim than contributory or contingent benefits, which limits the scope for simplification.

Second, because the government had sought to achieve simplification on a nil-cost basis, many supplementary benefit claimants stood to lose and it was therefore necessary in the short term to introduce a byzantine system of transitional allowances. The changes to Housing Benefit also resulted for many recipients in losses of benefit. These proved greater than had been anticipated (especially by back-bench Conservative MPs) and the government was panicked into adopting more generous capital disregard rules for Housing Benefit than for Income Support (thus undermining the alignment between the two benefits) and into introducing yet another transitional protection scheme.

Third, even allowing for the teething troubles of a new system and the complexity of the transition process, there is little evidence that the benefits system is any more comprehensible. Income Support may be simpler to administer than supplementary benefit, but for claimants, one set of complexities has been replaced by another. It may be easier to allocate a 'client group premium' than to determine an 'additional requirement' based on a specific need, but eligibility for such premiums is still subject to a system of rules which is not necessarily transparent to claimants, while the claim form which Income Support claimants are required to complete is a daunting twenty-page booklet. In some instances, what had been transparent has been rendered obscure: whereas supplementary benefit claimants had received a specific addition to meet water rates, and general rates were fully met through Housing Benefit, Income Support claimants must now take it on trust that their 'personal allowances' contain a notional element sufficient to meet 'average' water rates and 20 per cent of 'average' general rates/poll tax/council tax.

The government was also concerned to maintain work incentives for the unemployed, to enforce the obligations of liable relatives and to be seen to be preventing fraud and abuse. The many and various restrictions associated with these preoccupations (see Dean and Taylor-Gooby 1992) were calculated to increase and not reduce the complexity of the claiming process, particularly for groups such as lone parents and the unemployed. The introduction of the Social Fund, justified as a measure to instil greater budgetary discipline upon claimants, involved a return to far greater bureaucratic complexity and discretion than the supplementary benefit single payment scheme (see Becker and Silburn 1991).

Managerial reform

The OS was to have achieved the complete computerization of the DHSS by 1991, an objective which was substantially achieved, at a cost of some £2 billion (more than twice the original estimate) and with various elements of the system (including incapacity benefits) still to be integrated. The extended planning and procurement phase of the OS was fraught with difficulty and delay. While the government stopped short of contracting out the project entirely to the private sector, external consultants played a major part in designing the OS, often at the expense of end-user involvement (Dyerson and Roper 1991).

A Departmental Central Index, a Pensions Strategy Computer System and the major Local Office Project were all set up, the latter being introduced into pilot offices in 1988 and then progressively 'rolled out' to the majority of DSS offices between 1989 and 1991. However, political pressure to introduce the system on time and to achieve the cost-efficiency savings promised by the OS (including an estimated reduction of over 13,000 staff by 1999) necessitated 'a degree of compromise between service levels and systems capabilities' (ibid.: 1). This meant that staff were obliged to devise *ad hoc* methods to work around inflexibilities in the system (see SSSC 1991b: paras. 117–18), but more fundamentally, the extent of integration between different benefit schemes within the system was 'less than originally anticipated' (Dyerson and Roper 1991: 14).

Coincidentally, the 500 local social security offices were reorganized into a network of 159 districts, each with a single management team responsible for the local branch offices in their district. In the case of twenty-one London offices, work not requiring 'face-to-face' contact with the public was relocated to three large new Social Security Centres – in Glasgow, Belfast and Mackerfield – where staff recruitment and retention were easier. This was made possible by the OS and by an advanced new telecommunications system, known as CENTREX. The relocation exercise was regarded as an experiment in the use of technology to rationalize benefits administration. However, the experiment proved unpopular with claimants (see Towerwatch Report 1991). The relocation of work from other offices is an option which the Benefit Agency is keeping open, although cost-efficiency savings from the experiment have been slower than anticipated and, pending an evaluation, there are no plans to extend the scheme (SSSC 1991b: para. 363).

Between 1989 and 1993, the DSS was to be divided into five 'Next Steps' executive agencies, the biggest of which (with around 70,000 staff) is the Benefit Agency, created in 1991. The other agencies are: the Resettlement Agency, set up in 1989 to manage the DSS's nineteen surviving resettlement units for 'people with an unsettled way of life'; the Information Technology Services Agency, which absorbed the OS Directorate and related computer services; the Contributions Agency, responsible for the collection of NICs and maintaining contribution records; and the Child Support Agency, due to be established in 1993 to implement the provisions of the Child Support Act and which will, in the process, take over the 'liable relatives' work currently performed within the Benefit Agency. The agencies are charged with carrying out their respective functions within a policy and resources framework set by the DSS and are required to produce an annual business plan showing how targets and performance standards will be met.

The Benefit Agency is responsible for the assessment and payment of all claims for the full range of social security benefits and pensions. It is also responsible for the detection, investigation and prosecution of fraudulent 'customers'. The 159 district offices are each required to produce district strategic plans and annual business plans on the basis of 'market research' and public consultation. The attention so far given to consultation arrangements in different districts has been at best patchy, with some district managers actively promoting benefits liaison groups (involving voluntary groups, local authorities and claimants) and others exhibiting a 'marked reluctance' to engage in dialogue with outside organizations (Lakhani 1991).

As a result of the government's *Citizens' Charter* initiative, the Benefit Agency is additionally producing a 'customer charter', publishing its various targets at both national and district level and introducing Customer Service Managers in each office. While the emphasis required by the *Citizens' Charter* is upon 'quality of service', this has in the recent past been primarily interpreted – both within the DSS and beyond – in relation to such performance indicators as the standards of speed and accuracy in decision making (see NAO 1988; Adler and Sainsbury 1990). Thus, for example, the Benefit Agency's target in 1991–92 was to process all Income Support claims within an average clearance time of five days, with an accuracy rate of 93 per cent. The Benefit Agency's objective over the next two years is to move away from targets based on average clearance times and towards targets which require a set percentage of all claims to be processed within a definite time limit (see SSSC 1991: para. 292).

The impact of change: The emerging issues

Despite their extent, the changes described above have not so much defined new issues as a new context within which certain emerging issues of service delivery must be addressed.

Privatization

During the 1980s, the proportion of pension payments originating from the private sector (both personal and occupational) was rising as the proportion originating from the state was falling (from 53.1 per cent in 1978–79 to 43.2 per cent in 1987–88; see Barr and Coulter 1990: table 7.4). This was due in part to the slower growth in state spending arising from the indexation of pensions to prices rather than earnings, and partly to a continuing expansion of occupational pension provision (received by 29 per cent of elderly people in 1975, but 39 per cent in 1990; ibid.: table 7.5; OPCS 1992: table 4.14). The changes introduced by the Social Security Act 1986 were therefore building upon a well-established trend towards the privatization of pensions. There are, however, three major issues associated with this trend.

First, the spread of occupational and personal pension provision is uneven and there is evidence that, coupled with the declining value of the basic state pension relative to earnings, this is leading to greater inequality. There is considerable variability in the extent and standards of occupational pension provision. Although there has been a gradual trend towards the harmonization of provision as between men and women and as between non-manual and manual workers, significant discrepancies remain (see Papadakis and Taylor-Gooby 1987). Little is known as yet about which groups within the working population have participated in the substantial growth in PPPs, but it is higher earning and/or securely employed groups which are most likely to be attracted. Households Below Average Income (HBAI) statistics show that between 1979 and 1988 the proportion of pensioner households to be found within the poorest fifth of the population fell from 34 to 30 per cent and this was in part due to the expansion of occupational provision (SSSC 1991a). However, the statistics also show a very high risk of poverty among single as opposed to married pensioners, which indicates that recent trends have been to the particular disadvantage of women in retirement and to older pensioners who have never had the opportunity to contribute to occupational schemes.

Second, questions must be raised about the degree of risk associated with private pension funds, which may be vulnerable to maladministration and to adverse market forces. Occupational pension funds are subject to a limited degree of regulation by the Occupational Pension Board (OPB) and personal pension funds by the Securities and Investment Board (SIB) and, in 1991, the government also introduced a pensions registry and a pensions ombudsman. However, the Robert Maxwell affair (in which substantial sums had been siphoned from the Mirror Group Pension Fund in order to meet the proprietor's personal debts) drew attention to the absence of any effective protection for pensioners in company schemes (see SSSC 1992). What is more, even if the probity and competence of fund managers could be guaranteed, there can be no protection against the fluctuations and hazards of financial markets. The greatest threat to the stability of the private pensions industry arises from the very factor which the Conservative government had called in aid of its preference for promoting private provision, namely the effects of population ageing. Ermisch (1990) has argued that occupational and personal pension schemes will not necessarily be immune from the consequences of demographic change since, as the 'baby boom' generations reach retirement in the next century, the resulting rush by funded pension schemes to realize assets may provoke a crisis in capital markets and so prejudice the returns on pensioners' contributions.

Third, account must be taken of the full costs to the state of the expansion of private pensions and of how those costs are distributed. To the cost of the special incentive payments and the direct losses of revenue to the National Insurance Fund (see above) must be added the revenue lost to the Exchequer from tax relief on private pension contributions and from tax exemptions upon pension fund income/capital gains and upon lump-sum payments to pensioners. The total annual cost of these 'tax expenditures' has been calculated to have risen during the 1980s from £2.6 billion to £6.5 billion (NAO 1990). Like mortgage tax relief, such expenditures are demand-led and their distributive effect is regressive: higher-paid employees reap proportionately greater advantages than lower-paid employees. Private pensions under the present regime amount to a form of tax-free saving of particular benefit to the better off (Wilkinson 1986).

As with occupational pensions, the growth in occupational provision for short-term sickness represents a trend which predated the policy changes of the 1980s. The evidence suggests that the introduction of SSP had a minimal impact upon OSP coverage, which has been steadily expanding since the 1960s (from 57 per cent in 1961 to 91 per cent in 1988; see DSS 1988b; Dean and Taylor-Gooby 1990b). Like occupational pensions, OSP schemes are subject to considerable variation as to their terms and scope and, despite some trends towards the harmonization of entitlements, public sector employees and workers in large-scale service and new manufacturing industries tend to fare better than workers in small businesses and the older industries. Substantial numbers of part-time, casual and short-serving workers are excluded from OSP provision and the evidence for increasingly widespread occupational provision conceals a growing disparity between the conditions of service enjoyed by higher-paid 'core' workers and those endured by more vulnerable 'peripheral' workers. Analysis of data from the General Household Survey (GHS) before and after the introduction of SSP suggests that the scheme was reasonably successful in getting some income to the majority of sick or absent workers and in reducing the numbers who suffered a substantial drop in income (Dean and Taylor-Gooby 1990b). However, the same analysis also makes clear that those employees who suffer the biggest losses of income during sickness are concentrated among the semi- and unskilled workers, again suggesting the presence within the workforce of a vulnerable minority dependent on statutory minima without a recourse to higher levels of occupational provision.

The introduction of SSP was received by some employers as an opportunity to extend the monitoring and control of sickness absence in their workforces (Dean and Taylor-Gooby 1990a). SSP involved a significant shift of administrative power from the state to the private employer. The government's experiment with employer administered benefits, like its attempts further to promote private pensions, was most significant, not for net reductions in state spending, but for the roles it has conferred upon private institutions.

Administrative simplification

An exercise comparing the incomes of claimants coming onto Income Support in 1990–91 with those of supplementary benefit claimants in 1987–88 concluded that many claimants had become worse off in real terms (CPAG 1990). However, the distorting effect of transitional measures and the dearth of official statistics for more recent years make it difficult to assess the consequences of the 'simplifying' reforms for different groups. The immediate effect of the 1988 changes appears in relative terms to have benefited couples with children at the expense of lone parents, but also to have adversely affected pensioners (SSSC 1991a). Nevertheless, changes to the benefits system were but one factor contributing to a general trend towards greater inequality in the 1980s (see Townsend 1991) and the specific impact of administrative simplification is at present unclear.

Recent qualitative research upon the experiences of social security claimants found that less than a third of a sample of working age social security claimants considered the claiming process to be easy or straightforward (Dean and Taylor-Gooby 1992: 107). The advantages of such simplification as has occurred have been outweighed by the strengthening of administrative surveillance. Claimants are made to feel vulnerable and anxious and that the process is designed to catch them out or trip them up (ibid.: 111). There have been aspects of the benefits system where administrative simplification has been sacrificed in the interests of achieving greater administrative power; power that is deployed to enforce greater self-sufficiency on the part of welfare dependants. In particular, the tightening of the regime to which unemployed claimants are subject is intended to promote work incentives and to oblige the unemployed to accept less rewarding jobs; the elaborate rationing of loans from the Social Fund and the machinery of the proposed Child Support Agency are intended to promote greater dependency upon family members and liable relatives and to oblige claimants to maximize financial support from family and conjugal relationships. Such objectives are not only incompatible with administrative simplicity, they may actually be counterproductive if they run against the grain of popular cultural aspirations and expectations (ibid.: ch. 4).

Managerial reform

The operational efficiency which the OS and the reorganization of local offices were aimed to achieve was supposed to make possible more modern and congenial working practices, and a better and more coherent service. The actual impact, however, has fallen short of both goals. Civil service trade unions have argued in evidence to the SSSC that information technology and office networking has fragmented the work of social security staff:

> We believe that, in terms of job satisfaction to members of staff, the ideals are not being realised. The jobs are in fact becoming compartmentalised. The members are becoming button pushers. These are highly qualified, highly trained staff and we believe that they could be used much more ambitiously. (SSSC 1991b: para. 116)

The implication is that, in place of the old integrated local offices – which processed several benefits clerically in one location – the DSS have created a monolithic network of rigidly specialized information-processing points. Information technology and managerial reform have resulted not in the decentralization of decision-making processes and a greater flexibility and diversity of skills, but in the centralization of management control, a more rigorous separation of conception from execution and a tendency to staff 'deskilling' (as characterized in Braverman's classic critique of Taylorist management; see Braverman 1974; Cousins 1987).

According to welfare rights organizations like the National Association of Citizens' Advice Bureaux (NACAB) and the Central London Social Security Advisers' Forum (CLSSAF), this fragmentation of labour processes inside the DSS has been reflected in a failure to achieve the coherence of service implied by the much vaunted 'whole person concept'. Questioning the commitment of the DSS to the idea that local branch offices should be 'one stop shops', a CLSSAF spokesperson explained in evidence to the SSSC:

> There are some people in the Department who believe having a one stop shop means having a receptionist who can tell you where your case is: "'phone Glasgow about IS, 'phone Newcastle about pensions, 'phone Hastings about Liable Relatives position" and so forth. Some people in the Department feel that this will satisfy the Prime Minister's idea about the whole person concept. (SSSC 1991b: para. 191)

Following Mashaw (1983), Adler and Sainsbury (1991) have argued that there are three models of what good administration should comprise: the bureaucratic model, which values speed, accuracy and cost-effectiveness in decision making; the professional model, which is holistic and client-oriented; and the juridical model, which is concerned with the adjudication of disputed claims and the fairness with which benefits are allocated. Adler and Sainsbury's assessment of the way in which the OS has been implemented is that it has adopted a predominantly bureaucratic approach to managerial reform. This 'triumph of bureaucratic rationality', they say, 'has come about due to DSS taking a restricted view of what quality of service entails' (ibid.: 37).

The other major managerial reform in recent years has been the move to agency status. The Benefit Agency has been contrived ostensibly to create the appearance of a supplier–customer relationship in place of the state–claimant relationship fostered by a conventional government department. However, just as the creation in the 1930s of the Unemployment Assistance Board had been intended to deflect criticism of the benefits system away from the government (see Lynes 1975), so the creation of the Benefit Agency undeniably serves to distance present-day policy makers from the responsibility of implementing the distributive priorities which they determine.

Within months of the Benefit Agency coming into existence, its chief executive was expressing fears that, as a result of an unforeseen rise in unemployment, the workload of the agency and the resources allowed to it no longer matched (SSSC 1991b: para. 27). An additional £29.5 million had to be negotiated for the Benefit Agency, and describing the 'constructive tension' between the Secretary of State and himself, the chief executive explained: 'my first task . . . is to manage within the budget I am given and to try to provide the level of service which we have contracted to provide within that budget and it is only if that becomes impossible that I would want to renegotiate targets or resources' (ibid.: para. 353). This raises the first of three issues concerning the Benefit Agency's targets. Resources may prove insufficient to meet such targets and, if additional resources cannot then be secured from the

Treasury (as they were in 1991), a politically expedient dilution of standards might be negotiated instead.

The second issue concerns the terms in which performance targets are set. One of the complaints levelled by welfare rights groups has been that a target based, for example, upon the percentage of claims to be processed within a set time limit, offers no incentive to deal effectively with the remaining cases, which may in fact include those cases which are most difficult or urgent (SSSC 1991b: paras 221 and 293). While the Benefit Agency may be in a position to claim to have met or even exceeded its targets, it may none the less be providing a very poor service to a vulnerable minority among its 'customers'.

The third issue concerns the scope of the Benefit Agency's target. The performance targets set by the government do not include targets for promoting the take-up of benefits, but they do include targets for benefit savings from anti-fraud work (£382 million in 1991–92). Unlike a commercial enterprise, the Benefit Agency is not required to promote its services to potential customers and, when pressed upon this difference, the Permanent Secretary at the DSS has admitted, 'There are differences. For one thing, they are in it to make profits; we are in it to distribute taxpayers' money' (SSSC 1991b: para. 33). A National Association for the Care and Resettlement of Offenders (NACRO) working party, set up to examine the enforcement of the law relating to social security, once observed that there is an 'unavoidable tension' between the first duty of those who administer social security – 'prompt payment of benefits and relief of need with due consideration for people's dignity and welfare' – and their secondary function of 'combating abuse' (NACRO 1986: 16). That unavoidable tension has now been transferred to the Benefit Agency and has not in any way been ameliorated through the setting of targets which might guarantee a proper balance between these conflicting priorities.

International influences

Challenges arising from fiscal, labour market and demographic trends have required a reappraisal of income maintenance policies throughout the 'developed' world and the policy responses of the UK government should be viewed within a global context.

Privatization

To the extent that the underlying direction of policies on pensions and benefits during the Thatcher years amounted to an attempt partially to dismantle the social security system, the government would seem to have been influenced by ideas from the USA. The foremost US advocate of welfare retrenchment, Charles Murray, is known to have visited the UK and met with DHSS and Treasury officials and members of the Prime Minister's policy unit (Levy 1988). Murray's (1984) argument, which reflected a dominant strand in US welfare planning during the Reagan era, was that the state income maintenance policy was itself to blame for the persistence of poverty.

As it happens, the UK social security system was not dismantled, but benefit spending was restrained and a substantial shift of emphasis occurred in favour of private and occupational provision. In this, the UK stood in an 'exceptional position' in relation to other European Community (EC) countries (Chamberlayne 1992: 17). Within the EC, the UK government has sought consistently to resist the idea of a 'social dimension' to European union and to dilute the impact of 'social' measures directed to securing the harmonization of employment protection regimes (Low Pay Unit 1991, 1992). Most recently, the UK government opted out of the 'social chapter' of the Maastricht Treaty, which has none the less been adopted as a separate protocol by the other eleven member states and which includes provision relating to social security and minimum income protection.

However, one area in which the UK has been 'dragged along by the EC' relates to equal opportunities policy (Baldwin-Edwards and Gough 1991: 157). EC equal treatment directives and rulings of the European Court have resulted in changes to social security legislation, particularly in relation to invalid care allowances for married women and the statutory regulation of occupational pensions. At the time of writing, the issue of equal pension ages for men and women has been forced onto the agenda by EC directives. Although the latter relate specifically to occupational social security schemes, they have indirectly compelled the UK government to re-examine the question of the statutory pension age and the framework within which state and occupational schemes interrelate.

Administrative simplification

The UK government's commitment to administrative simplification was, as we have seen, ambiguous. Shifting the emphasis towards more minimal forms of income maintenance policy has entailed greater reliance on means-testing processes which remain complex, even when streamlined. Although never expressed as a long-term aim, the logical conclusion to the policy direction espoused by Conservative governments could be described as 'simplification' if indeed it were eventually to result in the dismantling of national insurance and some or all of the various contingent benefit schemes. To this extent, the UK has been subject to US rather than EC influences.

There are indications however that, in the long-term, the UK may be obliged to move back into line with other Western European countries in matters of income maintenance policy. By opting out of the social chapter at Maastricht, the UK was seeking to secure an advantage over its competitors in the world economy and to continue a trend towards an ever wider spread of earnings. However, Northcott (1991: 286) has argued that this trend will pose 'an increasingly insoluble dilemma'. The relative fall in earnings at the bottom of the UK earnings distribution will compel the government either to set means-tested benefit levels so low that they inflict acute hardship, or else to allow benefits to rise above the lower earnings range so that people will lose all incentive to work or save. It is inevitable, therefore, that the UK should revert to the use of social insurance and/or universal benefits and 'in particular, child benefit which can help cover the costs of bringing up children without at the same time reducing work incentives for their parents' (ibid.). This prophecy has already been partially fulfilled in so far that the UK government began to make concessions in this direction in its 1991 budget, when child benefit was uprated for the first time in four years.

Managerial reform

While policy makers may seek to emulate or eschew the examples of other national governments, the influences which ultimately exert themselves may in a more subtle sense be global rather than specific. This may yet prove to be true in the case of information technology-led innovations to the management of the UK social security system.

Information technology and the management culture associated with its application represents a phenomenon of trans-national provenance within the capitalist world. The input by external computer consultants was acknowledged by civil servants involved in the development and implementation of the OS to have 'sharpened' their management skills (Dyerson and Roper 1991: 6). However, the OS has failed to realize its potential in terms of the greater control and discretion it was to have conferred upon management at local or district level (ibid.: 7–8). More generally, as is observed above, the OS has been blamed for rendering benefits administration more rather than less 'Fordist' or 'Taylorist': it is alleged to have given rise to less flexibility and greater fragmentation in working practices, which perversely is the opposite trend to that conventionally associated with the computerization of production processes.

As the OS develops, this may change. The constraints upon such a process relate to the context of the managerial reform. The UK government has been resistant to the emphasis characteristic in France and Italy during the 1980s towards decentralization and consumer participation as ways to democratize income maintenance provision (see Chamberlayne 1992: 15). As in other areas of policy, it may be that in the course of the next decade European models will come to exercise more influence upon methods of service delivery in the UK. The very limited and patchy attempts at consumer consultation now being attempted by the Benefit Agency may portend the beginnings of a movement away from a highly bureaucratized approach to benefits administration.

Conclusion

Despite the changing policy context resulting from economic, social and political trends, three central issues continue to underlie the development of income maintenance provision: the necessary extent of state involvement; the balance between universalism and selectivity; the question of whether recipients of cash benefits are to be treated as citizens or as administrative subjects.

The trend towards private and occupational provision for income during retirement and sickness is well established and has been accelerated by recent changes in government policy. This chapter has argued that the distributive impact of this trend will itself have consequences for future state provision, especially if marginalized groups within the population are not to be seriously disadvantaged. In particular, the state will have a continuing role to play in regulating the standards of provision within the private/occupational sectors and in providing adequate safety-net provision for those whom mainstream structures cannot or will not accommodate.

The debate concerning the respective advantages of universal versus selective provision in social security is customarily conducted with reference to the competing principles of social justice and economic efficiency. This chapter has sought to highlight some of the technical considerations of that debate. Recent attempts to achieve a measure of simplification in benefits administration have demonstrated that simplification and selectivity are inherently incompatible. If administrative simplicity is valued as an end in itself, it would be better achieved by a shift towards universalism.

Recent managerial reforms within the DSS – the implementation of the Operational Strategy and the creation of the Benefit Agency – have failed to give expression to the 'whole person concept' in the administration of income maintenance. Neither have the reforms demonstrably increased the public accountability of that administration. So long as the administration of benefits remains so bureaucratized and so tied to the control of individual behaviour, then benefit recipients – whether they be described as 'claimants' or 'customers' – will not be constituted as citizens exercising rights, but as the subjects of administrative government.

7

The new educational settlement: National Curriculum and local management

Peter Taylor-Gooby

Over the past fifteen years, virtually every aspect of education policy in the UK has been remodelled. Curriculum, examinations, teacher training, management, finance, the roles of parents, potential employers, planners and professionals in the system, even the length of the school year and the age-range covered by compulsory schooling are affected. A major restructuring of post-school and university education is now in progress. The new education settlement represents the most substantial change in what is taught, to whom and under whose control for half a century.

The context

From the end of the war to the early 1980s, the education system in this country displayed four main features. First, the organization of the system represented an administrative compromise between broad central direction and local control so that local government had considerable influence on the planning, finance and management of schooling, further education and the polytechnic sector of higher education. Central government passed legislation, inspected schools, and produced reports and recommendations. Local authorities set budgets and took responsibility for schooling in their area. There was considerable scope for diversity between them in such matters as level of spending, selection at age eleven and provision for preschooling or for those over sixteen.

The second feature was that schools as institutions had become more similar, but provided diverse educational experiences. The private sector played a declining but still significant role, catering for some 5 per cent of children drawn almost entirely from the upper and middle classes by the mid-1970s. In the state sector, comprehensive schools had replaced the division between grammar and secondary moderns for over 90 per cent of students. However, despite the trend to comprehensive schooling, educational pathways within schools varied considerably for different groups. Curriculum was driven almost entirely by professional decisions, heavily influenced by teachers themselves and for secondary schools by the syllabuses of examining boards which were dominated by professional educators. A clear division existed between the curriculum of higher achieving students, leading typically to sixth-form schooling, A-levels and higher education, and that of less academically successful students, who tended to receive little education beyond the minimum school-leaving age of sixteen.

Taken together, the division of administrative control between central and local government and the curricular authority of professionals led to the third feature of educational policy in the UK. Since different interests were involved, change tended to follow from the slow evolution of consensus rather than from central direction. The limits to innovation were dictated by the willingness of different interests to compromise. Changes which threatened the vital interests of any group – for example, a reduction in professional power over the curriculum, the imposition of uniformity between areas, erosion of the privilege of advantaged groups – were virtually impossible to achieve.

The fourth feature was the division between academic (mainly middle-class) and vocational (mainly working-class) students, reflected in resource allocation, in the greater likelihood that the former group would receive extended education in sixth-forms and universities, and the different status of academic and practical education throughout the system. Vocational interests received less time, attention and money. An analysis of the distribution of educational resources by social class shows that the children of non-manual parents on average each receive substantially more in education spending than the children of manual workers (Le Grand 1982: 58). The most significant element in this is access to education after age sixteen: the statistics for 1985 show that the non-manual group received over four times more post-school education than did manual workers' children (Glennerster and Low 1990: 75). The emphasis on academic work by central government and local officials and by dominant interests in the teaching profession obstructed attempts to give greater priority to vocational training (Ainley 1988: 1–4).

Cross-national comparisons show that the UK spends a rather low proportion of its national wealth on education than most advanced countries, that it offers a shorter period of schooling or training to most members of the population and that vocational preparation is taken much less seriously (OECD 1975; Heidenheimer et al. 1990: 36–41). However, the academic education offered to a minority is as good as that available anywhere in the world. One of the few wide-ranging cross-national comparisons available ranks the UK bottom of a list of nine advanced countries in science and maths achievement scores for ten-year-olds and seventh for fourteen-year-olds, but top for eighteen-year-olds. At this stage, only some 20 per cent of selected students remain in the UK system (IAEEA 1988: table A.10; NFER 1992).

The policy debate

Three general issues have shaped recent policy debates. First, the poor economic performance of the UK compared to other advanced countries in the recessions of the mid-1970s, early 1980s and early 1990s has focused attention on the capacity of the education system to meet the needs of the economy. Of particular concern is the effect of skill shortages in limiting output, reported by over a quarter of firms in a recent Confederation of British Industry survey (CSO 1991b: table 4.36). Second, concern at the continuing high levels of unemployment, especially among young people, has raised the question of whether this group is adequately prepared and motivated for work. The proportion of school-leavers who became unemployed or entered training schemes topped 50 per cent in 1983 and has remained at that level for the rest of the decade (CSO 1991b: table 3.15). Third, the increased social inequality resulting from changes in patterns of employment, work and family life (Taylor-Gooby 1991a) has sharpened debate on the contribution of education to the enhancement of individual opportunity.

Economic crisis has given added urgency to policy debate over the last two decades. The key themes were first set out in a government-sponsored 'Great Debate' on education, initiated by the then Prime Minister, Jim Callaghan, in a widely publicized speech at Ruskin College, Oxford, in 1976 and nourished in a flurry of national conferences culminating in a Green Paper (DES 1977). The Ruskin speech signalled a major shift in Labour policy away from the egalitarian and pupil-centred approach of the 1960s. It stressed 'complaints from industry that new recruits . . . sometimes do not have the basic tools'; 'unease about the new informal teaching methods'; and counselled teachers that 'you must satisfy parents and industry that what you are doing meets their requirements' (quoted in Brooks 1991: 9, 14, 30). Throughout, responsiveness to the wishes of consumers and to the presumed needs of industry furnishes the touchstone by which schooling is to be judged – the central issue is the 'need for . . . teaching that will lead towards practical applications rather than academic studies'. Hitherto education had been discussed almost exclusively in the terms set by professionals – teachers, academics, civil servants and policy makers – the key players in the tradition of consensus formation between experts that had dominated educational policy. Although the Labour government fell before it could produce firm proposals for legislation, the Great Debate sets the tone for subsequent discussion. Professional judgements are swept aside: the views of those outside the educational experts' consensus – politicians, employers, parents and voters – become paramount. The education debate ceases to be a matter for teachers

and officials and becomes an issue in which government takes a decisive
interest.

Education reform moved rapidly up the political agenda in the 1970s.
The UK system was finding it increasingly difficult to reconcile conflicting
demands for vocational training, the socialization of young people and the
extension of individual opportunity in the context of recession. This raised
issues of the relationship between what went on in schools and the world of
work, the nature of the curriculum and who should control it, what standards
were attained, how they should be assessed and whether the teaching force was
adequately trained or motivated to meet the demands placed upon it. The
academic bias of the system made it especially vulnerable to searching enquiry
in these areas. In the 1980s and 1990s, these general issues have been focused by
the determination of Conservative governments to constrain state spending,
extend the use of markets as against bureaucratic and professional decision
making and restrict the role of local government; this made a collision with the
education system inevitable. In 1980, education accounted for about 5.5 per
cent of gross domestic product (GDP), comparable to health care and representing one-sixth of all state spending. It employed nearly 565,000 teachers,
over 120,000 further and higher education lecturers, 2500 officials in the
Department of Education and over 50,000 officials in local government (DES
1992a: table 30; CSO 1993: table 3.27). Education budgets made up more than
two-thirds of local government expenditure. The stage was set for a transition
in educational policy making from the slow development of consensus to the
imposition of a new paradigm, whether teachers and local government liked it
or not.

Policy change 1979–87: Clearing the ground

The changes of the early 1980s were piecemeal reforms, designed to restrict the
influence of local education authorities (LEAs), direct attention to vocational
education and strengthen controls over the teaching profession. They took
place in the context of increasingly vigorous attempts to control educational
spending. It is unlikely that a grand design for the restructuring of education
policy operated throughout the 1980s. However, the net effect of the changes
was to put in place the groundwork on which the new structure could be built
and, perhaps most significantly, deliver a number of defeats to the interests
which resisted change so that radical reform became politically possible. After
the 1987 election, legislation imposed central solutions to the problems of what
schools were to teach, how education was to serve the needs of the economy,
how standards were to be assessed and what the places of local government,
teachers and the consumers of the service were to be in the system. Through
these changes, a new structure based on central control of curriculum and
examinations, with resources allocated through a managed market, a substantial
enhancement of immediate consumer choice and a reduction in the influence
of local government and professional teachers emerged.

The erosion of local authority power

The central theme of the 1979 and 1983 Conservative election manifestos was the expansion of individual choice against bureaucratic state planning and professional authority. Education reforms were presented in these terms, the consumer being defined as parent or employer, not as school student. This approach led immediately to interest in a market based on education vouchers, which, in theory, makes the consumer sovereign over the service providers. Discussion of voucher systems in the UK was influenced by experiments in the USA in the 1970s, where limited voucher schemes had enhanced parental choice between a range of school programmes and facilitated the integration of different groups in an ethnically diverse school system (Cohen and Farrar 1977). In fact, these experiments used vouchers designed specifically to reduce the power of privileged groups in the educational market by the simple expedient of paying more for children from low-achieving groups, and were unlike the systems under discussion in the UK.

The Secretary of State, Sir Keith Joseph, described the idea as 'intellectually attractive' in an open letter to education lobbies in 1981 (Seldon 1986: xiii), and stated at the 1982 Party Conference: 'we want to extend choice to every person. That is what a properly constructed voucher scheme would do.' Twelve months later, at the 1983 conference, he repudiated the idea: 'the voucher . . . is dead'. Most commentators explain this reversal in terms of the capacity of Whitehall to moderate schemes for radical change. DES officials were able to defeat the key idea in the introduction of market principles into education by convincing Sir Keith that it would be expensive and unworkable (Seldon 1986: 17–35). They pointed out that under existing legislative arrangements, it would be necessary for government to bear the costs of the expansion of successful schools and the contraction of unsuccessful ones and to fund the transport of large numbers of pupils to the school of their choice. They also claimed that there was little demand for such schemes on the basis of studies such as the feasibility study carried out in Kent in 1976 (Kent County Council 1978: 32). Changes which reduced the responsibilities of LEAs for the allocation of places and brought home the costs of change to the schools themselves would be necessary before a variant of the voucher scheme could be contemplated in the UK.

The 1980 and 1986 Education Acts enhanced the powers of school governing bodies over school management and the curriculum and ensured that parents and local business people (in line with the theme of responsiveness to industry) formed a majority on them. Market mechanisms in the state sector were strengthened with the introduction of open enrolment and the requirement that schools recruited up to a 'standard number' of places. This severely limited the capacity of local authorities to protect recruitment at particular schools when places were available elsewhere, and was a step in the direction of a more open market.

A second innovation, the Assisted Places Scheme, was designed to extend choice by paying bursaries for low-income pupils at participating private schools. This proved to have a limited impact. By 1992, a relatively small group of pupils (some 34,000) were supported at 295 schools and there are no plans to expand the scheme further (DES 1992a: 14). In fact, the income from this scheme does not entirely make up the reduction in state finance of the private sector through local authority purchase of places which had declined as a result of general spending constraints (Papadakis and Taylor-Gooby 1987: 92). Although there is no official DES research into the operation of the scheme, the surveys that have been carried out show that the scheme has had little effect in enhancing opportunities for working–class children. Places are allocated by schools and somewhere between 70 and 90 per cent go to children from middle–class homes who have suffered a drop in income rather than to the children of manual workers (Whitty et al. 1986: 8; MORI 1992). The significance of the scheme lies mainly in the public endorsement of private schooling.

These developments took place against the background of the declining autonomy of local government. The increasing success with which central government was able to control local spending forced councils to limit budgets in education, their most costly service. New controls on capital expenditure cut building budgets by 60 per cent between 1979 and 1983. Penalties for high revenue spending were introduced in 1981. Rate-capping was introduced in 1985 and a new and restrictive system of local finance – the poll tax – in 1990 (Savage and Robbins 1990: 176–9).

The result was that education spending, which had risen more rapidly than national product in volume and cash terms throughout the previous three decades, ceased to expand from 1979 (Glennerster and Low 1990: 41). Current spending, mainly on salaries, rose slightly and capital spending fell to less than a third of the level of the mid-1970s, with serious implications for the quality of school buildings. The increasingly strict attempts to control local government spending resulted in a wider dispersion of expenditure between local authorities. Glennerster and Low (1990: table 3.13) calculate a 'coefficient of variation' between local authorities in spending on each pupil that increased by over a third between 1974 and 1985, reversing the trend of the previous 15 years.

Other changes weakened the capacity of DES officials in Whitehall to resist the new direction in education policy. Developments in vocational training showed that the government of the 1980s was determined to make radical changes.

Vocationalism and the encroachment of the MSC

Concern about the success with which schools prepared young people for work was a powerful motive for educational reform. Developments in this area allowed central government to play a stronger role in determining what went on in local authority schools and indicated that the capacity of DES officials to resist the changes desired by politicians was decisively weakened. The incursion of the 'new vocationalism' into education is described in more detail in

Chapter 8. Innovation in the UK was influenced by concerns derived from cross-national comparison. This is not a new issue. As Reeder (1979: 121) points out, anxiety about the capacity of the nation to sustain an imperial role had led reformers to compare British education with that available to students in rival countries, particularly Germany, from the 1890s onwards. In recent years, attention has focused on two main areas – the low proportion of young people staying on beyond sixteen in further education in the UK and the low status of business and applied studies. Such comparisons provide an impetus for expansion. Although the proportion of sixteen- to eighteen-year-olds in school or college (70 per cent) is comparable with other European Community (EC) countries, the USA, Australia and Japan, only just over half of these receive full-time education, whereas the proportion elsewhere ranges upwards from two-thirds (CSO 1993: table 3.16).

The evident weakness of the UK economy, the highest levels of youth unemployment for half a century and the skill mismatch in some key industrial areas put vocational education high on the agenda in the early 1980s (see Chapter 9). This enabled the Manpower Services Commission (MSC) to make a substantial incursion into the province of the Department of Education and Science. The MSC set up directly funded programmes which it and not the education authority controlled in local authority schools and colleges through the Training and Vocational Educational Initiative (TVEI) and through the links between the Youth Training Scheme (YTS) and further education. The strategy of funding TVEI through the transfer of resources from education budgets to the MSC, so that local authorities then had to bid against each other to get their own money back, was extremely successful in securing participation from the very authorities who were criticizing the scheme. The scheme was announced by the Prime Minister, Mrs Thatcher, in 1982 before the DES press office had even been informed of its existence (Hartnett and Naish 1986: 132).

The apparent capacity of outside agencies to trample on their patch had a powerful effect in focusing the minds of DES officials on the difficulty of resisting determined political direction. By 1987, the institutional colonialism of the MSC was rebuffed: TVEI was incorporated into the DES's territory as the technical and vocational education scheme, and technology became a foundation subject in the national curriculum after 1987. The DES also set up a pilot scheme (announced at the 1986 party conference) to found up to twenty City Technology Colleges (CTCs), which were to be run directly outside LEA control, to include a substantial amount of technology on their curriculum, to be located in urban areas and to be funded in the main by local business. This scheme was influenced by the apparent success of 'magnet' schools in US cities in achieving good results with students from deprived areas. However, it has proved difficult to attract independent finance. At the time of writing, fifteen colleges have been agreed with four-fifths of the finance coming from government (DES 1992a: 14). These colleges represent a snub to LEAs and are often seen as an attempt to introduce greater selectivity into the state system.

1988 and after: The new educational settlement

The direct impact of reform before the 1987 election was limited, although the changes had severely weakened the power of teachers, local government and central planners to influence policy. Teachers had been defeated in pay negotiations, and were under attack in their control of the curriculum and of professional training. Local government could no longer plan school size, was increasingly accountable to parents and employers, and was constrained by financial pressures. The incursions of the MSC into the province of the DES (although eventually rebuffed) and the reorganization of central government outlined in Chapter 1 eroded the confidence of Whitehall. The stage was now set for radical reform and this was embodied in the 1988 Education Reform Act.

The main points of the new legislation were outlined in the 1987 manifesto. After a brief consultation period (two months in the summer), during which the overwhelming majority of comments appear to have been hostile (for an analysis, see Haviland 1988), the Bill was published and passed within six months of the election. The ease with which the government felt able to press ahead with legislation is an indication of the extent to which opposing professional and organizational obstacles within the system had been overcome. Consensus policy making in education was dead and the way was open for a shift to managed markets in the delivery of education.

Schools: Imposed curriculum and consumer choice

The 1988 Education Reform Act dealt with schools, further and higher education and presaged thorough-going reform in each area. In relation to schools, the new system defines clearly the content of education, provides for the publication of information on school performance and decentralizes finance to the schools themselves. The result is a shift to resource allocation between schools through a market driven by consumer choice, rather than through local authority planning. The reduced role of government direction is summed up in the 1992 departmental name-change – from Department of Education and Science to Department for Education. The influence of local government is further eroded by provision for schools to opt out of the council system altogether.

The content of education is defined through an imposed National Curriculum reinforced by a system of attainment targets and testing. The National Curriculum is a new departure for UK education, which had previously relied on professional judgement supplemented by examination-led syllabuses. The curriculum lays down ten subject areas (plus Welsh language in Wales), with a core of English, mathematics and science. It is not compulsory for CTCs and the private sector. The curriculum is monitored by testing at four 'Key Stages' (7, 11, 14 and 16 years of age). The results of the tests are to be published for each school. From 1994, the principal school-leaving examination, the General

Certificate of Secondary Education (GCSE), is to be incorporated into National Curriculum testing. Teachers' professional judgements had played a major role in this examination through teacher-assessed course-work, which accounted for 100 per cent of the marks in some subjects. The influence of teachers will be sharply reduced. Course-work is to be cut back to a maximum of 30 per cent of the final mark in most subjects, a new grading scale with sharper distinction at the top end introduced and more use made of differentiated papers for different ability ranges.

Proposals backed by the teaching profession to broaden sixth-form schooling and to make it more accessible to less academically successful students have also been rejected. The A-level is to remain as the examination determining the curriculum for the minority of high-fliers, with the proportion of marks decided by teacher assessment limited to 20 per cent (Clarke 1992). Teachers' professional influence on what is taught in secondary schools and how standards are assessed is in decline. More recently, the government has launched an attack on the quality of teaching in primary schools, traditionally the area in which teacher-directed, child-centred learning is strongest (DES 1992b).

The system of central imposition of curriculum together with the publication of test results constitutes a major shift in power away from local government and teachers in two directions – upwards to central government and outwards to parents, who may use the information to guide their choice of school, as consumers acting in a market. The 1991 'Parents' Charter' for education is almost entirely concerned with establishing rights for parents to receive information about schools and about their children's education. In particular, test results will be published as a league table for all schools in a locality. Many commentators have pointed out that the level of achievement which these scores will show is influenced by other factors in addition to the quality of schooling. The test tables will thus show the success of the school in attracting able pupils as much as its success in teaching them. If good results attract advantaged children who tend to do well, they become a self-fulfilling prophecy and will enable successful schools to become increasingly selective. The test results are likely to be treated as the main index of quality in schooling. The government plans to run down the independent and highly professional Inspectorate, an arm of the DES which has expressed growing criticism of the impact of government spending policies on standards in schools (see, for example, HMI 1991). It will be replaced with a system of monitoring by inspectors selected from a centrally approved list and paid by schools themselves (DFE 1992). Such inspections may lack the weight of independent professional judgement.

The National Curriculum will determine the content of schooling and testing will provide the main indicator of standards to the consumer. Choice is to be exercised through an internal market which schools are encouraged to enter through the new system of local financial management. The control of funds is devolved to governing bodies which have radically extended powers over the hiring of teachers and other personnel, the tenant responsibilities of maintenance and effective autonomy in the purchase of books, equipment and other resources. The legislation requires that 85 per cent of the LEA budget is allocated by a formula that allows for at least 80 per cent to be distributed through a capitation allowance for pupils. Coupled with open enrolment, this arrangement effectively introduces paperless vouchers into the state sector, without additional funding for expansion or contraction or for transport to the school of one's choice. The success of professional and administrative interests in rebuffing Sir Keith Joseph's enthusiasm for vouchers in the early 1980s has been completely reversed. Schools are compelled to compete for resources by attracting pupils. Those that are unsuccessful lose resources and ultimately face the possibility of teacher redundancies and closure.

The shift of power away from local government is reinforced by provision for schools to opt out of local authority control completely on the strength of a simple majority in a parental ballot (regardless of the proportion who do not vote) subject to the Secretary of State's approval. Current spending in such 'grant-maintained' schools is financed directly through DES grants at the same level as comparable LEA schools. The value of the grants is deducted from LEA budgets. However, grant-maintained schools have been treated favourably for capital spending allocations and are awarded other subsidies. Capital grants for 1992–93 average £102,000 for each grant-maintained school, as against £28,000 for each maintained school (DES 1992a: table 2 and p. 13). The 1992 Technology Initiative offers an average of £50 a head to pupils in grant-maintained schools, but only £7.50 a head to those in state schools (*Guardian* 1992a: 5).

One result of preferential funding is that the move to grant-maintained status is gathering momentum after a slow start. At the time of writing, 609 schools (almost all secondary) have opted out from a total of about 4000 secondary schools eligible. A further 300 are seeking grant-maintained status. These schools are concentrated in areas with a tradition of low levels of local government spending on education, typically Conservative shire authorities – such as Kent, Essex and Leicestershire. About half of existing grant-maintained schools were under threat of closure or reorganization at the time they left the LEA. The 1992 election result has encouraged many more schools to opt out. The new Secretary of State, John Patten, states in his 1992 White Paper that he wishes to see grant-maintained status become the norm in secondary schooling and expects some 60 per cent of schools to have opted out by 1995 (DFE 1992). Whether parents of children at most schools will vote to pursue this path and whether a government committed to tax cuts will be able to maintain additional spending on these schools is unclear. The opportunity to opt out makes LEA planning of education, especially where this might involve school contraction or closure in the face of declining demand, impossible. In a speech to the Adam Smith Institute, the Prime Minister suggested that central government might intervene directly in the case of failing schools, imposing a management reshuffle and, if that did not work, closing the school, after the manner of a receiver dealing with a bankrupt business (Major 1992). These policies are included in the 1993 Act. The attack on local government was also carried forward by the abolition of the largest single education authority with the highest level of spending – the Inner London Education Authority.

Other developments reduced the professional autonomy of teachers. After a series of confrontations in the early and mid-1980s, the government in 1987 scrapped the salary-negotiating machinery and imposed new conditions of employment. Subsequently, there have been moves to erode national salary scales through an extension of the powers of governing bodies to set their own pay policy and to award discretionary additions. In 1993, a performance related element was included in all pay scales. Central control over the profession was tightened in 1983, when a new accreditation body for teacher-training courses was set up with the brief of inspecting colleges and monitoring the content of their courses. After 1988, the status of teaching as a graduate-only profession was undermined, and a new entry scheme permitted the training of 'licensed teachers' on the job. Proposals advanced in 1992 will shift the greater part of teacher training out of specialized institutions linked to higher education into schools themselves. Taken together, these moves are seen as a return to the nineteenth-century system of pupil-teachers trained as craft apprentices. Central government has taken decisive steps against teachers as a group with a professional status that will enable them to exert an independent influence on developments in education.

The 1988 Act, therefore, provides the foundations for a new education settlement, consolidated in the 1992 White Paper: central government controls curriculum, teacher training and examinations, while the strategy of open enrolment, local financial management and the publication of league tables ensures that schools compete directly for students. The role of the local authority is reduced to setting the overall budget within the strict limits implied by poll and council tax capping. As more schools become grant-maintained, the central Funding Agency for Schools will take over this role.

Further and higher education: Expansion, competition and spending constraint

The reform of further education follows the same themes as the reform of primary and secondary schooling to a logical conclusion. The LEA is required to devolve budgetary and staffing responsibilities to colleges. Governing bodies are now weighted towards the representation of employers, who take at least half the seats, with the LEA typically limited to a sixth of the membership. Student enrolment plays a large part in deciding the size of the budget, so that competitive pressures become stronger. There are additional opportunities to gain resources from such sources as Training Credits. Subsequent legislation grants colleges 'corporate status' and sets up a national funding council, the Further Education Funding Council, which will take the finance of this sector completely out of the hands of local government.

It is at present unclear how far the new council will involve itself in the determination of the range and level of subjects that colleges offer, impose a minimum viable size and structure or attempt to intervene directly in college closure and amalgamation. These issues may be left to the operation of the market in students. Colleges will compete with each other, and in many areas of work with local authority schools. Such competition is already apparent in the sharp expansion of state sector educational advertising, an activity hitherto almost entirely confined to the private sector, and in the enthusiasm of schools to develop courses in areas such as the vocationally oriented training accredited by the Business and Technical Education Council, which had previously been almost entirely the preserve of colleges. The divorce between further education and local government will be final.

The new legislation also takes local government out of higher education. It ends the distinction between the quasi-independent university sector and the LEA-run polytechnic sector by conferring corporate status on polytechnics and creating parallel funding arrangements for both – via the Universities Funding Council (UFC) and the Polytechnics and Colleges Funding Council (PCFC) – with strong representation from employers and the requirement 'to comply with any directions given . . . by the Secretary of State' (McIlroy 1989: 17). Universities had previously been funded through the University Grants Committee (UGC), which operated at arms length from government influence. Subsequent legislation (the Further and Higher Education Act 1992) merges the two councils into the Higher Education Funding Council and ends the binary divide. Policies imply a substantial increase in student numbers, to double the 1990 level by the end of the century – raising the participation rate among young people from about 19 to 30 per cent (Conservative Party 1992: 32). The costs of this increase are to be contained by replacing maintenance grants for those on higher education courses with loans, and by reductions in spending on each student.

Polytechnic education is currently cheaper than university education. The cost for each student fell rapidly as the system expanded in the 1980s, so that by 1986 it was just over £3000 in current terms as against £6000 in universities (Glennerster and Low 1990: 44). Over this period, universities were able to resist government pressures to reduce costs and underwent only a modest expansion. By the late 1980s, the position had changed radically. The UGC was replaced by the UFC and the basis of university funding was revised to encourage expansion and cut costs.

The official indices suggest that university unit costs fell by only 3 per cent between 1979 and 1990, but project a cut of 14 per cent by 1993. Costs in polytechnics fell steadily over the period and will reach 67 per cent of the 1979 level by 1993 (DES 1991: table 11.16; 1992a: table 17). Further developments are likely to intensify the pressure. Teaching resources are increasingly linked to student numbers and the new Funding Council initially has encouraged institutions to take extra unfunded students, by rewarding them with extra grant support in later years. However, in 1993 expansion was abruptly halted and fee levels cut back. New systems of selectivity in research funding make a clear distinction between universities which support research, those mainly concerned with teaching and those which sustain both activities. The result of these changes is a sharpening in the competition for students and for research funds. The allocation of resources in higher education increasingly operates as a market, managed by the policies of the HEFC. The previous assumption that all UK universities were equal as centres for the advance of knowledge has been overturned.

The changes reduce local authority influence as local government loses power over the polytechnic sector. They expand central control, since the new funding council is subject to government direction and may enhance consumer influence, to the extent that funding arrangements are more clearly driven by student numbers. The capacity of the universities to resist budget cuts and a redirection of their role has been undermined. Consequently, access to further and higher education will be widened at the price of greater inequality in provision.

The impact of the changes

The education reforms are far-reaching and it will be some years before their impact can be fully assessed. They introduce a managed market, with the diet of curriculum and examinations laid down by the centre and separate providers competing for the custom of service users. This involves a transfer of power away from local government and a diminution in the professional autonomy and hence the status of teachers. Tests and examinations are designed to produce simple performance indicators readily accessible to consumers. Managed markets also appear to be emerging in further and higher education, although the degree of central government intervention in the curriculum diminishes at the university level.

The new curriculum will ensure that many students will receive more teaching in science and a modern foreign language than in the past. These changes may go some way towards reducing the gender bias of the previous system, in which girls tended to choose humanities options and boys science and maths when these were choices. However, they will do little to remedy the inequality whereby girls tend to do less well in maths, physics and chemistry and boys in English and foreign languages, when both sexes take the same course, unless attention is given to the complex factors which influence achievement (McDowell 1989: 257–9). The new system ignores the serious problem of under-performance by ethnic minorities, especially by students of Afro-Caribbean origin (Smith and Tomlinson 1989: ch. 1).

The new mechanism of local management and open enrolment will enhance consumer choice. The system of testing and of the publication of results has been widely criticized because it will not take into account the social factors, completely outside the control of schools, that influence the level of students' achievement. The league tables of test results will provide good information on which schools succeed in attracting the students who perform best and in excluding those who are disadvantaged, although they will be less useful as indicators of the quality of schooling. Together with other factors, these procedures are likely to intensify the pressures towards selection and towards greater inequality in education. Schools will compete to take students who make the school more attractive. There is a strong risk that low-achieving students will be relegated to the least attractive schools, which will be locked into a downward spiral of disadvantaged students, poor test results and low resources as the weakest go to the wall in the educational market. There are already indications that some grant-maintained schools are seeking to exclude pupils who do not perform well in examinations, a policy which will enhance the school's test record, but do little for students who are hard to teach. Newspaper reports in mid-1992 detail the unusually high level of exclusions at grant-maintained schools in Barnet (*Guardian* 1992c: 21). These inequalities will continue to grow if successful schools pursue a strategy of excellence rather than expansion, skimming the market for high achievers rather than embarking on ambitious building programmes to cater for a wider range of pupils. Experience in the private sector indicates that, although the most prestigious schools could fill their places many times over with applicants willing to pay the fees, they tend to pursue a logic of status rather than growth (Glennerster 1987). High-status state schools will follow this path, leaving lower-status schools with the lower-achieving students. The 1992 government has already indicated that it will allow grant-maintained schools to select aspiring students (DFE 1992). As this sector expands, the old distinction between grammar and secondary modern schools will re-emerge initially in the contrast between grant-maintained and council schools, and, ultimately, as local authority schooling withers, through competition within the grant-maintained sector.

There are already indications that the shift to a managed market with a strong element of central control will not be achieved painlessly. Competition implies losers as well as gainers. One result is the creation of inefficient schools unable to attract sufficient pupils to maintain a full range of curriculum options. Under the current system, it is difficult to close such schools against parental resistance with the result that the Department of Education estimates that some 500,000 empty places are provided in schools at considerable cost. The 1993 Act allows central government to resolve the problem by direct action.

A second problem of parental choice concerns the co-ordination of admissions. A High Court ruling in 1989 established the right of a parent to apply for their child to be admitted to a school outside their area of residence. In any case, grant-maintained schools have a considerable degree of autonomy in admissions policy. The wise parent will apply to several schools, and may hold places at more than one, so that schools have no way of knowing who will actually turn up until the school year starts. For example, in the Borough of Bromley, where twelve out of seventeen secondary schools are grant-maintained, 225 pupils were left without a secondary school place when admissions were announced in April 1992. Some students were later offered places in another borough and were faced with a twelve-mile journey. How far the excess pressure on places is due to multiple place-holding and how far it is due to an influx from other areas is not clear until enrolment actually takes place in September. Similar problems have emerged in some areas of Kent (*Guardian* 1992b: 21). The government proposes to set up a clearing system to co-ordinate admissions (DFE 1992).

These developments indicate that the new settlement will require strong central control if it is not to create inefficiencies that are worse than those it is designed to eradicate. Reform so far has been pursued at minimal cost. The growing effectiveness with which central government has been able to control local spending over the past decade has contained pressures for more resources. However, the extension of teaching over a greater range of subjects for many students and the introduction of other innovations are likely to generate press-ure for greater spending. The backlog resulting from the attrition of main-tenance budgets over the 1980s will impose burdens at some stage in the future. Many schools call on parents for contributions to help with expenses. Under these circumstances, the more popular schools may be able to extract fees, whether they are described as such, or as 'voluntary contributions to the school fund'; similar top-up fees charged directly to the consumer are under discussion in higher education.

The influence of local government has been further weakened by the loss of further education and the polytechnic sector. In these areas, the reforms have also cleared away the obstacles to change, and expansion of the system has been achieved with very little in the way of additional resources. The impact of this expansion on standards cannot be judged at this stage, and the emphasis on consumerism and on central control in the 1988 Act is still working through the system. The direct link between resources and student numbers has facilit-ated an expansion in sixth-form schooling, further and higher education. Aided by the pressures of pupil-based funding on the supply side and continuing youth unemployment and the higher levels of qualification on the demand side, the proportion of sixteen- and seventeen-year-olds in schooling increased from 24 to 33 per cent between 1986 and 1992. Enrolment in further educa-tion has risen from 32 to 35 per cent of the age group (DES 1992a: table 7). Similarly, the policies of funding councils have led to an expansion of higher education.

At the beginning of this chapter, four features of the UK educational tradition were identified. The new settlement has upset the balance of power between teachers, civil servants and local and central government that made for consensus planning. It has imposed a uniform curriculum, but diversity in educational experience will continue between students in unequally successful schools. The division between academic and vocational routes is firmly entrenched after age sixteen. Political debate about education in recent years has centred on the claim that the education system is failing the nation because it is unresponsive to the demands of the consumers and the needs of the economy. The changes facilitate the expansion of post-sixteen schooling, al-though they offer a greater range of quality in a wider system. Consumer responsiveness is increased up to the point at which schools select students rather than students schools. By the millennium, policy may have re-established the divisions between secondary modern and grammar school edu-cation of half a century earlier, with the inequalities masked in a rhetoric of 'choice and diversity' rather than 'parity of esteem'.

8

The legacy of the Manpower Services Commission: Training in the 1980s

Pat Ainley

In time all those who can understand realise that nowadays things are being ordered differently.

(William Trevor (1991) *Reading Turgenev*)

The Manpower Services Commission (MSC) pioneered the new forms of contractual management that have permeated the new enterprise state. This chapter sets out the economic context of the MSC's activity and influence and tells the remarkable story of its rise and fall. It concludes by outlining likely future developments in the new mixed economy of a semi-privatized state sector and a state-subsidized private sector.

Context

During the 1970s, tripartism in the UK ran into a dead end. The consensus for a mixed economy of private and state monopoly capital sustained by successive governments collapsed as the long, faltering post-war boom finally fell into recession following the 1973 oil crisis. The policies of planned growth under Keynesian demand management with which Labour justified its claim to be the natural party of government had failed to modernize the economy and reverse Britain's steady industrial decline. Among mainstream political parties, only the Liberals manifestly advanced an alternative policy of national wage bargaining. Labour, despite (or because of) its organic relation with the trades unions, was repeatedly unable to incorporate the organized workforce into the setting of wage norms. Only the Labour left advocated a programme of wholesale nationalization for domination of the economy by state capital. The Conservatives meanwhile had learnt the lessons of the defeat of Edward Heath's government in the 1974 miners' strike. Under a new leader, they prepared to implement what their then chief strategist, Keith Joseph, called 'a law-abiding free enterprise reconstruction of Britain's social relations of production' (quoted in Coates and Hilliard 1986: 354). After 1979, Conservative governments openly repudiated the commitment to full employment shared by all parties since the war but already abandoned surreptitiously by Labour under Healey's Chancellorship. The object of Mrs Thatcher's 'British experiment' was to demonstrate that 'Trade Union power can be curbed within a free society and that inflation can be eradicated within a democracy' (Lawson, quoted in Ainley and Corney 1990: 53). It was ironic that the MSC, an organization associated with the tripartite policies of the previous period, was to play such a large part in this process. This chapter examines its role.

Comprehensive manpower policy

The Training Services Agency (TSA) that became the MSC in 1974 was established by the Conservatives in the 1973 Employment and Training Act. This executive agency was hived-off from the Department of Employment in the manner recommended by the 1968 Fulton Committee on Civil Service reorganization as revived by Prime Minister Heath's 'Businessman Team' of advisers. The TSA was later split into two operating arms, one administering the newly revamped benefit offices, while the other ran special employment and training programmes. Initially, only forty civil servants strong, this was 'the tiny spore' from which what Low (1988: 215) called 'a great fungus' was to grow.

The intention, as Maurice Macmillan, Heath's Employment Minister, told Parliament, was 'to set up a Manpower Services Commission representative of employers, trades unions and other interests which would have direct responsibility to me for employment and training services' (House of Commons Debates 1972: Vol. 846, col. 1293). This was not strictly a quango (quasi-autonomous non-governmental organization), since the elected Minister held a crucial directive role over the Commissioners he appointed. Labour and the Trades Union Congress (TUC), who had long been proposing something similar along the lines of the Swedish Labour Market Board, though without its wage-fixing powers, welcomed the proposal. Partly it was intended as a sweetener for Heath's own attempt at incomes policy.

The previous system of training organized through Industrial Training Boards and partly financed by a levy had met with opposition from employers. The numbers on the traditional apprenticeship schemes it supported fell rapidly in the recession of the late 1960s. The trades unions were divided between urging greater state planning of training to benefit all workers while hanging on to the relatively advantageous conditions they had secured for their craft members. Shop-floor activists were coming to see that the crisis of industrial restructuring highlighted by dramatically rising unemployment could only be met by a programme of comprehensive education and training for all, using new technology to overcome traditional divisions between hand and brain (e.g. the Lucas Aerospace Workers' Corporate Plan in Cooley 1987; Trades Union Resource Centre 1987).

This vision was partially shared by many who contributed to the growing debate on education and training in Britain, not least by the economists and planners who became the driving force behind the MSC. They too recognized that new technology was undermining the immemorial divisions between mental and manual labour and could contribute to a new industrial revolution. In this modernization of the British economy, a new training culture of lifelong learning would overcome the demarcations associated with obsolete heavy industry between managers and managed, office and plant, skilled and un-skilled, manual and non-manual, blue- and white-collar. In their place, a new, flexible and multiskilled workforce would combine the mental skills of diag-nosis and programming with the manual abilities to effect repairs and maintain production. However, this radical vision was characteristically posed in class neutral terms. It was to be implemented by individual skill acquisition and ownership that took no account of the class cultures by which tacit knowledge and the theoretical abstractions based upon it are developed as they are handed down the generations (e.g. Hayes 1983). The problem of skill shortage, for example, which was exacerbated by rapid technological change and which yet came to co-exist with mass unemployment aggravated by the application of that same new technology, was therefore conceived as a purely technical and not a social problem. Nevertheless, as expressed in the MSC's (1976) espousal of Comprehensive Manpower Policy, the importance of the labour force was elevated to an unprecedented level as the Commission assumed for itself a strategic role in the labour market, extending from schooling through to facilit-ating labour mobility via housing policy (see Ainley and Corney 1990: 36).

The task which the MSC was set of linking job creation with training for employment was unparalleled in peacetime. Yet Labour, which returned to power in 1974, could not accept that the recession, with unemployment rising beyond one million by 1975, was not cyclical and temporary but permanent and structural. Consequently, under Michael Foot at Employment, the MSC embarked upon a series of job creation and make-work schemes. These soon created at ever-mounting cost what became widely known as an alphabet soup of rapidly changing acronyms aimed at counter-cyclical training. They were intended to placate the trades unions, as Labour in its turn attempted its own social contract on wage restraint with the TUC. This was the source of the much repeated criticism, made for instance by Benn and Fairley in 1986, that the MSC was 'blown off course' from its intended purpose into 'fire fighting' unemployment, particularly that it abandoned adult retraining in favour of youth unemployment.

First, however, the Quango − as it was widely known − had to win the right to administer these successive programmes from its parent Department of Employment's long-time rival, the Department of Education and Science (DES). The DES had been heavily criticized by a 1975 OECD international comparison of England's dismal performance in vocational education and training. On the strength of this, the MSC's (1975) *Vocational Preparation for Young People* initiated the so-called 'Great Debate on Education'. In his Ruskin College speech, the new Prime Minister Callaghan signalled his party's abandonment of the policy of 'equal opportunities' through comprehensive schooling which it had pursued since 1965 in favour of the new watchword of 'relevance' to the needs of industry (see Ainley 1988, 1990a). Still, it was only after prolonged Cabinet wrangling that Albert Booth, who replaced Foot in the reshuffle following Harold Wilson's sudden resignation (see Wright 1987), won the agreement of Shirley Williams at Education to a pilot programme of Unified Vocational Preparation. This was to be run jointly by both ministries, while the idea of a vocational preparation scheme for all young people – first suggested by the MSC in 1974 – was shelved.

MSC officials meanwhile had been dispatched to Canada to study the means by which the central government there bypassed the federal authorities to channel funds straight into the hands of local agents managing a Youth Opportunities Programme (YOP) for the unemployed. The MSC's Annual Report for 1974–75 noted the immediacy and flexibility of this approach which 'can be introduced and terminated speedily' as required. Following this model, Booth announced a British YOP as 'a new deal for the nation's unemployed' (on such 'New Deals' generally, see Finn 1987). YOP began by offering work preparation and pre-vocational training to one in eight of all sixteen-year-old school leavers, 80 per cent of whom graduated to employment or further full-time training. As numbers on the scheme rose to 500,000 by 1982, when half of all sixteen-year-old school leavers joined, the pattern that was to be repeated by the Youth Training Scheme (YTS) was established as training quality and placement rates fell.

Despite its success in delivering a programme of the size of YOP, plus its own growth to 26,450 staff in regional centres, area boards and a new headquarters in Sheffield, the seemingly irresistible rise of the MSC was threatened by Mrs Thatcher's unexpected 1979 election victory. The tripartite Commission suddenly seemed a relic of the eccentricity of beer and sandwiches at Number 10, so that rumours spread that the new regime would abolish it along with other quangos. There could be little room for a Department of Employment, let alone its creature Quango, in a government that eschewed employment policy. Cuts of £186 million were ordered in special employment programmes, including YOP, following Sir Geoffrey Howe's first budget.

The monetarist solution of allowing unemployment to find its 'natural' level meant that the dole queue quickly rocketed towards three million. Even Frederick Hayek (1984), the monetarist inspiration of Sir Keith Joseph's Institute for Economic Affairs, doubted 'that any government could persist for two or three years in a policy that meant 10 per cent unemployment for most of that period'. So although the MSC was censured by the Pliatsky Report on Non-Departmental Public Bodies, its abolition was postponed. The government took a grip of the Commission by sacking its Chairman, Sir Richard

O'Brien, associated by them with Labour's consensual approach, replacing him with their own man. David (later Lord) Young was a former property developer returned from the USA to head the Conservative Party's research unit and to advise Sir Keith (later Lord) Joseph. They had met through their mutual interest in the narrowly utilitarian Organization for Rehabilitation and Training that ran trade schools in France and elsewhere. The Quango was also given back £183 million in 1980 with which to add 40,000 places to the YOP. This was not enough, however, to avoid the widely predicted outbreak of rioting or 'Uprising' by inner-city youth during the spring of 1981, following which Mrs Thatcher announced a £500 million expansion of the programme.

In addition, the Central Policy Review Staff (1980) published a report recommending a 'modernised apprenticeship for all'. This would reclassify all occupational tasks to facilitate the flexible transfer of labour and replace trades union control which it saw as another means of maintaining restrictive practices. This was sufficiently similar to the vision held by leading members of the MSC for its Director, Sir John Cassels, to reveal in an interview that the most important factor in his decision to think again about the country's training institutions was what was happening in the industrial relations arena (Ainley and Corney 1990: 50). Significantly, he soon moved to the Cabinet Office to be succeeded as Director by Sir Geoffrey Holland, author of *Young People and Work* (MSC 1977), which had prepared the ground for the YOP.

In the run-up to the 1983 election, Norman Tebbit announced a task force to implement a £1 billion YTS of training and vocational preparation leading to 'recognized qualifications' for sixteen- to eighteen-year-olds. This was but a part of the MSC's New Training Initiative, which was to replace the statutory structure of the Industrial Training Boards and the levy/grant system that had characterized the two previous attempts at training reform. Instead of the £40 initially paid on YOP, Tebbit offered youngsters £15 (later raised to £25 after protest) for the 'high-quality training' that it was promised YTS would provide to distinguish it from 'Son of YOP' as critics soon called it. Given such concessions, the TUC's representative on the MSC told the Congress's Youth Conference that 'The new scheme is fully consistent with TUC policy on training for all' (reported in the *Times Educational Supplement* 25 February 1983). However, the threat of compulsion by withdrawal of benefits for those under eighteen (previously suggested by Labour's Albert Booth) was only narrowly averted. In 1985, 250,000 school students walked out of classrooms all over the country to protest against compulsory YTS in the largest such strike in Britain's history. Compulsion was only finally introduced after the 1987 election.

The Thatcher government now directed its attention at the 'enemies within' – ranging from the National Union of Mineworkers to DES officials tainted with 1960s egalitarianism. The latter had so frustrated Mrs Thatcher during her office under Edward Heath that she actually sanctioned the replacement of more grammar schools by comprehensives than any other Minister of Education. 'Now', as Norman Tebbit at Employment gleefully told the *Financial*

Times (15 October 1982), with 'Keith Joseph at the DES and David Young at the MSC I think you will soon find the Vandals stabling their horses in the temples'. Indeed, Young was 'the only man', Mrs Thatcher declared, 'to bring me solutions not problems', while Joseph was widely recognized as her *eminence grise*. So for the next six years, until the departure of Sir Keith and the subsequent feuding between Tebbit and Young, this Gang of Four really made policy in the crucial area of education and training. Under their aegis, the MSC rose to the height of its power and influence, playing a large part in the permanent transformation of economy and society that is Mrs Thatcher's legacy to the nation.

The Ministry for Training

Lord Young made no secret of his intention to take over the DES and merge it with the MSC/Department of Employment to create a new Superministry of Education and Training. The methods which had launched first YOP and then YTS (extended in 1985 from a one-year to a two-year scheme) were now applied to schools and colleges. The Technical and Vocational Education Initiative (TVEI) – a scheme to develop a new technical training curriculum in schools financed and controlled directly by the MSC – was announced to Parliament in 1982 (see Chapter 8). It showed the characteristically precipitate action of the Gang of Four, typically bypassing conventional channels of procedure and funding. Lord Young even threatened the local education authorities that if they did not volunteer to run TVEI, then the MSC would set up its own schools to do so, which he proposed calling Young Schools!

As well as elbowing aside local democracy, TVEI also demonstrated the way policy was now made on the hoof. This resulted in contradictory statements of its intentions by Thatcher, Tebbit and Young, who had not even consulted Joseph on the initiative, let alone Sir Geoffrey Holland – or so Holland claimed. Money saved from cuts elsewhere was to be thrown at a problem in a 'pilot' phase that was quickly declared a success and extended further (eventually, though spread much more thinly, to all secondary schools). Sir Keith Joseph was proved right that given cash incentives most local authorities would soon cooperate. However, like the City Technology Colleges (CTCs) that succeeded TVEI and the YTS that went before it, central funding was intended as 'pump priming' and employers were supposed to pay for the programme later when they saw its benefits to them. This they never did. When the money ran out, the purpose of TVEI, which received only a two-line mention in the 1988 Education Reform Act, was redefined into one of supporting the 'national' curriculum imposed upon local authority schools by the Tories' new education policies. By that time, another consequence of the MSC's method of operation was that teachers and lecturers had taken the money and spent it to bring new technology into schools and colleges, updating and integrating their teaching for their students' benefit. Similar unintended consequences were later to result from the higher education equivalent of TVEI – the Enterprise Initiative (discussed below).

By 1986, the Quango was at the height of its power. With £3000 million forecast for its 1987–88 budget, a million unemployed sixteen- to eighteen-year-olds were anticipated on YTS and on the Community Programme to which they graduated at eighteen-plus. Employed workers were also subsidized by the MSC through the New Workers' Scheme, as was Non-Advanced Further Education in colleges and TVEI in schools, for which the MSC also supplied special teacher training. The youth service and voluntary sector working with the unemployed also largely depended on MSC funding, as did a hundred-odd TUC-sponsored Centres for the Unemployed. Adult Training, Information Technology Centres and training for small business were also part of its empire. In many places, the MSC was the biggest local employer, taking over the function of previous regional aid. In others, more and more statutory local authority services were coming to depend upon its support and it was also linked to Inner City Task Forces. In 1986–87, the Quango spent £16.5 million on advertising alone – half the government total, which that year surpassed for the first time the amount spent by any individual private company. Its final fling was a £100 million Enterprise in Higher Education Initiative. Meanwhile, the Quango continued to enjoy all-party, CBI and TUC support. They had to agree with Sir Geoffrey Holland that 'If the two year YTS fails then we are at the end of the road. There is nowhere else to go' (*Times Educational Supplement* 2 December 1985).

However, the MSC's rapid series of initiatives were running out of steam as government interest turned again. Even the Quango could not run fast enough to keep up with its critics and Young left it for the House of Lords and the Department of Trade and Industry, faced with opposition from the ten-man Commission over a plan to transfer £220 million from further education to the MSC's budget. The measure was only forced through by Young's casting vote as Director backed up by a directive from the Employment Minister. Young's replacement, Sir Bryan Nicholson, quickly compromised with the LEAs and even prepared for an accommodation with a possible Labour government, writing in 'The New Statesman' (13 May 1985) and the NUT's journal *The Teacher* (31 April 1986). Meanwhile, Sir Keith Joseph, who had virtually surrendered the independence of the DES to the strategic domination of Young and Tebbit, ran into a similar impasse as Young in his long-running dispute with the teachers' unions. He had been 'more than anyone else', as Mrs Thatcher acknowledged in her letter answering his resignation, 'the architect who shaped the policies that led to victory in two elections'. So in the run-up to the 1987 election, with Tebbit carpeted for the lack-lustre campaign, there was no-one left to press upon Mrs Thatcher the virtues of a combined system of education and training for economic modernization. Instead, as the election progressed, her ear was left open to new appeals from educational traditionalists who confirmed her own belief that a return to grammar school excellence was the way to prepare the nation to enter the next millennium.

In 1986, the DES took the initiative from the MSC for the first time with the announcement of its own CTC as a solution to the nation's training crisis.

However, it was unlikely that the planned 'twenty beacons of excellence', 'halfway houses between the independent and state sectors' announced by Education Minister Baker to a standing ovation from that year's Conservative Party Conference could actually do much to close Britain's skill training gap. The CTC proposal represented a bridge between the 1976–87 vocational phase of education policy and the new education reforms then being drawn up. Concentrating all resources in a few technical schools was an admission that the effort to bring vocational education to all schools through TVEI was too expensive to continue without the private employer funding that had not been forthcoming. At the same time, CTCs presented a model for the way to run schools which opted out from local authority control. Eventually all schools could follow under their own financial management, thus unleashing competition, increasing diversity and creating 'opportunities to be unequal', as Mrs Thatcher translated Labour's old slogan. The prototype was in turn taken from the method used by the MSC for per capita funding to the private training agencies which provided its youth and other training programmes and which it had borrowed from the Canadians.

The DES appropriated the MSC's style as well as substance, issuing a glossy brochure with accompanying video to launch the initiative. It was not the only government department at which profound changes in policy were being put into effect. A review of social security spending had been going on for some time at the DHSS under Norman Fowler. The aim was to retarget benefits at 'those most in need', distinguishing once again between the deserving and the undeserving poor. The latter were to be set to work to earn their maintenance by the state until they developed the qualities of enterprise enabling them to break free from dependence. The reforms thus ran contrary to the spirit of the MSC's efforts, which had begun as a process of job creation, though they had gone on through a series of schemes to subsidize existing low-paid jobs. It was always intended that employers would come to appreciate the value for them of a training revolution. The voluntary principle was of cardinal importance in this process, not only to sustain its credibility, but also because forced training was clearly impossible (though forced labour was not).

The MSC had been criticized for its poor accounting and wastefulness by the Auditor-General in 1985. His report even suggested that YTS had contributed to the unemployment it was supposed to alleviate by substituting permanent adult employees with temporary trainees. Now the ground was cut further from under the Commission's feet by a temporary recovery in the economy. Together with the demographic fall in the proportion of young people entering the labour market, the government now actually began to believe its own rhetoric that a training revolution in British industry and commerce had been achieved. The rapid boost to MSC programmes to reduce further the unemployment total prior to the 1987 election was thus the Quango's last gasp. Like its many schemes, the MSC had outlived its usefulness to government and could now be disbanded.

The planned changes followed swiftly after the election victory. The first reductions in MSC grant-in-aid since 1981 were made while the Job Centres and Enterprise Allowance Scheme were returned to the Department of Employment. The 1987 Employment Act proposed the establishment of a new employer-dominated Training Commission. Employers were also given predominance over the nominally tripartite local Area Manpower Boards, renamed Labour Advisory Boards to reflect the more marginal training role of the new Commission. The government then introduced a £10-plus-benefit Employment Training scheme that they knew the unions, committed to the principle of the rate for the job, could not accept. The government used the refusal of the 1988 Trades Union Congress to cooperate with Employment Training to wind up the Commission after only ten days in existence. In its place, the once-mighty Quango was relegated to the ignominious position of a Training Agency (later Training, Enterprise and Education Directorate) within the Department of Employment.

The new enterprise state

'The story of the MSC is important because it amounts to *the* major attempt at large-scale social engineering in Britain since the post-war wave of measures' (Roberts 1990). Yet what can be made of the Conservative claim that the Quango had achieved the long-sought training revolution to create an enterprise culture when Mrs Thatcher could declare to her last party conference that the battle for the economic future would be won, not by relating education to employment and training, but 'in Britain's classrooms' by teaching the future generations of workers to spell properly? Conservative education policy changed little after she left. State-subsidized training was returned to employers, whose failure to train had previously led to the creation of the Industrial Training Boards, the last of which was abolished in 1991. Yet, as Frank Coffield (1990) pointed out, it was still the case that 'training is perceived by many employers as a disposable overhead dropped at the first sign of lowering profit margins', as the MSC had noted a decade earlier.

Employers do not see themselves as responsible for either education or for retraining the unemployed, which they regard as social problems not of their concern. As a *Financial Times* (5 December 1990) editorial put it, 'Successful businessmen are not educators. Businessmen are necessarily driven by short-termism.' These were the people now charged with spending locally, through the Training and Enterprise Councils (TECs) that replaced the national structures of the MSC, its £3 billion training budget to solve long-term skill problems. Despite the obsession with identifying skill shortages and attempting to eradicate them, there was still a 'skills crisis' in the British economy. As soon as the economy recovered somewhat, 'skills mismatch' was again held to account for the bottleneck that held back industrial advance and the full use of new technology. This, in turn, contributed to the weakness of the recovery and its vulnerability to the next world slump. As that recession deepened, the OECD 'Economic Outlook' once more reported 'chronic skill shortages and inadequate training of the labour force' in Britain (July 1991). The report echoed an earlier World Competitiveness survey, which ranked the UK bottom among OECD countries for standards of compulsory education, availability of skilled labour and qualified engineers. The country was also ranked last for in-company training (reported in Unemployment Unit 1991). Training was once again the first casualty of recession as redundancies suddenly succeeded skill shortages. It is predictable that, in the event of any recovery, skill shortages and 'overheating' will set in at an even earlier stage than after the last recession (see Ainley 1993).

To put employers in charge of the situation for which they were responsible may not merely be, as Coffield (1990) suggested, a 'triumph of political preference over experience'. The enterprise solution has been seen as a form of modernization which offers a way out of the intractable crisis of Keynesian welfare capitalism. 'State induced enterprise', as Wallace and Chandler (1989) called it, is coming to 'permeate the franchise sections of the welfare state' from youth training managing agents, to schools, colleges, the health and social services, along with whatever other public services can be put out to contract. As an organizational principle, it means that 'problems can be privatised too' and 'whilst responsibility is decentralised, power is further centralised'. This mirrors the model of the state as a 'holding-company which subcontracts parts of itself at different levels'. Independently, Randall (1992: 4) came to the same conclusion when he wrote that TEC managing boards 'have the sort of freedom which business people gain through franchising from a Pizza Hut multinational'.

> A clear advantage of this government by quango is that the government can retain firm control of policy development but distance itself from the detailed day to day management of programmes. Additionally, civil service bureaucracies can be expanded and disbanded 'to task', according to the exigencies that arise. This new flexibility of response had allowed government to by-pass and eradicate the remnants of Britain's corporatist and tripartite past. (Ainley and Corney 1990: 128)

In this new 'mixed economy' of private and state capital, not only are former services provided by the local or national state taken over and sold off to private companies, other public services are retained by the state as semi-independent agencies to be run at a profit. Consumers are then redefined as 'citizens' with individual rights enshrined in the contractual relations of 'charters'. The 'citizens' of Mr Major's 'charters' do not participate collectively as informed individuals in democratic decisions about which goods and services should be provided by society at what cost to its members. They merely choose passively between the different commodities that the market offers term so that their 'equality' is only that of the marketplace. In the market, the only common value of commodities is their relative price. As the tool of all tools in which all qualities are represented as quantities, money appears as the universal medium, a measure which is not itself measured (see Simmel 1978). Public issues of health, education and welfare that should be the subject of informed debate and democratic decision are reduced by the mechanical routines of cost accounting to simple certainties that can easily be measured. Once established, monetary measures of 'value added' form a closed, apparently concrete and completely self-sufficient system of reference exclusive of all external considerations. The end result is a new Benthamism in which profit is the only measure of utility so that, as was said of a previous indictment of such 'Hard Times', 'As the issues are reduced to algebraic formulation they are patently emptied of all real meaning' (Leavis 1972: 265). This, and not any illusory 'training revolution', is the real cultural revolution to which the MSC contributed.

Training for the future

The MSC has been presented 'as a paradigm of new state agencies' (Baron 1989: 119). It may have been unique, but in a wider perspective Paolo Garonna and Paul Ryan (1991) note that such training proposals as it initiated can be seen as part of the revision of the post-war regulatory system or 'labour accord' in a number of advanced economies, but particularly the USA and UK. The eighty-two local TECs in England and Wales and the twenty-two Local Enterprise Companies (LECs) in Scotland which by 1991 had taken over the national administration of training from the Department of Employment, were widely seen as modelled on the US Private Industry Councils (PICs). As Evans (1993) notes, 'This reflected ideological bonds between the Thatcher and Reagan administrations', a world-view that saw the USA as, in Mrs Thatcher's phrase, 'the flagship of enterprise'. Moreover, Lord Young had returned from numerous visits to the land of the free to express an interest in the PICs and when Norman Fowler succeeded him as Secretary of State for Employment he visited the Boston PIC which ran the Compact scheme there. As a consequence, Kay Stratton, a member of Governor Dukakis's gubernatorial office responsible for the so-called Massachusetts miracle, advised the Department of Employment on formulating the 1988 White Paper *Employment for the 1990s*, which announced the new TEC policy. She subsequently performed the same role for the National Training Task Force (NTTF) given a four-year life-span to advise Fowler on the transfer of the former Quango's functions to the self-appointed groups of local businessmen hastily cobbled together out of Local Employer Networks, or, where they did not exist, local Chambers of Commerce.

As Evans (1993) records, 'It became clear by the beginning of 1990 that the NTTF was falling apart as many of its members . . . appeared to lose interest in its work', so that 'In reality it was departmental and TA officials who approved the applications for TEC status.' Meanwhile, the government cut the training budget, earmarked for specific purposes, which was to be handed over to the TECs from £2.9 billion to £2.4 billion in 1991, with a further £110 million reduction proposed for 1992–93. The TEC boards were thus involved in a three-way struggle to get more money out of government, while the

Training Enterprise Education Division (TEED) tried to prove its enduring usefulness by setting the standards to monitor this spending. This struggle was intensified by the rise in unemployment during the longest slump since the 1930s when, with 75 per cent of funding still tied to youth training and employment training, employers on the TECs found themselves responsible for lower-level skill training and unemployment programmes rather than able to train for their own firms' higher skill requirements as they might have preferred. Several TECs refused to agree contracts with the Department of Employment and some, already in deficit, may soon become insolvent. Indeed, according to an internal Department of Employment report, 'relations between the government and the TECs are unsustainable without a fundamental review' (reported in the *Financial Times* 9 July 1991). For, while nominally private companies, the TECs remain dependent on state funding and while less centralized they are no more independent than the old MSC. In fact, given the other commitments of the businesspersons (mostly men) who have volunteered, been cajoled or merely appointed their (originally excluded) personnel managers into serving on the TEC boards, TECs are also staffed and run by civil servants who have been drafted in from the old regional and area structures of the MSC.

The TECs were set up on voluntarist principles to return training to the *laissez-faire* situation that existed before 1964. They have been much criticized because that approach of relying upon persuasion alone did not work in the past and there are no compulsory financial levies upon employers as in France and Sweden, nor legal compulsion to train as in Germany. TECs are not accountable to the local communities they are supposed to serve and make no claim to represent the 'social partners' incorporated, for instance, in the German Chambers of Commerce. They are not even representative of local employers, for large manufacturers (where they exist) tend to predominate overall. The local focus of the TECs does not necessarily correspond with local labour markets and makes national co-ordination of education and training impossible, especially as schools, sixth-form and further education colleges, polytechnics and possibly the Careers Service have also been cut loose into the marketplace. All of these are dependent upon bidding for short-term contracts from the TECs and LECs. In this 'contract culture', according to one college principal quoted in the *Times Educational Supplement* (21 February 1992), 'Nothing is shared since everything has its price'. Indeed, the paper added that a highly critical report by the Bridge Group of 15 large voluntary organizations had identified the potential for widespread financial abuse of this bidding system. For as Tony Christopher (1992) of NACRO recorded, 'the monitoring of actual delivery on the ground by the Employment Department is limited and remote'. As a result, 'TECs are diverging further and further from each other and from any concerted approach to raising the skills of those with fewest qualifications'.

Under control of the TECs, YTS (imaginatively renamed YT in April 1990) no longer even pretends to present itself as a coherent national programme and several large employers have withdrawn from it altogether, unwilling to make 104 separate agreements with individual TECs and LECs. Since 1991, the TECs have been unable to meet the guarantee of a YT place for every school leaver by Christmas and the Unemployment Unit and Youthaid's 'Working Brief' has been detailing the rising numbers of young people left without any income as a result. One report estimated that more than 50,000 young people were still without training places in early 1992 (Unemployment Unit 1992). Despite this, TECs have piloted training credits for YT planned to go national after only a four-month trial period. Credits have been seen as another attempt to introduce vouchers that subsidize private schooling but their more likely extension is to further and higher education. Yet with the atrophy of LEA powers, the TECs are fast becoming the only major planning body for training and education at local level. Meanwhile, with the White Paper *Employment and Training for the Twenty-first Century* (DES 1991b) focused almost exclusively upon young people, the 70 per cent of the workforce with no recent education or training and the 3.4 million adults enrolled in further and adult education have been abandoned.

The Conservative's 1992 election manifesto promised to look further at the machinery of government, perhaps heralding the final dismemberment of the Department of Employment. Already the substantial Business Enterprise Programme and the Small Firms Service have gone to the Department of Trade and Industry and the TEED (or parts of it) may follow Sir Geoffrey Holland's transfer to the Department for Education. At the time of writing, as unemployment looks set to exceed 3 million in early 1993, future directions are unclear. It is likely that what remains of the MSC's training and employment efforts will be tied yet more closely to social security and unemployment relief, and will become part of a 'workfare' programme, offered under whatever guise.

This may seem a negative summary of the results of nearly thirty years of training reform, let alone for the billions that were spent by the MSC and its successors. Perhaps the best that can be said is that the training system – if anything so organized can be said to exist – has been driven into such incredible confusion that it at least offers the opportunity for a thorough reorganization. In place of the moribund market modernization attempted by the Conservatives, there is the potential for an alliance between what is left of British industrial capital and a government that would attempt a real modernization of the economy and society. As a first step, the full employment goal of economic policy must be reasserted. The right to work must be reaffirmed as well as the 'right to training' which has been substituted for it. With the relative decline of British industry and the growth of multinational companies reducing the influence that any government can exercise over its national economy, education and training policy has come to substitute for discussion of more fundamental problems facing society. Nevertheless, due to all the talk about training there is at least now an awareness of the problem, though still no consensus on how to deal with it.

Although the situation is better in Scotland (see Raffe 1991), the vocational education debate in Britain remains polarized between the North

American model of general education to eighteen with transition via local community colleges to a mass system of higher education thereafter and the German dual system which separates the vocational from the academic at an early age. In the British cultural context, where the two routes do not enjoy parity of esteem, this would deepen the division in the workforce between an academic minority and the majority who are failed by the schools system. The YTS apprentice-boy model of training would be preserved and the labour market further segmented. To overcome the still lingering Victorian legacy of early school-leaving, the normality and desirability of full-time education to eighteen and recurring returns to learning full- and part-time thereafter has to be established. Instead of cutting them loose into the marketplace where the lecturers' union NATFHE estimates between a quarter and a third of colleges may close, further education colleges could then become the link between schools and higher education. Further education has always been well-integrated with skill training in local labour markets and through TVEI and other 'bridging' arrangements with their local secondary and special schools. Colleges also increasingly franchise the lower levels of higher education courses so that the two years which many youngsters – together with adults on 'access' courses – already spend in further education before moving on to higher education can become the basis for a new two-plus-two degree structure. This would require a broad-based and flexible qualification structure embracing both academic and vocational – or general and specific – skills.

Paradoxically, one relic of the MSC's period of domination over education and training may offer a means to achieve this. In 1977, the MSC began the development of an Occupational Skills Inventory which claimed to record all possible tasks required in every occupation in the economy. At first narrowly behaviouristic, this classification developed to form the basis for the National Council for Vocational Qualification's matrix of vocational qualifications. Qualified recently by the addition of General NVQs to assess 'underpinning knowledge' as well as practical competencies, this is an attempt to introduce coherence and progression into the maze of vocational qualifications and to make them continuous with academic and professional qualifications. There are many problems associated with this approach (for a preliminary discussion, see Ainley 1990b: 69–78), not least of which is that it sits very uneasily alongside the grammar-school based 'National' Curriculum for schools and the A-level 'gold standard' which government insists on retaining for qualification to higher education. NVQs are however seen as a means of effecting the proposed 'harmonization' of all qualifications across the European Community.

The Conservative government set admirable targets for raising the numbers in higher education but contradicted them by introducing loans to pay for courses that in a market-driven system would be raised to their full cost. The expansion of higher education may then accommodate only those who can afford it, while the widely predicted separation of research from teaching, together with the introduction of two-year degree courses, will create a new binary divide between the more or less privatized antique universities and the rest of the colleges of higher education striving to imitate them. In this competition, the distinctive contributions of the former polytechnics would be lost, just as the ideals of the comprehensive schools are being submerged in the academic competition engendered by the 1988 Act.

This marketing of education and training is in contradiction with technological development and the demands placed upon society by continuing international economic crisis, the social and environmental consequences of which are imposing physical limits on further growth. The resolution of this crisis can no longer be limited by national boundaries. The accelerating pace of change demands new skills and new ideas developed from existing knowledge to enable people to cooperate in using the latest technology for collective ends. Such a necessity does not enter the agenda of current policy making.

Acknowledgements

I am indebted to Professor Brendan Evans of Huddersfield University for his careful commentary on the draft and also to Sarah Vickerstaff and Phil Brown of Kent University for their comments.

9

Where we go from here: The new order in welfare

Peter Taylor-Gooby and Robyn Lawson

The job of the Welfare State is to organize the production of a range of goods and services and distribute them to particular groups in the population, according to policies laid down by government. Traditionally, provision has been administered through the bureaucracies of central and local government. The new approach analysed in this book stresses two themes: at an organizational level the everyday management of services is decentralized to the lowest practicable layer, and at a distributional level markets are used to match provision to consumer demand. In theory, the approach is agnostic both as to whom the providers who are managed may be – public, private-for-profit or voluntary sector – and as to who counts as a consumer – individual citizens, groups of individuals, professionals acting on their behalf, private and voluntary agencies, are all treated as consumers in different reforms. In practice, the government of the 1980s and 1990s has used the new policies to shift the balance of provision away from public agencies and encouraged consumers to use private services for political reasons.

The radicalism of the new paradigm differs from that of the drive to budgetary constraint and privatization, understood as denationalization, that marked the reforms of the early 1980s. It does not necessarily imply spending cuts – in fact, many of the innovations (opt-out schools and hospitals, privately managed social housing, personal pensions) appear to cost government more than the previous equivalents or to offer less extensive provision at the same price. The same techniques could be used to manage expansion. Advocates claim that it allows a more responsive system to emerge, and critics suggest that the use of welfare to monitor and regulate the behaviour of groups such as unemployed or homeless people will become more stringent.

The changes discussed here are likely to prove the most significant force shaping welfare policy – who gets what, how and from whom, and who pays for it, as well as which groups are denied benefits and what conditions are attached to receipt – well into the next century. Many of the themes of the new state managerialism – consumerism, opposition to professional power, suspicion of large bureaucracies, enthusiasm for markets, determination to improve cost-efficiency – are common ground between many on the political right and on the political left. Decentralization, responsiveness to consumers and the use of markets figure prominently in the 1992 election manifestos of all major parties, and in the publications of opposition think-tanks or left-of-centre academics (Conservative Party 1992: 13–16; Labour Party 1992: 7; Liberal Democratic Party 1992: 48–51; Institute for Public Policy Research 1992: 4–6; Le Grand 1990: 14). The key difference is the stress on the use of the new methods to realize goals of cost-efficiency, selectivity and the expansion of choice on the right, while left-wing writers are more concerned with equality and the tailoring of services to meet need among all groups in society. However, practical experience indicates that the new policies are used mainly to justify contraction. A recent review of the new developments in European countries concludes: 'the current direction of social policy almost everywhere [is] . . . largely an attempt to limit some central aspects of all our citizenship rights by claiming in questionable ways to extend or protect others' (Baldock and Evers 1991: 123–4).

We will review the main changes in relation to the new philosophy of managerialism and markets, examine the constraints that have affected its implementation, and then consider explanations of the forces that underlie the new welfare settlement and the impact of the changes.

The new paradigm: Managerialism

The approach distinguishes between the aspects of a service essential to effective control and those that are of secondary importance. Power over the essentials is retained centrally while management of inessentials is decentralized. In this way, government can keep a tight grip on provision, while allowing the service to be run in a way that is responsive to local circumstances. Power thus moves in two directions: upwards to central government, and downwards and outwards to units closer to consumers. The intermediate institutions of the state (local government and regional bodies), of the services (professional organizations and trade unions) and of the wider society (independent community groups and advocacy agencies) lose influence.

These developments reflect a new philosophy of management that has spread through much of the private sector over the past three decades. The vertically and horizontally integrated firm which strives to include all aspects of its operation from the production of raw materials to the marketing of the final product within its own structure is increasingly being replaced by a complex network of subcontracting, interdependency and exchange. Particular firms may occupy the commanding heights of the system, but they still tend to contract particular aspects of their operation out to subsidiaries or independent contractors. Their power is expressed in their capacity to determine the terms of the contract. The point is that new technology and new managerial techniques mean that it is no longer necessary to incorporate a particular process in order to be able to control it, and there are real advantages in terms of flexibility and responsiveness to circumstances in the contract system, which allows the dominant firm to shed subsidiaries, relocate or redirect its endeavours at little cost to itself. Such a system is appropriate to modern conditions in which technical advance is rapid, in which the demands of consumers are becoming ever more complex and in which capital operates in a global market which no one participant can hope to control (Offe 1985; Lash and Urry 1987).

Over the last decade, and particularly since 1987, similar ideas have been imported into the welfare sector. One result is that some of the distinctions common in the welfare debate over recent years have lost much of their significance. The division between local and central government service weakens as control over the essential features of local government is tightened, while day-to-day management of central government services is localized. Similarly, claims based on professional expertise lose their effectiveness as central government establishes commonsensical measures of performance. New distinctions are in the process of emerging. These include the use of contractual rather than bureaucratic and professional mechanisms to achieve policy goals, the evaluation of quality by consumers rather than experts located within the service and, crucially, the separation of purchasing and providing agencies within a state-financed service. Only if the purchasing division of a state agency (care managers in social services; the local authority setting the pupil unit price for locally managed schools; the council contracting for refuse disposal; the fund-holding GP purchasing clinical services) is distinct from the providing agency (voluntary, private and in-house care providers; locally managed and grant-maintained schools; in-house and private contractors; trust, health authority and private hospitals) can real competition take place.

Decentralization makes far greater flexibility in the detail of service delivery possible, so that individual providing agencies may operate independently from each other. There is no reason why such agencies need to be part of the government system, and they may include the private or voluntary sector. The new welfarism is often analysed in terms of a 'core–periphery' relationship, rather than the hierarchical 'top-to-bottom' pyramid of the traditional bureaucratic structure with its direct chains of command and accountability down through the layers of officialdom to the street-level providers (Handy 1984: 57–64; Kanter 1985: 42–58; Hoggett 1990: 28).

In this model, the core functions are strategic thinking, policy making, setting objectives and standards, co-ordinating the purchase of services and overall budgetary control. It may be necessary to retain direct control over some areas for particular reasons: because they relate to basic state policing functions (such as probation work); because they are politically sensitive (such as child care); or because it is hard to find plausible peripheral providers (such as provision for elderly people who are severely mentally infirm). It is not yet clear how far it is possible to go in decentralizing control – the limits are set by cost, by the availability of information systems which allow the centre to evaluate work at the periphery and by what is politically acceptable. At the periphery, the providers can be left to manage budgets and organize service delivery, so long as a mechanism for checking their work exists. Again, the ultimate limits to what may count as satisfactory monitoring are technical feasibility and political acceptability, so that the issues of what groups in the population are affected by failure in the service becomes of considerable importance.

In the services we have considered, the increasing stringency of central budgetary control is one of the most striking features of the 1980s. In the local government services – social housing, education, the personal social services (PSS) – the autonomy of local government to make budgetary decisions has been circumscribed by new financial arrangements. As Chapters 4 and 6 show, the introduction of new technology in the NHS and in social security admin-istration enables the centre to monitor local spending more effectively. One of the main obstacles in the way of progress towards a core–periphery relation in PSS is the slow pace of investment and development in new management information systems.

State services differ from the private sector because there is a direct relation to the political system, and this leads to a dualism in the mechanism for checking on the success with which services are delivered. This must be acceptable both to government and to the public on whom the government depends for support. Government is able to monitor the progress of the re-forms through agencies such as the Audit Commission which, as Chapter 1 shows, has played a powerful role in spreading the new management culture. New mechanisms are to be made available through the cluster of reforms associated with the *Citizens' Charter* (Cabinet Office 1991a). This promotes a range of methods for improving basic standards, the availability of choice, the quality of provision and value for money in the public sector, including com-petition, contracting out, privatization, performance-related pay and the other techniques discussed in this book (Cabinet Office 1991a: 4–5).

The Charter also emphasizes the use of systems which relate to the second aspect of monitoring – supervision by the public rather than by govern-ment. Performance indicators designed to be accessible to ordinary people include test results for schools, waiting times for treatment in different hospi-tals, the proportion of claims resolved in a specified period in social security offices and so on. The measures chosen are highly controversial, and there is considerable concern that the desire to meet the standards as defined will skew resource allocation and stifle innovation within services, damaging the aspects not included in the measures (Millward 1982; Bartlett 1991b: 20; Patel 1991). However, the new approach has the effect of co-opting the public onto the side of the centre in the surveillance of performance at the periphery. At the time of writing, more than 40 'Citizens' Charters' have been published for services, including the NHS, education and council housing, and more are in preparation (Conservative Party 1992: 13). It is unclear whether the public are impressed by the paperwork. Much will depend on perceptions of the standards of services that are actually delivered.

The new paradigm: Markets

The new regime combines decentralized management with increased reliance on markets. Markets allocate resources through a price mechanism. Advocates claim four general advantages over planned allocation systems: greater choice, better communication, improved efficiency and greater political acceptability for controversial decisions.

First, markets allow consumers to choose between competing suppliers and to combine different packages of goods and services as suits themselves, rather than the suppliers. This argument is often associated with the Chicago School of Political Economy (Friedman 1960: chs 1 and 2). Second, they transmit information about what those who are in a position to pay for a service actually want swiftly and effectively. One tradition in social science sees the historical success of market capitalism as based on the superior quality of markets as opposed to command economies in allowing providers to balance what they can provide with effective demand. This is the central argument of the Vienna School of Political Economy. Von Mises (1962) provides the classic statement of the argument, refined by von Hayek (1949). Third, markets are seen as a spur to efficiency. Competitive pressures ensure that all providers strive to offer a service that is as good as that available from others, and ensure that those who do not move on to something else. Competition can take place on quality or price or a combination of the two, depending on what consumers value and who they are (Knight 1933; a succinct summary of these three arguments is contained in Gray 1992: 5–30). The fourth point is that markets provide a powerful mechanism for political legitimation. It is argued that market outcomes are neither fair nor unfair, but simply the result of the operation of impersonal forces, so that it is as pointless for the loser to protest about market allocations as it is for cyclists to complain about the steepness of hills (von Hayek 1976: 65; Offe 1984: 56–8, 267–70). To the extent that people hold this view, market systems offer the possibility of allowing politicians to hold responsibility for the welfare outcomes of government policies at arms length. These arguments are, of course, hotly contested (for a summary of the debate, see Plant 1991: 80–107).

All four features combine to make the extension of markets in welfare an attractive policy for those convinced by these arguments. In welfare, officials and professionals are often accused of managing services in their own interest; welfare needs are often complex and require the sophisticated combination of different services; financial stringency and rising demand place a heavy burden on the system; over recent years, government has been increasingly vulnerable to attack over policy failure, as the outcry over untreated NHS patients (Chapter 4) and the 'Great Debate' about education and the needs of the economy (Chapter 7) illustrate.

Throughout most of the 1980s, the main policy introducing markets into welfare was privatization. The most significant changes involved the sale of council houses to sitting tenants and the substitution of state for private earnings-related pensions (see Chapters 3 and 6). The lack of public complaint (indeed, the grudging acceptance by opposition parties of the right to buy for council tenants) indicates that these policies are successful from the viewpoint of legitimacy, whatever their effect in terms of choice, communication and efficient provision in the areas of housing and poverty in old age. The cost of private schooling, medical and social care suggests that further welfare denationalization in the immediate future would be unpopular, and such policies do not figure prominently in the 1992 Conservative election manifesto, which devotes half a side to privatization, against four pages to the *Citizens' Charter* and the new managerialism (Conservative Party 1992: 10, 13–16).

From the late 1980s onwards, interest in welfare markets has centred on the use of internal markets, financed by government and used to allocate resources between providers. The most developed instances are the system of compulsory competitive tendering within the NHS and local government, and local management of schools. Competitive tendering was initially introduced in the NHS for portering, catering and cleaning services. After union struggles involving lengthy industrial action at four hospitals, the system was established throughout the NHS. A variety of potential providers was permitted to tender for the provision of these services, according to a tight specification drawn up by hospital management. The result of the exercise has been that in about 84 per cent of cases, contracts are won in-house (Cabinet Office 1991b: 17), the previously directly employed division of the NHS taking the contract.

The chief effect has been to drive down wages and conditions of service, so that provision becomes cheaper, and large savings are achieved, estimated at £626 million between 1984 and 1991. Similar results emerge in local authorities which have used competitive tendering to organize school meal or cleaning services. There is considerable concern about the extent to which the process emphasizes competition on price in circumstances of tight budgets, to the exclusion of competition on quality, determined by the specification and the effectiveness with which the contract is monitored. Such policies are to be extended to cover between 12 and 25 per cent of civil service jobs by 1995 (Waldegrave 1992). The effect of 'market testing' on wages and conditions of work will depend on the labour market in the relevant areas. High levels of unionization had enabled NHS and local government manual workers to drive up wages compared with those in the private sector. The new policies imply the end of national pay bargaining. However, professional workers in the civil service often work in a labour market context where pay scales outside are higher, and may succeed in bidding their pay up under the new arrangements.

In other areas of welfare, the market principle is substantially modified. In the NHS and PSS, professionals are increasingly taking the role of managers of service provision, acting on behalf of clients. Thus patients may choose a GP and the mechanisms allowing people to shift between GPs have recently been strengthened. However, in the case of fund-holding GPs, it is the doctor and not the patient who then makes a decision between the various opportunities for treatment available. Similarly, the objective of the current reform of the PSS is to allow case managers to make choices on behalf of clients, assembling a care package tailored to meet their needs. The term 'quasi-market' has been coined to take account of the difference in status of the consumer in these situations. Many commentators have pointed out that the old problem of professional power is likely to re-emerge in the relation between the quasi-market actors and the consumers whose best interest they serve. The responsibility of the budget-holder is to consult with the consumer, but such consultation may be limited by professional authority and by financial constraint.

In addition, fund-holding GPs are at once providers and proxy purchasers of services. The same applies to Social Services Department (SSD) case managers in authorities where the two functions are not clearly demarcated. This may lead to a conflict of interest, especially at a time of resource constraint, that may put an additional burden on professional standards. Thus the new paradigm simultaneously downgrades professionalism, by elevating the position of managers and consumers, and demands increased professional objectivity in areas where professionals are both purchasers and providers in a competitive market. If GPs protect their funds by substituting their own treatment for necessary but costly hospital care or case managers deny access to expensive residential accommodation when this is what clients would prefer, the legitimacy of the new system may be called into question.

Quasi-markets pose especial problems of choice, communication, efficiency and legitimacy. The restrictions placed by government on freedom of referral and on hospital specialization in the NHS and the likelihood that initially the new PSS arrangements will not operate to shift existing recipients of the service out of residential accommodation (see Chapters 4 and 5), indicate that the new system will be developed with caution.

The system of open enrolment plus local financial management of schools (see Chapter 7) introduces a market into state education. Resources follow pupil demand. Here discussion about efficiency has centred on concern about the extent to which declining schools can provide a full range of education at a high standard. Information passes effectively to providers from fluctuations in pupil numbers and budgets. It is unclear what the balance between selection of pupils by schools and selection of schools by pupils will be. The legitimacy of the arrangements may depend ultimately on the extent to which the system is seen to deliver freer choices to a substantial and politically influential group in the population. Similar issues apply in further and higher education.

In other areas, market choices that have strong implications for others are to be made by groups of individuals, or by private agencies. A group of council tenants or of parents of children currently at a particular school may elect to take their estate or school out of local government management by a simple majority, although there is no complementary procedure for taking the institution back if they change their mind. Private landlords or housing associations may also initiate the process in the case of housing. Those who might hope to have access to the housing or use the school in the future are not consulted.

The new paradigm: Problems, constraints and distortions

The chief criticisms of the new approach concern the emphasis on cost-efficiency, the limitations imposed on choice, the channelling of innovation towards increased economy, the practice of selectivity and the problems of constructing collective outcomes through the aggregation of individual choices. Discussion of these issues indicates that the detail of implementation is of considerable importance in determining the outcome of the reforms.

The term 'efficiency' refers to the use of the fewest resources to achieve a particular goal. It is therefore concerned with the means by which ends are achieved and cannot be an end in itself (Le Grand 1991: 29). Common sense values efficiency as the antithesis of waste, but requires that the object of policy be distinguished from the efficiency with which it is achieved. However, current practice, which stresses financial restriction and the zero-cost implementation of reform, tends to valorize economy as the goal by which efficiency is to be measured, rather than quality of service. Thus compulsory competitive tendering rules insist that the lowest tender is accepted. The problem is well illustrated in the White Paper entitled *Competing for Quality*, which asserts the virtues of 'market-testing' in the NHS and central and local government services as a 'fundamental management reform' to obtain 'the best standards achievable within a given budget' (Cabinet Office 1991b: 2). This statement is backed up by detailed evidence of cost-savings (ibid.: 17, 19, 23, 26–35), but nothing on ways of measuring the impact on quality. The adequacy of the new system in improving efficiency is uncertain, and the net effect may be to substitute cheapness for quality, driving down standards to the lowest common denominator. In addition, some aspects of the new policies require additional expenditure: plural services may not be able to achieve the economies of scale available to large providers; the new monitoring methods require expensive management information systems; regulation involves inspection and the specification and negotiation of contracts; and participation in a market requires extra spending on advertising, market research and self-presentation. For example, a recent study of the plural system of commercial medical insurance in the USA indicates that administrative costs ran at 33.5 per cent of the amount paid in claims in 1988 – a proportion 14 times as high as in the state-run Medicare (Brandon *et al.* 1991: 265). In addition, 'many of the regulatory interventions characteristic of a mixed economy act as deterrents to competition by creating entry barriers and offer the prospect of monopoly profits to those who successfully negotiate their way through' (Rowley 1982).

Second, choice requires adequate public knowledge of alternatives and the opportunity to choose between them. The measures of quality available to the public may be misleading: Chapter 7 points out that the key stage tests used in education are likely to reflect the quality of student intake rather than the quality of schooling; average hospital waiting times or case clearance rates in social security administration may measure the extent to which resources are focused on the simplest cases (Chapters 4 and 6). In areas like medicine and PSS, the consumer may not be a good judge of his or her own need and must then rely on the decisions of the GP or case manager. The burden thrown on professional integrity by the transformation of professional workers into budget-holders has already been discussed. In general, freedom of choice is weakened by the degree to which specialist knowledge is essential to the exercise of consumer choice. Choice also implies alternatives. For some groups, realistic choices are unavailable. This is most obvious in relation to the most vulnerable groups of users – for example, unemployed and unskilled young people, who are unable to receive training places because of the shortfall in provision, those patients or school students who are least mobile or least skilled in self-advocacy, tenants who are unable to buy, those with inadequate work records or pay too low to command a personal pension. This problem is compounded by the incentives for providers, who are in a position to do so to discriminate against unattractive consumers.

Third, the new system places a high premium on innovation to meet new and developing needs. In some areas, innovation took place mainly in the state sector; for example, most of the curricular innovation in education in the 1960s and 1970s originated in state schools and state social security was able to escape the straitjacket of actuarially sound pension calculation. In other areas, innovation was located in private and voluntary agencies, for example, in housing management and welfare rights advocacy. The new system imposes a more rigid definition of the task on the state sector – the National Curriculum in education, insistence that the National Insurance fund must balance its books – and more stringent contractual controls on private agencies. Innovative energies are directed towards cost-efficiency. One obvious strategy is to develop new ways of circumventing performance indicators – teaching to the test, rather than the needs of the pupil; excluding awkward cases from the medical practice; concentrating on straightforward claims for benefit. The burden of ensuring quality is thrown back onto the monitoring apparatus. An official study of contractual arrangements in community care concludes: 'if criteria other than generating choice guide the implementation of the reforms, choice may be reduced rather than extended' (Flynn and Common 1990b: 26).

Fourth, there is real concern about the position of the more vulnerable groups in the system. The pressures for selectivity among schools and GPs have been discussed at length. Whether similar pressures will force those groups with the most expensive needs to the back of the queue – for example, pupils with learning difficulties, disabled housing association tenants, those with complex social security claims – remains to be seen. As a result of changes in social security benefits, as well as shifts in the economy leading to greater dispersion of pay rates and changes in family structure, leading to more single-parent families relying on benefit, British society is growing more unequal. The most recent official statistics show that the proportion of people living below half average income increased from 9 to 22 per cent between 1979 and 1988–89. The real income of the poorest 10 per cent had fallen by 6 per cent in real terms (after housing costs are taken into account), while average incomes had risen by over 30 per cent (Department of Social Security 1992b). In the context of growing income inequality, the trend to selectivity within state services and the residualization of groups such as council tenants is an especial cause for concern.

Finally, the new approach relies on the aggregation of individual choices to produce the best overall outcome, using three main mechanisms: quasi-ballots in the case of grant-maintained schools and Tenants' Choice; internal markets in local authority schooling, health and much of the PSS; and the managerial compilation of information in core–periphery administrative structures. In the case of the first device, many of those affected by the decision are excluded from the process. In the case of the other two, choice is constrained by knowledge and by the availability of alternatives. Since some crucial factors – most importantly overall budget and policy objectives – are decided at a political level, some possibilities are necessarily ignored by the system. It is not possible for schooling outside the National Curriculum or health care at a standard more costly than that allowed for by the contract to enter the internal market. Pressure for development in these directions is thus contained.

These criticisms do not imply that the new approach is wrong-headed. They do indicate that the detail of implementation in terms of spending levels, monitoring apparatus, measures of the standard of provision and the responsibilities laid on providers and the political choices which shape the freedom of the operation of markets and the actions of managers are of fundamental importance. We now turn to the context in which the new paradigm was introduced in the UK in the 1990s.

Implementation: the political context

The new approach to welfare has been implemented in a political context marked by concern about spending constraint, antagonism to local government and the normal desire of the party of government to strengthen its own political base worked out in the peculiarities of the UK's constitutional arrangements. These factors have shaped the way in which the new policies were developed and have introduced a number of distortions.

First, spending constraint has resulted in the implementation of reform at zero cost in most areas. Competition has been increasingly directed at price rather than quality. There has been considerable concern about the standards of competitively tendered services, and the evidence that most people would prefer to pay more tax for better welfare services has been ignored (Taylor-Gooby 1991b: 41). The new monitoring mechanisms have been starved of resources. In social security, the determination to set up a system that would allow the efficient monitoring of local offices has taken precedence over policies that would allow for the treatment of individual claimants as whole people with a plurality of interacting needs (see Chapter 6). In the NHS and PSS, implementation of the new management information systems has been delayed due to cost constraints (Perrin 1991: 154).

Hostility to local government is expressed in the increasingly stringent controls that have curtailed the freedom of action of councils in service provision. Local authorities have lost control of further education to a national body and of schooling to the schools themselves – partly in the case of locally managed schools, completely in the case of grant-maintained schools. Much of social housing has been transferred to housing associations. Only PSS are as yet relatively unscathed, and it is often suggested that antagonism to the idea of letting local authorities act as the 'lead agency' in community care delayed acceptance of the Griffiths proposals (see Chapter 5). Increasingly, SSDs are under pressure to transfer work to the voluntary and private sectors (Kelly 1991).

The political context of change operating in a context of financial constraint and government commitment to tax reductions, at least in the case of the highly visible income tax, have led to the implementation of changes in a way that distributes benefits and burdens unevenly. The denationalizations of the 1980s were driven by carrots and sticks – discounts for 'right to buy' council tenants and rent increases for those who remained, subsidies for people switching to personal pensions and cuts in benefits for those who stayed in the state scheme. The net effect of these changes was a shift in state subsidy upwards. Thus tenants who are in a position to buy are able to obtain discounts of up to 70 per cent of the value of the property, while the cost of the main subsidy to buyers – mortgage interest relief – rose from £3.2 to £7.8 billion (at 1991 values) between 1979 and 1991 (CSO 1992: table 8.26). Tax relief subsidies for private pensions rose to £13,340 million by 1990–91 (including £1100 million direct subsidy to personal pensions), while the Exchequer subvention to the National Insurance fund, running at about 10 per cent of the annual cost of the benefits in the mid-1980s, was entirely removed by 1990 (Her Majesty's Treasury 1991: table D1).

The new paradigm of the 1990s has been implemented in a way that ensures that advantage remains with the privileged groups who contain the highest proportion of supporters of the party of government. This appears in the division between grant-maintained and council schools and the extra subsidy to the former group, the increasing discrimination between different classes of patients in a cost-conscious health service, and the probability that similar judgements may be made in relation to PSS clients in relation to expensive services like residential care. One approach to the Welfare State makes a crude division between the mass services, such as education, the NHS and pensions, used by the majority, highly valued and less vulnerable to cuts in the financial constraint of the past two decades, and the minority services, such as cash benefits for unemployed and low-paid people and single-parent families, and social housing, directed at the poor, viewed with suspicion and subject to the heaviest cuts. In the former area, policy is concerned to meet need within political constraints, whereas in the latter, it is also concerned to regulate behaviour, so that the effect of welfare on work incentives, parental willingness to support children and the desert of those who seek social housing become significant.

The reforms of recent years sharpen the distinction between mass and minority services. People in council housing who could possibly afford home ownership are given every incentive to buy, provision for homeless people is policed more strictly, and the mechanisms for enforcing availability for work and child support are strengthened, so that the Welfare State for the poor is more tightly focused. The subsidies available to comfortable groups within mass services are also enlarged through pension subsidies and housing relief. At the same time, the new decentralized mechanisms enable finer distinctions to be drawn and give providers every incentive to do so. In education, schools compete for pupils who will produce good test records. GPs have an incentive to court healthier people and those with private medical insurance. Of course, not all will succeed. However, the logic of the internal market is a logic of inequality and selectivity, since some consumers are more attractive to providers than others. One result may be the emergence of a welfare system which disengages the provision enjoyed by supporters of the party of government from that for the rest of the population and thus buttresses political advantage.

It is possible to envisage the new paradigm being applied to achieve goals of greater equality and more widespread access to state services. Differential subsidies such as the contribution to personal pensions or the 'right to buy' discount could be removed, the confused implementation of the purchaser–provider split in PSS and fund-holding GPs resolved, and the opportunities for selection and discrimination between consumers by providers in services like education abolished where there is excess demand through the allocation of places by ballot. The current party of government, however, has distorted the new technology of management to serve electoral interests.

Accounting for the new paradigm

The changes of the new paradigm are fundamental and command considerable support across political parties, although the particular implementation expresses Conservative ideology. Similar changes are proceeding in other countries; indeed, Baldock and Evers (1991: 111) note a 'growing enthusiasm over the last decade or so for the use of the price mechanism' throughout Europe. So far-reaching a change demands explanation, and explanation must be sought beyond the level of party politics.

The four main currents in explanation stress the role of economic problems, the impact of social change on demand for welfare and on expectations, the limitations of welfare bureaucracies, and the impact of new technology on the political economy of the Welfare State. In considering these explanations, it must be borne in mind that decentralization and flexibility are powerful strands in management thinking outside the state sector, but that there are particular features of the Welfare State – to do with its commitment to meeting the needs of groups who are unable to enter the market, its social control functions and its relation to politics – that distinguish it from private enterprise.

The first strand in explanation concerns economic pressures. Traditional bureaucratic structures aided by influential professionals represented a good mechanism for organizing services to meet social need at a time of expansion, but are less useful at a time of constraint. The problems of growth concern the identification of new needs and the devising of appropriate systems to meet them. Priorities are an issue, but not of such overriding importance as they are when it is necessary to decide which services to cut first. Resource constraint demands an overriding emphasis on cost-efficiency, and the making of tough decisions about priorities. Large bureaucracies with professional advice are good at maintaining an existing routine structure of provision and incorporating new needs into it through incremental growth. They are less good at divorcing decisions about priorities from the professional advocacy of influential client groups or from the commitment to satisfying existing rights. The new system offers the opportunity to centralize decisions about priorities in the hands of a small group who can initiate radical policies with the minimum of interference from vested interests within the service. The new managerialism also appears as politically neutral and offers the possibility of separating unpopular decisions from politics and representing them as technical matters.

Social change has two important aspects. The first strengthens the above argument: a number of shifts increase social need so that the pressure on services grows more intense. Most importantly, inequalities are growing wider, poverty, homelessness and unemployment are far higher than in the 1970s, and the increasing number of elderly people places growing demands on pensions, health and social care. Most of these trends seem likely to continue over the next decade. An alternative view suggests that the claim that these pressures require new policies is overstated; while inequalities are severe they will not necessarily grow worse, and the greater part of the burden of demographic change will be absorbed by an increase in women's paid employment and by improving health among elderly people (Falkingham 1989: 227; Ermisch 1990: 43). However, most official planning is informed by the more pessimistic view (DHSS 1985a: para. 5.2; 1989: para. 1.4). Thus anticipated pressures on welfare form a further reason for establishing a structure fitted to curb the post-war growth of welfare spending.

The second aspect of social change concerns expectations. Average living standards have risen and higher living standards are linked to a growth of consumerist demands on services. People have more realistic opportunities for exit from the state sector; they are better educated and the gap between service users and state professionals has narrowed, so that they are more willing to question official decisions. The development of new social movements outside the traditional politics of class has led to a questioning of the role of the government in maintaining the interests of advantaged groups through welfare services in relation to ethnic minorities and women (Pierson 1991: 69–95). This change forms part of a growing mistrust of government across the whole range of its activities.

The third strand concerns the critiques of the unresponsiveness and inefficiency of state bureaucracies developed by public choice theorists over the past thirty years and more recently adopted by mainstream welfare writers. This critique has two parts. First, many writers have argued that monopoly providers, especially those backed by the power of the state to obtain resources through compulsory taxation, have little incentive to pay close attention to consumer demands. Most consumers have few alternatives but to take what is offered – after all, they have already paid for it anyway (Hirschman 1970: 102–106). Second, it is argued that the incentives that face bureaucrats encourage them to expand their own domain (Niskanen 1973). The result grosses up to over-supply and in terms of individual agencies leads to an in-built tendency to inefficiency – people will try to maximize resource use in relation to a given task rather than minimize it because their own career prospects are directly related to the size of their budgets. The theory of non-market failure is developed at greater length by Wolf (1979; for a clear commentary, see Goodin 1988: 242–6). The new managerialism alters this by providing a direct route for the expression of consumer preference through a market or quasi-market, by placing a premium on cheap service at the periphery and by establishing information systems that allow the centre to know when they are getting it.

The fourth strand takes all these points and develops a new political economy of organizational change. The central point is that new technology changes the nature of managerial control. At one time, it was necessary for an organization to own every aspect of its operation directly in order to be able to control it. The logical result is the integrated firm, including raw material supply, manufacture and marketing within one consolidated organization. Welfare bureaucracies on the post-war model mimic this approach. Developments in computing and information systems means that an organization can now check on any part of its activities rapidly so that a much more flexible system is possible. The pressures of rising demand and resource constraint make flexibility desirable. In welfare, the core–periphery model where the centre retains the essentials and contracts out tasks to a plurality of providers is the outcome. Hoggett (1990) develops this account into a political economy of welfare management based on the marxist insight that changes in the forces and relations of production are the motors that lie behind social change, so that the origins of the new paradigm are to be found in innovations in communications and knowledge processing in the field of welfare production.

None of the four explanations offered is entirely convincing. It is not clear that traditional management structures cannot handle problems of priorities rationally, although they may permit stronger cases against change to be made and may allow more space for stronger professional advocacy through the multitude of agencies that exist between the base and the centre. From this perspective, the changes must be seen in a political context: as a convenient approach for an administration that wished to cut back provision and to weaken the capacity of service providers to resist such cuts.

Similarly, the claim that social change has imposed ineluctable burdens on welfare in the last quarter of the twentieth century may be misleading. As has already been noted, some new developments will not increase welfare burdens. Many of the policy reforms – cuts in benefits, abolition of wage protection, a shifting of the tax burden from better- to worse-off groups and the failure to provide support for informal social care – result from political decisions rather than social factors, and could certainly be reversed while retaining the new paradigm. The new consumerist citizenship is a trend noted and welcomed in many quarters. However, the extension of consumer rights is not incompatible with the traditional welfare structures, and may be achieved through other means than the expansion of markets. One response on the left argues for a citizenship expressed in equal access to services realized through democratic participation in welfare institutions (Alcock *et al.* 1989: 269; Lister 1990: 464).

The debate about public choice is unresolved at a theoretical and an empirical level (Mueller 1979: 270; Dunleavy and O'Leary 1987: 159–64, 345). It is by no means certain that private services are any more responsive than public ones. Much depends on the ability of consumers to contest the decisions of service providers and the availability of viable alternatives, which requires genuine competition (Letwin 1988). Market costs such as the external regulation of standards, advertising and the devising of strategies to attract consumers may wipe out cost-efficiency gains from the competition. New technology provides opportunities for a restructuring of state welfare as of private enterprise because management can now control the front-line providers more easily, without having to take on the costs of incorporating them into its own organization. However, possibility does not necessitate action. The changes must be understood in their context as policies pursued by a particular government and crucially affected by its ideology and its conception of its own electoral interests. New technology provided an opportunity. Determination to cut spending demanded that the opportunity be grasped in a particular way. Economic crisis, social change and public choice arguments provide convenient justifications for change.

From this perspective, the appeal of the new paradigm may be understood in terms of a changed agenda of political legitimation. The traditional Beveridgean Welfare State faced the contradiction that Turner (1986: 132–3) identifies in all state bureaucracies. The system seeks to guarantee individual citizen rights. However, the process used to value rights reduces citizens to the status of clients trapped in the 'iron cage' of the framework of rules, which does not recognize individuals, only cases. The Welfare State attempted to resolve the conflict between rights as rules and individual citizenship through the regulation of state bureaucracies by a political system which represented individual grievances. This process was certainly imperfect, and the reaction against its imperfections is one of the principal forces compelling change. The philosophy of rolling back the state and expanding markets championed by the New Right faces the opposite contradiction: in a free market, actors have strong incentives to combine whenever they can to bias the market in their own favour. Free markets can only be sustained by vigorous state action to abolish monopoly, cartel, trade unionism and all collective organization of interest. As Gamble (1979) points out, this poses a problem of legitimation: the market is justified as a domain of individual freedom, but it requires determined state action to restrict the exercise of freedom so that competition on equal terms is possible. Just as the solution to the problem of the dominion of bureaucracies was to place the bureaucracy within a political system, so the solution to the problem of maintaining market freedom is to insert the market within the state, so that the terms of trade can be regulated at will by politicians and citizens/consumers. The new system makes the world safe for the market as the previous system attempted to make it safe for bureaucracy.

The impact of the new paradigm

The impact of the new approach can be considered on two levels: First, what are the likely effects of the changes described in this book both on service users and on those working within welfare services over the next few years? Second, what are the likely effects on society as a whole – the relation between state, polity and citizen – of the changes?

The impact of changes on service workers is fairly clear: the key division is between managers and those in the front line. The influence of the intermediate levels of professionals and of bureaucracy is diminished across the board. This has powerful effects on work practices, job security and pay inequalities. The move away from large quasi-monopolistic purchasers (monopsonists) of labour also exposes pay and working conditions much more to market forces. Wages and conditions will depend on factors outside the control of the welfare service more than in the past. Much will depend on the operation of the labour market as a whole, and particularly on social changes affecting the supply of women workers on whom most welfare services have relied. Greater inequalities in pay will emerge within services like the NHS, as workers with scarce skills bid up the cost of their labour while routine workers are unable to resist downward pressures. Le Grand (1990: 11) illustrates the point using the example of income differentials in the decentralized US medical system (see Robinson 1988). This argument suggests that the new approach will erode the solidarity of unions in the Welfare State as it has outside it, and make it possible for government to replace national scales with locally negotiated performance-related pay.

State services may reduce their commitment to training if they are no longer the chief employer of skilled labour in a particular area. Fluctuations in labour supply are likely to make the situation less stable. Those whose skills are in demand may be able to reassert professional power if they choose to do so. Since the accreditation of specialist workers may create opportunities for some groups to restrict entry and inflate pay, the issue of training and licensing approving workers for particular skilled tasks raises difficult political questions for the new system.

At the periphery, private and voluntary sector agencies will be drawn more tightly into the structure of service delivery according to policy laid down by the centre and monitored through contracts which can be terminated if performance is unsatisfactory. This change will erode the capacity of voluntary agencies to innovate or to take on an advocacy role for clients. Whether it will be possible for a 'second front' of voluntary organizations to develop beyond those whose scope for action is regulated by contracts with state agencies is unclear. Much will depend on the terms of trade between purchasers and providers. In general, there are likely to be fewer suppliers for the most complex, difficult and specialized needs, so that contracts will tend to be more flexible in these areas.

For service users, the changes are likely to mean greater inequality in provision – the capacity of providers to select users in education, health care and some areas of PSS is an obvious source of discrimination in these areas. Cuts in funding for social housing and in the real levels of benefits indicate that these services will decline for the remaining state sector users, while the encouragement of private alternatives through schemes such as the right to buy and personal pensions makes state provision increasingly distant for the mass of the population.

Longer-term prospects are uncertain. The implementation of the new structure may lead to the fragmentation of provision, with the costs of management information, the duplication of peripheral administration, market research and advertising outweighing savings and government failing to find providers for some needs, e.g. special needs schooling or provision for homeless young people who are denied benefit. In this case, pressures towards a more unitary system in which government directly controls services may reappear. Alternatively, competition could improve standards, encourage greater diversity in provision and contain costs. The most likely outcome is that both processes will emerge in relation to different services as experienced by different groups in society. The services directed at the poorer groups in the population are most likely to remain in the ambit of the directly providing Welfare State, and the diversity of provision and effective choice between alternatives will increase higher up the social class scale. This discussion indicates that the outcome depends primarily on the political context in which its implementation develops. If the emphasis is on cost constraint and middle-class advantage, the system will deliver cheap, unequal services, with little room for advocacy and innovation. If high standards and broad access are strong priorities, the new structure may facilitate competition that drives up the quality of common provision.

Britain in the 1990s combines a strong centralized state apparatus with a government committed to residualism. Many of the reforms of the past decade have been concerned with the further tightening of central control. However, as Chapter 2 shows, the best examples of strong central government elsewhere are to be found in the Scandinavian countries – Esping-Andersen's paradigmatic social democratic welfare regimes (1990: ch. 2) – but here powerful government is linked to interventionism and universalism. Plural systems have arisen in countries where there was no central commitment to welfare precisely because there was no consensus at the level of government on the provision of services to meet common social needs. The result in countries like Germany – Esping-Andersen's exemplar of a corporatist welfare regime – is that a diversified welfare sector develops which provides a base for pressure to expand provision, and which is not integrated into the state apparatus in a way which permits effective control of spending. In Britain, the drive to pluralism is accompanied by centralization of power and a determination to limit provision.

The real question is whether central government, having unleashed both providers and service consumers from the restrictions of a bureaucratic state, will succeed in using the new managerial techniques to contain demands on the system. The strategy of undermining universalism by allowing wider divisions to appear between the services enjoyed by comfortable and poorer groups in the new competitive economy of welfare may help, because it will be easier to satisfy the more influential constituency if middle-class services are clearly separated from those for weaker groups. However, European experience indicates that the success of the centre in imposing its objectives on a plural system is not a foregone conclusion. Instead of taking welfare out of politics, the new managerial dispensation may simply construct the next arena for conflict.

References

Abrahamson, P.E. (1991). 'Welfare and poverty in the Europe of the 1990s: Social progress or social dumping?', *International Journal of Health Service*, 21(2), 237–64.

Adler, M. and Sainsbury, R. (1990). *Putting the Whole Person Concept into Practice*. Final Report: Part 1. Department of Social Policy and Social Work, University of Edinburgh.

Adler, M. and Sainsbury, R. (1991). 'Administrative justice, quality of service and the operational strategy', in M. Adler and R. Williams (eds) *The Social Implications of the Operational Strategy*. New Waverley Papers, Social Policy Series No. 4, University of Edinburgh.

Ainley, P. (1988). *From School to YTS: Education and Training in England and Wales, 1944–87*. Milton Keynes, Open University Press.

Ainley, P. (1990a). *Training Turns to Enterprise: Vocational Education in the Market Place*. London, Tufnell Press.

Ainley, P. (1990b). 'Vocational education and training', in T. Wragg (ed.) *Education Matters*. London, Cassell.

Ainley, P. (1993). *Class and Skill: Changing Divisions of Knowledge and Labour*. London, Cassell, forthcoming.

Ainley, P. and Corney, M. (1990). *Training for the Future: The Rise and Fall of the Manpower Services Commission*. London, Cassell.

Alcock, P., Gamble, A., Gough, I., Lee, P. and Walker, A. (eds) (1989). *The Social Economy and the Democratic State* (the Sheffield Group). London, Lawrence and Wishart.

Alexander, A. (1991). 'Managing fragmentation – democracy, accountability and the future of local government', *Local Government Studies*, 17, 63–76.

Association of Directors of Social Services (1989). *Community Care: Agenda for Action: Response to Sir Roy Griffiths' Report*. Manchester, ADSS.

Association of Directors of Social Services (1992). *Private Residential Care in England and Wales: Report of a Survey by the ADSS*. Manchester, ADSS.

Audit Commission (1984). *The Impact on Local Authorities' Economy, Efficiency and Effectiveness of the Block Grant Distribution System*. London, HMSO.

Audit Commission (1986). *Making a Reality of Community Care*. London, HMSO.

Audit Commission (1990). *Rationalising Primary School Provision*. London, HMSO.

Audit Commission (1992a). *Managing the Cascade of Change*. London, HMSO.

Audit Commission (1992b). *The Community Revolution*. London, HMSO.

Bacon, R. and Eltis, W. (1978). *Britain's Economic Problem: Too Few Producers*. London, Macmillan.

Baldock, J. and Evers, A. (1991). 'Citizenship and frail elderly people: Changing patterns of provision in Europe', in N. Manning (ed.) *Social Policy Review 1990–91*. Harlow, Longman.

Baldock, J. and Evers, A. (1992). 'Innovations and care of the elderly: The cutting edge of change for social welfare systems', *Ageing and Society*, 12(3), 289–312.

Baldwin-Edwards, M. and Gough, I. (1991). 'EC social policy and the UK', in N. Manning (ed.) *Social Policy Review 1990–91*. Harlow, Longmans.

Ball, M., Harloe, M. and Martens, M. (1988). *Housing and Social Change in Europe and the USA*. London, Routledge.

Ball, M., Gray, F. and McDowell, L. (1989). *The Transformation of Britain*. London, Fontana.

Barclay, P. (1982). *Report of the Working Party on Social Workers, Their Role and Tasks*. London, Bedford Square Press.

Baron, S. (1989). 'Towards a self-sustaining regime: The Manpower Services Commission and the Scottish universities', in A. Brown and J. Fairley (eds) *The Manpower Services Commission in Scotland*. Edinburgh, Edinburgh University Press.

Barr, N. and Coulter, F. (1990). 'Social security: Solution or problem', in J. Hills (ed.) *The State of Welfare: The Welfare State in Britain since 1974*. Oxford, Clarendon Press.

Bartlett, W. (1991a). *Quasi-Markets and Contracts: A Market and Hierarchies Perspective on NHS Reform*. Studies in Decentralisation and Quasi-Markets No. 3, School for Advanced Urban Studies, University of Bristol.

Bartlett, W. (1991b). *Privatisation and Quasi-markets*. Studies in Decentralisation and Quasi-Markets No. 7, School for Advanced Urban Studies, University of Bristol.

Becker, S. and Silburn, R. (1991). *The New Poor Clients*. Nottingham, Nottingham University/Community Care.

Bell, P. and Cloke, P. (1989). 'The changing relationship between the private and public sectors: Privatisation and rural Britain', *Journal of Rural Studies*, 5, 1–15.

Benn, C. and Fairley, J. (eds) (1986). *Challenging the MSC on Jobs, Training and Education*. London, Pluto.

Bennett, F. (1987). 'What future for social security', in A. Walker and C. Walker (eds) *The Growing Divide: A Social Audit 1979–1987*. London, CPAG.

Bertelsen, O. and Platz, M. (1991). *The Impact of Social and Economic Policies on Older People in Denmark*. Report to the European Community Observatory on Older People, Commission of the European Communities, Directorate General V, Brussels.

Blackstone, T. and Plowden, W. (1988). *Inside the Think Tank: Advising the Cabinet 1971–83*. London, Heinemann.

Booth, T. (1990). 'Taking the plunge: Contracting out?', *Community Care*, 26 July, 23–5.

Bosanquet, N. (1981). 'Sir Keith's reading list', *Political Quarterly*, 52, 324–41.

Brandon, R., Podhorzer, M. and Pollak, T. (1991). 'Premiums without benefits: Waste and inefficiency in the commercial health insurance industry', *International Journal of Health Services*, 21(2), 265–83.

Braverman, H. (1974). *Labor and Monopoly Capital*. New York, Monthly Review Press.

Brazier, J., Hutton, J. and Jeavons, R. (1990). *Analysing Health Care Systems: The Economic Context of the NHS White Paper Proposals*. York, Centre for Health Economics, University of York.

British Market Research Bureau (1989). *Housing Tenure*. London, Building Societies Association.

Brittan, L. (1988). *A New Deal for Health Care*. London, Conservative Political Centre.

Brooks, R. (1991). *Contemporary Debates in Education*. Harlow, Longman.

Bulpitt, D. (1983). *Territory and Power in the United Kingdom*. Manchester, Manchester University Press.

Butler, E., Pirie, M. and Young, P. (1985). *The Omega File*. London, Adam Smith Institute.

Butler, J.R. (1992). *Patients, Policies and Politics*. Buckingham, Open University Press.

Butler, J.R. and Vaile, M.S.B. (1984). *Health and Health Services: An Introduction to Health Care in Britain*. London, Routledge and Kegan Paul.

Cabinet Office (1991a). *The Citizens' Charter: Raising the Standard*. Cm 599. London, HMSO.

Cabinet Office (1991b). *Competing for Quality*. Cm 1730, London, HMSO.

Central Policy Review Staff (1980). *Education, Training and Industrial Performance*. London, HMSO.

Central Statistical Office (1991a). *Regional Trends*, Vol. 26. London, HMSO.

Central Statistical Office (1991b). *Social Trends*, Vol. 21. London, HMSO.

Central Statistical Office (1992). *Social Trends*, Vol. 22. London, HMSO.

Central Statistical Office (1993). *Social Trends*, Vol. 23. London, HMSO.

Chamberlayne, P. (1992). 'New directions in welfare? France, West Germany, Italy and Britain in the 1980s', *Critical Social Policy*, No. 33.

Chambers, G.R. (1988). *The Health Systems of European Community Countries*. Luxembourg, Directorate General for Research, European Parliament.

Child Poverty Action Group (1980). *No Way to Treat the Sick*. London, CPAG.

Child Poverty Action Group (1990). *Holes in the Safety-Net: Falling Standards for People in Poverty*. London, CPAG.

Christopher, T. (1992). 'Countering disadvantage now', *Policy Studies*, 13(1): 'Training and enterprise councils: The story so far'. London, Policy Studies Institute.

Clarke, K. (1992). 'Sixth form schooling', *Press Release*, February.

Coates, D. and Hilliard, J. (eds) (1986). *The Economic Revival of Modern Britain: The Debate Between Left and Right*. London, Elgar.

Cochrane, A.L. (1972). *Effectiveness and Efficiency*. London, Nuffield Provincial Hospitals Trust.

Coffield, F. (1990). 'From the decade of the enterprise culture to the decade of the TECs', *British Journal of Education and Work*, 4(1), 59–78.

Cohen, D. and Farrar, E. (1977). 'Power to the parents', *Public Interest*, No. 44.

Comptroller and Auditor-General (1985). *Vocational Education and Training for Young People*. Cmnd 9474. London, HMSO.

Conservative Party (1992). *The Best Future for Britain*, 1992 Election Manifesto. London, Conservative Central Office.

Cooley, M. (1987). *Architect or Bee? The Human Price of Technology*. London, Chatto.

Corfield, A. and Rippon, G. (eds) (1965). *The Conservative Opportunity*. London, Batsford.

Cousins, C. (1987). *Controlling Social Welfare*. Brighton, Wheatsheaf.

Davies, A. and Willman, J. (1991). *What Next?: Agencies, Departments and the Civil Service*. London, Institute for Public Policy Research.

Dean, H. and Taylor-Gooby, P. (1990a). 'Statutory sick pay and the control of sickness absence', *Journal of Social Policy*, 19(1), 47–68.

Dean, H. and Taylor-Gooby, P. (1990b). 'Inequality and occupational sick pay', *Policy and Politics*, 18(2), 145–50.

Dean, H. and Taylor-Gooby, P. (1992). *Dependency Culture: The Explosion of a Myth.* Hemel Hempstead, Harvester Wheatsheaf.

Dean, M. (1991). 'What happens after the election?', *Lancet*, 337, 965–6.

Dekker, W. (1987). *Bereid tot Verandering: Rapport van der Commissie Structuur en Financiering.* The Hague, Ministry of Health, Welfare and Cultural Affairs.

de Kok, A. (1987). 'Savings through innovative care provision in the Dutch welfare state', in A. Evers, H. Nowotny and H. Wintersberger (eds) *The Changing Face of Welfare.* Aldershot, Gower.

Department for Education (1992). *Choice and Diversity: A New Framework for Schools.* Cm 2021. London, HMSO.

Department of Education and Science (1977). *Education in Schools.* Cmnd 6069. London, HMSO.

Department of Education and Science (1991a). *The Government's Expenditure Plans, 1991–2 to 1993–4.* Cm 1511. London, HMSO.

Department of Education and Science (1991b). *Employment and Training for the Twenty-first Century,* Cm 1536. London, HMSO.

Department of Education and Science (1992a). *The Government's Expenditure Plans, 1992–93 to 1994–95.* Cm 1911. London, HMSO.

Department of Education and Science (1992b). *Curriculum Organisation and Classroom Practice in Primary Schools.* London, HMSO.

Department of the Environment (1977). *Housing Policy: Technical Volume,* Part 1. London, HMSO.

Department of Health (1989a). *Caring for People: Community Care in the Next Decade and Beyond,* Cm 849. London, HMSO.

Department of Health (1989b). *Income Generation: A Guide to Local Initiative.* HM(89)9. London, Department of Health.

Department of Health (1991). *The Health of the Nation – A Consultative Document for Health in England,* Cm 1523. London, HMSO.

Department of Health and Social Security (1976). *Sharing Resources for Health in England.* London, HMSO.

Department of Health and Social Security (1979). *Patients First.* London, HMSO.

Department of Health and Social Security (1980). *Income During Initial Sickness: A New Strategy.* Cmnd 7864. London, HMSO.

Department of Health and Social Security. (1981). *Growing Older.* London, HMSO.

Department of Health and Social Security (1982a). *Social Security Operational Strategy: A Framework for the Future.* London, HMSO.

Department of Health and Social Security (1982b). *Health and Personal Social Services Statistics for England, 1982.* London, HMSO.

Department of Health and Social Security (1983a). *Competitive Tendering in the Provision of Domestic, Catering and Laundry Services.* HC (83) 18. London, DHSS.

Department of Health and Social Security (1983b). *Report of the National Health Service Management Enquiry.* London, HMSO.

Department of Health and Social Security (1985a). *The Reform of Social Security* (Green Paper). Cmnd 9517. London, HMSO.

Department of Health and Social Security (1985b). *The Reform of Social Security: Programme for Action* (White Paper). Cmnd 9691. London, HMSO.

Department of Health and Social Security (1985c). *Social Security Statistics 1983*. London, HMSO.

Department of Health and Social Security (1989). *Working for Patients*. Cm 555. London, HMSO.

Department of Social Security (1988a). *The Business of Service* (the Moodie Report). London, HMSO.

Department of Social Security (1988b). *Occupational Sick Pay Schemes* (Research Report). London, HMSO.

Department of Social Security (1991). *Benefits Agency Business Plan 1991/1992*. London, HMSO.

Department of Social Security (1992a). *Social Security: The Government's Expenditure Plans 1992–93 to 1994–95*. Cm 1914. London, HMSO.

Department of Social Security (1992b). *Households Below Average Income: A Statistical Analysis, 1979–1988/9*. London, HMSO.

Diderichsen, F. and Lindberg, G. (1989). 'The Swedish Public Health Report, 1987', *International Journal of Health Services*, 19(2), 221–55.

Dieck, M. (1989). 'Long-term care for the elderly in Germany', in T. Schwab (ed.) *Caring for an Ageing World: International Models for Long-term Care*. New York, McGraw-Hill.

Dieck, M. (1992). *Redistribution of Political and Economic Influence of Relevant Actors within the System of Social Security and Service Provision in Germany*. Hasseludden Conference Papers, European Centre for Social Welfare Policy and Research, Vienna.

Disney, R. (1987). 'Statutory sick pay: An appraisal', *Fiscal Studies*, 8(2), 58–76.

Drewry, G. and Butcher, T. (1991). *The Civil Service Today*, 2nd edn. Oxford, Blackwell.

Dunleavy, P. (1991). *Democracy, Bureaucracy and Public Choice*. London, Harvester Wheatsheaf.

Dunleavy, P. and O'Leary, B. (1987). *Theories of the State: The Politics of Liberal Democracy*. London, Macmillan.

Dwelly, T. (1991). 'Tender moments', *Roof*, May–June, 19–21.

Dyerson, R. and Roper, M. (1991). 'Implementing the operational strategy at the DSS: From technical push to user pull', in M. Adler and R. Williams (eds) *The Social Implications of the Operational Strategy*. New Waverly Papers, Social Policy Series No. 4, University of Edinburgh.

Efficiency Unit (1988). *Improving Management in Government: The Next Steps*. Report to the Prime Minister by K. Jenkins, K. Cairnes and A. Jackson. London, HMSO.

Efficiency Unit (1991). *Making the Most of the Next Steps: The Management of Ministers, Departments and Their Executive Agencies*. London, HMSO.

Enthoven, A.C. (1985). *Reflections on the Management of the National Health Service*. London, Nuffield Provincial Hospitals Trust.

Ermisch, J. (1990). *Fewer Babies, Longer Lives*. York, Joseph Rowntree Foundation.

Esping-Andersen, G. (1990). *The Three Worlds of Welfare Capitalism*. Oxford, Polity Press.

Evandrou, M., Falkingham, J. and Glennerster, H. (1990). 'The personal social services: "Everyone's poor relation but nobody's baby",' in D. Hills (ed.) *The State of Welfare: The Welfare State in Britain since 1974*. Oxford, Clarendon Press.

Evans, B. (1993). *The Politics of the Training Market*. London, Routledge, forthcoming.

Evers, A. and Olk, T. (1991). 'The mix of care provisions for the frail elderly in the Federal Republic of Germany', in A. Evers and I. Svetlik (eds) *New Welfare Mixes for the Elderly*, Vol. 3. Vienna, European Centre for Social Welfare Policy and Research.

Evers, A. and Svetlik, I. (1992). *Balancing Pluralism: New Welfare Mixes in Care for the Elderly*. Frankfurt/Boulder, Campus Verlag/Westview Press.

Evers, A., Nowotny, H. and Wintersberger, H. (eds) (1987). *The Changing Face of Welfare*. Aldershot, Gower.

Falkingham, J. (1989). 'Dependency and ageing in Britain', *Journal of Social Policy*, 18(2), 211–334.

Finn, D. (1987). *Training Without Jobs: New Deals and Broken Promises*. London, Macmillan.

Flora, P. (1986). *Growth to Limits: The Western European Welfare States since World War II*. Berlin, de Gruyter.

Flynn, A.C., Gray, A.G. and Jenkins, W.I. (1990). 'Taking the Next Steps: The changing management of government', *Parliamentary Affairs*, 43(2), 159–78.

Flynn, N. and Common, R. (1990a). *Contracts for Community Care*. Caring for People Implementation Document CCI 4. London, Department of Health.

Flynn, N. and Common, R. (1990b). *Caring for People*. London, HMSO.

Forrest, R. (1991). 'The privatisation of collective consumption', in C. Pickvance and M. Gottdiener (eds) *Urban Life in Transition*. New York, Sage.

Forrest, R. and Murie, A. (1990a). 'A dissatisfied state? Consumer preferences and council housing in Britain', *Urban Studies*, 27, 617–35.

Forrest, R. and Murie, A. (1990b). *Residualisation and Council Housing: A Statistical Update*. Working Paper No. 91, School for Advanced Urban Studies, University of Bristol.

Forrest, R. and Murie, A. (1991). *Selling the Welfare State*. London, Routledge.

Fowler, N. (1984). 'The enabling role of SSDs'. Speech to the Joint Social Services Annual Conference, Buxton, 27 September.

Friedman, M. (1960). *Capitalism and Freedom*. Chicago, Ill., Chicago University Press.

Fulton, Lord (1968). *Report of the Committee on the Civil Service*. Cmnd 3638. London, HMSO.

Gamble, A. (1979). 'The free economy and the strong state', in J. Saville, and R. Miliband, (eds) *Socialist Register, 1979*. London, Merlin Press.

Gamble, A. (1988). *The Free Economy and the Strong State*. Basingstoke, Macmillan.

Gardiner, K., Hills, J. and Kleinmann, M. (1991). *Putting a Price on Council Housing: Valuing Voluntary Transfers*. Discussion Paper WSP62, Suntory-Toyota International Centre for Economics and Related Disciplines, London School of Economics.

Garonna, P. and Ryan, P. (1991). 'The problems facing youth', in P. Ryan, P. Garonna and R. Edwards (eds) *The Problem of Youth, the Regulation of Youth Employment and Training in Advanced Economies*. London, Macmillan.

Ginsburg, N. (1992). *Divisions of Welfare: A Critical Introduction to Comparative Social Policy*. London, Sage.

Glasman, D. (1991). 'First the dream – now comes the reality', *Health Service Journal*, 14 February, 14.

Glennerster, H. (1987). 'Goodbye Mr Chips', *New Society*, 9 December.

Glennerster, H. and Low, W. (1990). 'Education: Does it all add up?', in J. Hills (ed.) *The State of Welfare*. Oxford, Clarendon Press.

Goodin, R. (1988). *Reasons for Welfare*. Princeton, N.J., Princeton University Press.

Gray, A.G. and Jenkins, W.I. (1982). 'Policy analysis in British government: The experience of PAR', *Public Administration*, 60(4), 429–50.

Gray, A.G. and Jenkins, W.I. (1985). *Administrative Politics in British Government*. Brighton, Harvester Wheatsheaf.

Gray, A.G. and Jenkins, W.I. (1991), 'Administering local government', in W. Jones *et al.* (eds) *Politics UK*. London, Philip Alan.

Gray, A.G. and Jenkins, W.I. with Flynn, A.C. and Rutherford, B.A. (1991). 'The management of change in Whitehall: The experience of the FMI', *Public Administration*, 69(1), 41–59.

Gray, J. (1992). *The Moral Foundations of Market Institutions*. Choice in Welfare Series No. 10, Institute of Economic Affairs, London.

Griffiths, Sir R. (1983). *NHS Management Inquiry*. London, DHSS.

Griffiths, Sir R. (1988). *Community Care: Agenda for Action*. London, HMSO.

Guardian (1992a). 'School spending', 17 February.

Guardian (1992b). 'Opting out and losing out', 4 August.

Guardian (1992c). 'A poor choice for some', 4 August.

Guillemard, A.-M. and Frossard, M. (1992). *Caring for the Dependent Elderly: French Old Age Policies and the Welfare Mix*. Hasseludden Conference Papers, European Centre for Social Welfare Policy and Research, Vienna.

Ham, C. (1982). *Health Policy in Britain*. London, Macmillan.

Hambleton, R. (1988). 'Consumerism, decentralisation and local democracy', *Public Administration*, 65(2), 161–77.

Handy, C. (1984). *The Future of Work*. Oxford, Blackwell.

Hartnett, A. and Naish, M. (1986). *Education and Society Today*. Lewes, Falmer Press.

Haviland, J. (1988). *Take Care Mr Baker!* London, Fourth Estate.

Hayek, F. (1984). *1980s Unemployment and the Unions*. Hobart Paper No. 87, 2nd edn. London, Institute of Economic Affairs.

Hayes, C. (1983). *Training for Skill Ownership in the YTS*. Brighton, Institute for Manpower Studies.

Hearn, B. (1989). 'Research notes', *Community Care*, 12 October, 18.

Heclo, H. and Wildavsky, A. (1981). *The Private Government of Public Money*, 2nd edn. London, Macmillan.

Heidenheimer, A., Heclo, H. and Adams, C. (1990). *Comparative Public Policy*, 3rd edn. New York, St Martin's Press.

Hennessy, P. (1989). *Whitehall*. London, Secker and Warburg.

Her Majesty's Inspectors (1991). *Standards in Education, 1989–90*. London, HMSO.

Her Majesty's Treasury (1979). *The Government's Expenditure Plans, 1979–80 to 1981–2*. Cmnd 8494. London, HMSO.

Her Majesty's Treasury (1991). *Public Expenditure Analyses to 1993/4: Supplementary Tables*. London, HMSO.

Her Majesty's Treasury (1992). *Public Expenditure Analyses to 1994/5: Supplementary Tables*. London, HMSO.

Hills, J. (ed.) (1990). *The State of Welfare*. Oxford, Clarendon Press.

Hills, J. (1991). *From Right to Buy to Rent to Mortgage: Privatisation of Council Housing since 1979*. Discussion Paper WSP/61, Welfare State Programme, London School of Economics.

Hirschman, A. (1970). *Exit, Voice and Loyalty*. Cambridge, Mass., Harvard University Press.

Hoffenberg, R., Todd, I.P. and Pinker, G. (1987). 'Crisis in the National Health Service', *British Medical Journal*, 295, 1505.

Hoggett, P. (1990). *Modernisation, Political Strategy and the Welfare State: An Organizational Perspective*. Studies in Decentralisation and Quasi-Markets No. 2, School for Advanced Urban Studies, University of Bristol.

Hood, C. (1991). 'A public management for all seasons?', *Public Administration*, 69(1), 3–19.

House of Commons, Treasury and Civil Service Select Committee (1982) *Efficiency and Effectiveness in the Civil Service: Government Observations on the Third Report*, Session 1981–82. London, HMSO.

Housing (1990). 'Private lessons', June–July, 47–50.

Howe, G. (1965). 'The waiting list society', in *The Conservative Opportunity*. London, Batsford.

Hunt, M. (1989). *Cost of Caring: A West Yorkshire Study about Pay and Conditions of Care Workers in Private Old People's Homes*. Leeds, West Yorkshire Low Pay Unit.

Institute for Public Policy Research (1992). *Next Left: A New Agenda for the 1990s*. London, IPPR.

International Association for the Evaluation of Educational Achievement (1988). *Learning Mathematics and Science*. Slough, NFER.

Islington, London Borough of (1991). *Social Security – Dislocation of Service*. Islington Council Anti-Poverty Strategy Briefing No. 4, Islington Council, London.

Johnson, N. (1990). *Reconstructing the Welfare State: A Decade of Change 1980–1990*. Hemel Hempstead, Harvester Wheatsheaf.

Jones, J. (1991). 'GPs agree to truce in dispute over NHS', *The Independent*, 20 June.

Jowell, R., Brook, L. and Taylor, B. (eds) (1991). *British Social Attitudes*, Eighth Report. Aldershot, Dartmouth.

Kanter, R. (1985). *The Change Masters: Corporate Entrepreneurs at Work*. London, Unwin.

Kavanagh, D. (1987). *Thatcherism and British Politics: The End of Consensus?* Oxford, Oxford University Press.

Kelly, A. (1989). 'An end to incrementalism? The impact of expenditure restraint on social services budgets 1979–1986', *Journal of Social Policy*, 18(2), 187–210.

Kelly, A. (1991). 'The new managerialism in the social services', in P. Carter (ed.) *Social Work and Social Welfare Yearbook*, Vol. 3. Harlow, Longman.

Kent County Council (1978). *Education Vouchers in Kent: A Feasibility Study*. Canterbury, KCC.

Key, T. (1988). 'Contracting out ancillary services', in R. Maxwell (ed.) *Reshaping the National Health Service*. Hermitage, Berks, Policy Journals.

Klein, R. (1989). *The Politics of the NHS*. London, Longman.

Kleinmann, M. (1992). 'Large-scale transfers of council housing to new landlords: Is British social housing becoming more "European" ', *Housing Studies*, forthcoming.

Knight, F. (1933) *Risk, Uncertainty and Profit*. London, London School of Economics.

Knipscheer, C.P.M. (1992). *Historical Structuration and Recent Shifts in the Dutch Welfare State*. Hasseludden Papers, European Centre for Social Welfare Policy and Research, Vienna.

Kraan, R.J., Baldock, J., Davies, B., Evers, A., Johansson, L., Knapen, M., Thorslund, M. and Tunissen, C. (1991). *Care for the Elderly: Significant Innovations in Three European Countries*. Frankfurt/Boulder, Campus Verlag/Westview Press.

Labour Party (1985). *Conference Report*. London, Labour Party.

Labour Party (1992). *Its Time to Get Britain Working Again*. 1992 Election Manifesto. London, Labour Party.

Lagergren, M. (1982). *Time to Care*. Oxford, Pergamon Press.

Lakhani, B. (1991). 'The Benefits Agency – A better deal for claimants?', *Welfare Rights Bulletin*, No. 104.

Lash, S. and Urry, J. (1987). *The End of Organised Capitalism*. Oxford, Polity Press.

Lawson, R. (1991a). 'The impact of the new community care policy: The development of supply'. Paper given at the British Society of Gerontology Annual Conference, September.

Lawson, R. (1991b) 'From public monopoly to maximum competition: One authority's approach', *Bulletin*, No. 8, PSSRU, University of Kent at Canterbury.

Layfield, F. (1976). *Report of the Committee on Local Government Finance*. Cmnd 6453. London, HMSO.

Leat, D. (1990). *For Love and Money: The Role of Payment in Encouraging the Provision of Care*. York, Joseph Rowntree Foundation.

Leathley, A. (1989). 'Whatever happened to income generation?', *Health Service Journal*, 99, 1492.

Leavis, F. (1972). 'Hard times: The world of Bentham', in F. Leavis and Q. Leavis, *Dickens the Novelist*. Harmondsworth, Pelican.

Le Grand, J. (1982). *The Strategy of Equality*. London, George, Allen and Unwin.

Le Grand, J. (1990). *Quasi-Markets and Social Policy*. Studies in Decentralisation and Quasi-Markets No. 1, School for Advanced Urban Studies, University of Bristol.

Le Grand, J. (1991). *Equity and Choice*. London, Harper Collins.

Letwin, O. (1988). *Privatising the World – A Study of International Privatisation in Theory and Practice*. London, Macmillan.

Leutner, B. and Jensen, D. (1988). 'German Federal Republic', in H. Kroes, F. Ymkers and A. Mulder (eds) *Between Owner-Occupied and Rented Sector: Housing in Ten European Countries*. De Bilt, Netherlands, NCIV.

Levitt, R. (1976). *The Reorganised National Health Service*. London, Croom Helm.

Levy, D. (1988). 'The welfare revolution: Moore's American cure for Britain's "dependency" habit', *Listener*, 18 February.

Local Government Training Board (1988). *Managing Tomorrow*. Luton, LGTB.

Liberal Democratic Party (1992). *Changing Britain for Good*. 1992 Election Manifesto. London, Liberal Democratic Party.

Lister, R. (1990). 'Women, economic dependency and citizenship', *Journal of Social Policy*, 19(4), 445–68.

Little S. (1990). 'Experts fear a bleak future for income generation'. *Health Service Journal*, 100, 829.

Low, G. (1988). 'The MSC: A failure in democracy', in M. Morris and C. Griggs (eds) *Education – The Wasted Years? 1973–1986*. Lewes, Falmer Press.

Low Pay Unit (1991). *The New Review of the Low Pay Unit*, No. 11. London, LPU.

Low Pay Unit (1992). *The New Review of the Low Pay Unit*, No. 14. London, LPU.

Lynes, T. (1975). 'Unemployment assistance tribunals in the 1930s', in M. Adler and A. Bradley (eds) *Justice, Discretion and Poverty*. Abingdon, Professional Books.

Lynes, T. (1991). 'Next Steps!', *Welfare Rights Bulletin*, No. 105.

Mackintosh, S., Leather, P. and Means, R. (1990). *Housing in Later Life: The Housing Finance Implications of an Ageing Society*. School of Advanced Urban Studies, University of Bristol.

Major, J. (1992). 'Privatising choice', speech on 15th Annual Dinner of the Adam Smith Institute, 15 June.

Malpass, P. (1991). *Reshaping Housing Policy*. London, Routledge.

Malpass, P. and Murie, A. (1990). *Housing Policy and Practice*. 3rd edn. London, Macmillan.

Manpower Services Commission (1975). *Vocational Preparation for Young People*. London, MSC.

Manpower Services Commission (1976). *Towards a Comprehensive Manpower Policy*. Sheffield, MSC.

Manpower Services Commission (1977). *Young People and Work*. Sheffield, MSC.

Marinker, M. (1984). 'Developments in primary health care', in G. Teeling Smith (ed.) *A New NHS Act for 1996?* London, Office of Health Economics.

Market Opinion Research International (1992). *Opinions on Vouchers*. London, MORI.

Mashaw, J. (1983). *Bureaucratic Justice*. New Haven, Conn., Yale University Press.

Maud, J. (1967). *Report of Committee on Management in Local Government*. London, HMSO.

Maud, Lord Redcliffe (1969). *Report of the Royal Commission on Local Government in England*. Cmnd 4040. London, HMSO.

Maud, Lord Redcliffe (1982). *Efficiency and Effectiveness in the Civil Service*, Cmnd 8616. London, HMSO.

McDowell, L. (1989). 'Divisions in education', in M. Ball, F. Gray and L. McDowell, *The Transformation of Britain*. London, Fontana.

McIlroy, B. (1989). 'The Great Education Reform Act', in M. Brenton and C. Ungerson (eds) *Yearbook of Social Policy*. Harlow, Longman.

McKie, D. (1987). 'Mounting resistance to NHS cuts: Disaster inevitable', *The Lancet*, 2, 752.

Means, R. (1986). 'The development of social services for elderly people: Historical perspectives', in C. Phillipson and A. Walker (eds) *Ageing and Society: A Critical Assessment*. London, Gower.

Merrett, S. (1979). *State Housing in Britain*. London, RKP.

Millar, B. (1989). 'What about a little self-control', *Health Service Journal*, 99, 70.

Millar, J. (1992). 'Lone mothers and poverty', in C. Glendinning and J. Millar (eds) *Women and Poverty in Britain: The 1990s*. London, Harvester Wheatsheaf.

Millward, R. (1982). 'The comparative performance of public and private ownership', in Lord Roll of Ipsden, *The Mixed Economy*. London, Macmillan.

Ministry of Health and Social Affairs (1988). *The Government's Care for the Elderly Bill*. Ministry of Health and Social Affairs, Stockholm, Sweden.

Ministry of Welfare, Health and Cultural Affairs (1988). *Changing Health Care in the Netherlands* (the Dekker Report). Ministry of Welfare, Health and Cultural Affairs, The Hague, Netherlands.

Mishra, R. (1990). *The Welfare State in Capitalist Society*. Brighton, Wheatsheaf.

Moore, W. (1988). 'Beating private hospitals at their own game', *Health Service Journal*, 98, 904.

Moore, W. (1990). 'East Anglian RHA blazes the internal market trail', *Health Service Journal*, 100, 540.

Moroney, R. (1976). *The Family and the State: Considerations for Social Policy*. Harlow, Longman.

Mueller, D. (1979). *Public Choice*. Cambridge, Cambridge University Press.

Murie, A., Forrest, R., Partington, M. and Leather, P. (1989). *The Implications of the Housing Act 1988 for Low Income Consumers*. Working Paper No. 77, School for Advanced Urban Studies, University of Bristol.

Murray, C. (1984). *Losing Ground: American Social Policy 1950–1980*. New York, Basic Books.

Murray, F. (1983). 'The decentralisation of production: The decline of the mass collective worker', *Capital and Class*, 19, 25–46.

National Audit Office (1988). *Department of Health and Social Security: Quality of Service to the Public at Local Offices*. HCP 451, 1988–89. London, HMSO.

National Audit Office (1990). *The Elderly: Information Requirements for Supporting the Elderly and Implications of Personal Pensions for the National Insurance Fund – Report by the Comptroller and Auditor General*. London, HMSO.

National Audit Office (1991). *The Elderly: Information Requirements for Supporting the Elderly and Implications of Personal Pensions for the National Insurance Fund*. London, HMSO.

National Association for the Care and Resettlement of Offenders (1986). *Enforcement of the Law Relating to Social Security*. London, NACRO.

National Federation of Small Employers and Small Businesses (1980). *Income During Initial Sickness: A Prescription for Disaster*. London, NFSESB.

National Foundation for Educational Research (1992). *Learning Mathematics and Science: The Second International Assessment*. Windsor, NFER-Nelson.

Niskanen, W. (1973). *Bureaucracy: Servant or Master?* London, Institute of Economic Affairs.

Northcott, J. (1991). *Britain in 2010*. London, Policy Studies Institute.

Offe, C. (1984). *The Contradictions of the Welfare State*. London, Hutchinson.

Offe, C. (1985). *Disorganised Capitalism: Contemporary Transformations of Work and Politics*. Oxford, Polity Press.

Office of Population Censuses and Surveys (1990). *General Household Survey for 1989: Preliminary Results*. OPCS Monitor SS 90/3. London, HMSO.

Office of Population Censuses and Surveys (1992). *General Household Survey for 1990*. London, HMSO.

Organization for Economic Cooperation and Development (1975). *Education and Working Life*. Paris, OECD.

O'Sullivan, J. (1991a). 'District short of cash for patient referrals', *The Independent*, 20 June.

O'Sullivan, J. (1991b). 'Health commission must face century-old problems', *The Independent*, 10 October.

Papadakis, E. and Taylor-Gooby, P. (1987). *The Private Provision of Public Welfare*. Brighton, Wheatsheaf.

Parker, G. (1990). *With Due Care and Attention: A Review of Research on Informal Care*, 2nd edn. London, Family Policy Studies Centre.

Parliamentary Debates (1988a). *House of Commons Official Report 1987–8*, Vol. 24, Col. 1094. London, HMSO.

Parliamentary Debates (1988b). *House of Commons Official Report 1987–8*, Vol. 125, Cols 833–4. London, HMSO.

Patel, C. (1991). 'How can the industry mature in the 1990s?', paper presented at the *Laing and Buisson Conference on Community Care*, London, March.

Perrin, J. (1991). *Resource Management in the NHS*. London, Chapman and Hall.

Peters, T. and Waterman, R. (1982). *In Search of Excellence: Lessons from America's Best-run Companies*. New York, Harper and Row.

Pfaller, A., Gough, I. and Therborn, G. (eds) (1991). *Can the Welfare State Compete: A Comparative Study of Five Advanced Capitalist Countries?* London, Macmillan.

Pfeffer, N. and Coote, A. (1991). *Is Quality Good for You? A Critical Review of Quality Assurance in Welfare Services*. Social Policy Paper No. 5, Institute for Public Policy Research, London.

Pierson, C. (1991). *Beyond the Welfare State?* Oxford, Polity Press.

Pijl, M. (1991). 'Care for the elderly in the Netherlands', in A. Evers and I. Svetlik (eds) *New Welfare Mixes for the Elderly*, Vol. 2. Vienna, European Centre for Social Welfare Policy and Research.

Pike, A. (1989) 'Hospitals weigh prognosis for opting out', *Financial Times*, 24 January.

Pirie, M. (1985). *Privatisation*. London, Adam Smith Institute.

Plant, R. (1991). *Modern Political Thought*. Oxford, Blackwell.

Pollitt, C. (1990). *Managerialism and the Public Services*. Oxford, Blackwell.

Raffe, D. (1991). 'Scotland v. England: The place of "home internationals" in comparative research', in P. Ryan (ed.) *International Comparisons of Vocational Education and Training for Intermediate Skills*. Lewes, Falmer Press.

Randall, C. (1992). *Training and Enterprise Councils – An Exercise in Illusion, Exclusion and Class Elision*, Centre for a Working World Discussion Paper No. 6, The Centre for a Working World, Sheffield.

Raynsford, N. (1991). 'Management at arms length', *Housing*, June–July, 13–17.

Reeder, D. (1979). 'A recurring debate: Education and industry', in G. Bernbaum (ed.) *Schooling in Decline*. London, Macmillan.

Rees, A.M. (ed.) (1985). *T.H. Marshall's Social Policy*, 5th edn. London, Hutchinson.

Richards, J. (1992). 'Getting it right', *Housing*, February, 23–5.

Roberts, H. (1990). 'Preface', in P. Ainley and M. Corney, *Training for the Future: The Rise and Fall of the Manpower Services Commission*. London, Cassell.

Roberts, T. (1992). 'The money monster', *Roof*, January–February, 27–9.

Robinson, J. (1988). 'Market structure, employment and skill mix in the hospital industry', *Southern Economic Journal*, 55, 315–25.

Robinson, R. and Judge, K. (1987). *Public Expenditure and the NHS: Trends and Prospects*. London, King's Fund Institute.

Rose, R. (1985). *The State's Contribution to the Welfare Mix*. Studies in Public Policy No. 140, University of Strathclyde, Glasgow.

Rowley, C. (1982). 'Industrial policy in the mixed economy', in Lord Roll of Ipsden, *The Mixed Economy*. London, Macmillan.

Royal Commission on the National Health Service (1979). *Report*. Cmnd 7615. London, HMSO.

Saltman, R.B. (1991). 'Emerging trends in the Swedish health system', *International Journal of Health Services*, 21(4), 615–23.

Saltman, R.B. and von Otter, C. (1992). *Planned Markets and Public Competition: Strategic Reform in Northern European Health Systems*. Buckingham, Open University Press.

Saunders, P. (1990). *A Nation of Home Owners*. London, Unwin Hyman.

Savage, S. and Robins, L. (eds) (1990). *Public Policy under Thatcher*. London, Macmillan.

Schick, A. (1990). 'Budgeting for results: Adaptation to fiscal stress in industrial democracies', *Public Administration Review*, 50(1), 26–34.

Secretaries of State for Health, Wales, Northern Ireland and Scotland (1989). *Working for Patients*. Cm 555. London, HMSO.

Seebohm, F. (1968). *Report of the Committee on Local Authority and Allied Social Services*. Cmnd 3703. London, HMSO.

Seldon, A. (1986). *The Riddle of the Voucher*. London, Institute of Economic Affairs.

Sheaff, R. (1991). *Marketing for Health Service*. Milton Keynes, Open University Press.

Sheldon, T. (1990). 'When it makes sense to mince your words', *Health Service Journal*, 100, 1211.

Simmel, G. (1978). *The Philosophy of Money* (ed. D. Frisby; trans T. Bottomore and D. Frisby). London, Routledge.

Smith, D. and Tomlinson, S. (1989). *The School Effect*. London, Policy Studies Institute.

Smith, J. (1991a). 'The public service ethos', *Public Administration*, 69(4), 515–23.

Smith, J.R. (1991b). 'The BMA in agony', *British Medical Journal*, 303, 74.

Smith, T. (1988). 'New year message', *British Medical Journal*, 296, 1–2.

Social Security Consortium (1987). *Of Little Benefit: An Update*. London, Association of Metropolitan Authorities.

Social Security Select Committee (1991a). *Low Income Statistics: Households Below Average Income Tables 1988*. HCP 401, 1990–91. London, HMSO.

Social Security Select Committee (1991b). *The Organisation and Administration of the Department of Social Security – Minutes of Evidence* (5 volumes), HCP 550 (i) and (ii), 1990–91 and HCP19 (i), (ii) and (iii), 1991–92. London, HMSO.

Social Security Select Committee (1992). *The Operation of Pension Funds*. HCP 61-II, 1991–92. London, HMSO.

Social Services Committee (1986). *Fourth Report 1985–6. Public Expenditure on the Social Services*. HC 387. London, HMSO.

Social Services Committee (1988). *First Report 1987–8. Resourcing the National Health Service: Short Term Issues*. HC 264-1. London, HMSO.

Social Services Inspectorate (1987). *From Home Help to Home Care: An Analysis of Policy, Resourcing and Service Management*. London, SSI.

Social Services Inspectorate (1988). *Managing Policy Change in Home Help Services*. London, SSI.

Social Services Inspectorate and National Health Service Management Executive, (1992). 'Implementing caring for people', letter to local and health authorities and trusts, 11 March.

Stewart, J. (1986). *The New Management of Local Government*. London, Allen and Unwin.

Stewart, J. and Clarke, M. (1987). 'The public service orientation: Issues and dilemmas', *Public Administration*, 65(2), 161–77.

Stoker, G. (1991). *The Politics of Local Government*, 2nd edn. London, Macmillan.

Svenson, M. and MacPherson, S. (1988). 'Real losses and unreal figures', in S. Becker and S. MacPherson (eds) *Public Issues, Private Pain*. London, Social Services Insight Books.

Taylor-Gooby, P. (1991a). *Social Change, Social Welfare and Social Science*. London, Wheatsheaf.

Taylor-Gooby, P. (1991b). 'Attachment to the Welfare State', in R. Jowell, L. Brook and B. Taylor (eds) *British Social Attitudes: The Eighth Report*. Aldershot, Gower.

Thorslund, M. (1991). 'The increasing number of very old people will change the Swedish model of the welfare state', *Social Science and Medicine*, 32(4), 455–64.

Thorslund, M. and Parker, M.G. (1992). *The Changing Swedish Welfare State: Abandoned Ideals or a Response to Escalating Needs?* Hasseludden Papers, European Centre for Social Welfare Policy and Research, Vienna.

Timmins, N. (1987). 'Hospitals want payment for treating outsiders', *The Independent*, 30 April.

Timmins, N. (1988a). 'DHSS study urged end to tax-funded health care', *The Independent*, 8 February.

Timmins, N. (1988b). *Cash, Crisis and Cure*. London, Newspaper Publishing plc.

Towerwatch Report (1991). *Shame About the Service*. London, Archway Claimants' Action Group with Islington Council.

Townsend, P. (1991). *The Poor are Poorer*. Bristol, Statistical Monitoring Unit, University of Bristol.

Trades Union Resource Centre (1987). *Report of the National Labour Movement Inquiry into Youth Unemployment and Training*. Birmingham, TURC.

Treasury and Civil Service Committee (1982). *Efficiency and Effectiveness in the Civil Service*, Third Report, HC.236, Session 1981–2. London, HMSO.

Treasury and Civil Service Committee (1990). *Progress in the Next Steps Initiative*, Eighth Report, HC.481, Session 1989–90. London, HMSO.

Treasury and Civil Service Committee (1991). *The Next Steps Initiative*, Seventh Report, HC.496, Session 1990–91. London, HMSO.

Trevor, W. (1991). *Reading Turgenev*. New York, Viking.

Turner, B. (1986). *Citizenship and Capitalism*. London, Allen and Unwin.

Unemployment Unit (1991). *Working Brief*, August–September.

Unemployment Unit (1992) *Working Brief*, April, p. 1.

Ungerson, C. and Baldock, J. (1991). 'What d'ya want if you don' want money?: A feminist critique of paid volunteering', in M. McLean and D. Groves (eds) *Women's Issues in Social Policy*. London, Routledge.

Usher, D. (1987). *Housing Privatisation: The Sale of Council Estates*. Working Paper No. 67, School for Advanced Urban Studies, University of Bristol.

von Hayek, F. (1949). *Individualism and Economic Order*. London, Routledge and Kegan Paul.

von Hayek, F. (1976). *Law, Legislation and Liberty*, Vol. 2. London, Routledge.

von Mises, L. (1962). *The Free and Prosperous Commonwealth*. Princeton, N.J., van Nostrand.

Waerness, K. (1992). *Bettering the Public Care Services: The Only Realistic Alternative for the Welfare of Ordinary People*. Hasseludden Papers, European Centre for Social Welfare Policy and Research, Vienna.

Waldegrave, W. (1992). 'The future of the Civil Service', speech reported in *Guardian*, 1 June.

Walker, A. (1984). 'The political economy of privatisation', in J. Le Grand and R. Robinson (eds) *Privatisation and the Welfare State*. London, Unwin Hyman.

Walker, P. (1977). *The Ascent of Britain*. London, Sidgwick and Jackson.

Wallace, C. and Chandler, J. (1989). 'Some alternatives in youth training: Franchise and corporatist models'. Unpublished paper, Polytechnic South West.

Walsh, K. (1991). 'Citizens and consumers: Marketing and public sector management', *Public Money and Management*, 11(2), 9–16.

Warburton, M. (1991). *The Role of Local Authorities in Housing*. School for Advanced Urban Studies, University of Bristol (Mimeo).

Ward, S. (1985). 'Introduction: The political background', in S. Ward (ed.) *DHSS in Crisis*. London, CPAG.

Webb, A. and Wistow, G. (1983). 'Public expenditure and policy implementation: The case of community care'. *Public Administration*, 61, 21–44.

Webb, A. and Wistow, G. (1986). *Planning, Need and Scarcity: Essays on the Personal Social Services*. London, Allen and Unwin.

Welsh Housing Quarterly (1992). 'Competitive tendering: The new challenge', Spring.

Whittington, C. and Bellaby, P. (1979). 'The reasons for hierarchy in SSDs: A critique of Elliott Jaques and his associates', *Sociological Review*, 27(3), 513–39.

Whitty, G., Fitz, J. and Edwards, T. (1986). 'Assisting whom?', paper presented to the *British Educational Research Association Conference*, University of Bristol, 4 September.

Wilkinson, M. (1986). 'Tax expenditures and public expenditure in the UK', *Journal of Social Policy*, 15(1), 23–50.

Wilson, T. and Wilson, D. (eds) (1991). *The State and Social Welfare*. Harlow, Longman.

Wistow, G. (1989). 'Open forum', *Insight*, 11 October.

Wistow, G. and Henwood, M. (1991). 'Caring for people: Elegant model or flawed design?', in N. Manning (ed.) *Social Policy Review 1990–91*. Harlow, Longman.

Wistow, G., Knapp, M., Hardy, B. and Allen, C. (1992). 'From providing to enabling: local authorities and the mixed economy of social care', *Public Administration*, 70(1), 25–45.

Wolf, A. (1979). 'A theory of non-market failure', *Journal of Law and Economics*, 22, 107–140.

Woodward, R. (1991). 'Mobilising opposition: The campaign against Housing Action Trusts in Tower Hamlets', *Housing Studies*, 6, 44–56.

Wright, P. (1987). *Spycatcher*. Victoria, Australia, Heinemann.

Wyatt, S. (1991).'Webs of welfare: The Social Security Office gets networked', in M. Adler and R. Williams (eds) *The Social Implications of the Operational Strategy*. New Waverley Papers, Social Policy Series No. 4, University of Edinburgh.

Young, H. (1990). *One of Us*. London, Pan Books.

Index

IMPLEMENTING THATCHERITE POLICIES
AUDIT OF AN ERA

David Marsh and R.A.W. Rhodes (eds)

The politics and policies of the Conservative government under Prime Minister Margaret Thatcher constituted an undeniably distinctive phase in the history of post-war British politics. Her government claimed to have a radical policy agenda and placed a great deal of emphasis on achieving their objectives. This book examines the true extent of policy change in the 1980s, forsaking the conventional personalities and party rhetoric to focus on the hard question of 'What changed, by how much and why?' It compares the degree of policy change over a range of areas and explains why the extent of change was greater in some areas than others. The areas studied include: economic policy, industrial relations, local government finance, housing, social security, health, environment, agriculture and the European Community. The authors unearth a record of policy failure rather than transformation and argue that this failure was due to a lack of attention to implementation.

This important book will be of interest to policy makers, students and lecturers in social policy, politics, public administration and political economy.

Contents
'Thatcherism': an implementation perspective – Economic policy – Industrial relations – Local government finance – Housing – Social security – The National Health Service – Environmental policy – CAP and agricultural policy – The European Community – The implementation gap: explaining policy change and continuity – References and bibliography – Name index – Subject index.

Contributors
Jonathan Bradshaw, Peter M. Jackson, Peter Kemp, David Marsh, John Peterson, R.A.W. Rhodes, David Samways, Martin J. Smith, Hugh Ward, Gerald Wistow.

224pp   0 335 15682 7 (Paperback)   0 335 15683 5 (Hardback)

BRITISH AID AND INTERNATIONAL TRADE
AID POLICY MAKING: 1979–89

Oliver Morrissey, Brian Smith and Edward Horesh

This book argues that British aid did little to achieve developmental or commercial objectives in the years of the Thatcher government. Economic aid affects four areas of public policy: promotion of exports to developing countries, state-business relations, foreign policy and overseas development. In discussing aid policy making the authors examine the attitudes of, and relations between, four administrative departments – the Treasury, the Department of Trade and Industry, the Foreign and Commonwealth Office and the Overseas Development Administration. They also examine the role of Parliament, committees of the House of Commons and the influence of big business pressure groups. The book provides a comprehensive analysis of the economics and politics of UK aid policy, and the implications for public policy on trade, foreign relations and international redistribution. It will be an invaluable resource for students and professionals in political economics, development, public policy, politics and business.

Contents
Introduction – The objectives of aid policy – Parliament and lobbies – Whitehall and aid policy – Trends in the British aid budget 1978–89 – The impact of British aid disbursements – The Aid and Trade Provision, 1978–89 – Aid, employment and international trade – Summary and conclusion – References – Index.

192pp   0 335 15652 5 (Hardback)